# DREAMS GONE WRONG

## LINGG BREWER

**PEACE, WAR, AND MURDER AT MICHIGAN STATE UNIVERSITY**

Dreams Gone Wrong
by Lingg Brewer

Copyright © 2013 by Lingg Brewer

All rights reserved. No part of this book may be reproduced, stored in a retrieval system, or transmitted in any form or by any means—electronic, mechanical, photocopying, recording, or other—without written permission from the publisher, except in the case of brief reviews for critical articles.

Published by Lingg Brewer
Mason, Michigan 48854

5  4  3  2  1    13  14  15  16  17

ISBN: 978-09910424-0-1
Library of Congress Control Number: 2013919247

Book design by Julie Taylor
Cover design by Angela Brewer
Historical photos used with permission of the MSU archives.

Printed in the United States of America
by Versa Press | Peoria, Illinois.

To My Children:

Angela, Gideon, Kate, and Miriam, and their mother Marjorie, for tolerating my dreams—even believing in them and furthering them.

# Table of Contents

Chapter 1: At The Union Grill . . . . . . . . . . . . . . . . . . . . . . . . . . . 1
Chapter 2: Charlie Barke Tells the Story . . . . . . . . . . . . . . . . . . 3
Chapter 3: In The Beginning . . . . . . . . . . . . . . . . . . . . . . . . . . . 5
Chapter 4: Doesn't Kick or Bite . . . . . . . . . . . . . . . . . . . . . . . . . 7
Chapter 5: A Child Is Born . . . . . . . . . . . . . . . . . . . . . . . . . . . 11
Chapter 6: The War Ahead . . . . . . . . . . . . . . . . . . . . . . . . . . . . 13
    Isolationists before Pearl Harbor . . . . . . . . . . . . . . . . . . . . 14
    War Preparation Continues, In The Country, In Michigan,
    In Lansing. Money Is An Issue . . . . . . . . . . . . . . . . . . . . . . 15
    East Lansing Stays Peaceful . . . . . . . . . . . . . . . . . . . . . . . . 18
Chapter 7: George Hall Remembers Pearl Harbor . . . . . . . . . 19
Chapter 8: After Pearl Harbor, Back in Lansing . . . . . . . . . . . 20
Chapter 9: Meanwhile, Back in the South Pacific . . . . . . . . . . 23
Chapter 10: The Enclave of East Lansing . . . . . . . . . . . . . . . . 25
Chapter 11: Rick Fowler is Born . . . . . . . . . . . . . . . . . . . . . . . 29
Chapter 12: John Hannah Builds MSU . . . . . . . . . . . . . . . . . 30
Chapter 13: Rick . . . . . . . . . . . . . . . . . . . . . . . . . . . . . . . . . . . 35
Chapter 14: George Hall Takes a Dive . . . . . . . . . . . . . . . . . . 44
    Korea . . . . . . . . . . . . . . . . . . . . . . . . . . . . . . . . . . . . . . . . . . 49
    George Hall, Trained To Kill By The US Government. Was
    He On His Way To Korea, Or Some Place Worse? . . . . . . 51
Chapter 15: Back In Lansing as a Boomtown . . . . . . . . . . . . . 54
Chapter 16: East Lansing and MSU . . . . . . . . . . . . . . . . . . . . 56

Chapter 17: George Hall Goes Bad ..................... 59
   George Hall In Prison Was Not In the Belly Of The Beast, Initially ........................................... 60
   No More Croquet ................................ 61
   George Continues Down The Wrong Road ........... 62

Chapter 18: Rat-face likes His Drugs ................... 63

Chapter 19: Where's Viet Nam? ........................ 66

Chapter 20: MSU's Foreign Policy ...................... 70
   Wesley Fishel from MSU, Kingmaker ................ 73
   Fishel Takes Diem Around ......................... 76
   Mr. Fishel Leaves East Lansing And Goes To Saigon. It's Not Sleepy ......................................... 79
   MSU Faculty Live Well In Saigon ................... 81
   Not All of MSU's, And The USA's Efforts Were Involved With Policing. They Didn't All Live Like Aristocracy. They Weren't All "Yes" Men .............................. 82
   An Embarrassment of Riches For MSU ............... 85
   MSU Faculty Supervisors Close Their Minds And Their Eyes And "Soldier On" .............................. 87
   See No Evil, Hear No Evil .......................... 91
   If It Walks Like a Duck, And Talks Like a Duck ........ 92
   Nobody in Here but Us Chickens .................... 94
   Parlez-Vous Francais? .............................. 94
   I Broke Up With You First .......................... 94

Chapter 21: Back at the Union, Way Back ................ 97
   The Grill — The Bumboys .......................... 98

Chapter 22: George Hall Mostly Stays Out Of Trouble .... 109

Chapter 23: Rick Fowler, Better Than Bubba? ............ 111

Chapter 24: First Beer, Then MSU ...................... 114
   Bob Vee .......................................... 118
   Sports ........................................... 123

Chapter 25: Diem Comes Back to Town ................. 125

Chapter 26: JFK Gets Us in Deeper .................... 128
    Somebody's Lying................................. 130
    A Buddhist Monk Burns In Saigon ................. 131
    The Coup against Diem............................ 132
    Waist Deep In The Big Muddy ..................... 135

Chapter 27: The Union Grill after 1961 ................. 138
    Athletes At The Grill, Beginning With Biggie ........ 141
    More "Cornbeefing" [Scams] ..................... 149

Chapter 28: Assassination of President John F. Kennedy .. 151
    The Gulf of Tonkin Resolution..................... 152

Chapter 29: George Hall Has An Idea ................... 156

Chapter 30: Times Were A-Changing ................... 157
    A Blind Eye ...................................... 159
    The Eastern High Guys Weren't Rats ................ 160
    A House Divided ................................. 162
    Communists Not Just Under The Bed, But In The Bed 163

Chapter 31: Politics? For the Bumboys?.................. 166
    The Bumboys Start To Listen; Bumboy Sherb Had No Choice............................................ 168

Chapter 32: The Wallaces, Of "Old East Lansing" ........ 174
    Don't Go Near The Union ........................ 175
    The Enemy is Us ................................. 176
    Protest Begins With Green, And White All Over East Lansing .............................................. 177
    Cassandra Speaks. The Bumboys Don't Know or Care About Cassandra.................................. 178
    Marchers For Peace Find It a Slog .................. 181
    Jane Munn and Louise Holmes Slog On Too ......... 181
    To The Ramparts................................. 182
    What was the CIA doing on campus? ............... 184
    Radicals in Our Mist, that is, Midst................. 184
    East Lansing's Own Dave Lawson .................. 185

Chapter 33: Bob Vee Stands for Traditional Values . . . . . . . 188
   Bob Vee Gets A Little Political — Look At Those Fascist
   Pigeons Strut . . . . . . . . . . . . . . . . . . . . . . . . . . . . . . . . . . . 190
   In Lansing—Starting In "The Shop" . . . . . . . . . . . . . . . . . 191
   Oldsmobile and the East Lansing Life . . . . . . . . . . . . . . . 194
   Princess Nancy Attends Marcia's Party . . . . . . . . . . . . . . 200
   Nancy Gets Engaged, Eleanor Too . . . . . . . . . . . . . . . . . 203
   More Political Leaders Are Assassinated . . . . . . . . . . . . . 204

Chapter 34: The Guys Go See Their State Representative . . 206
   The Guys Play Some Cards, And Other Games . . . . . . . 214

Chapter 35: MSU Gets Un-Radical . . . . . . . . . . . . . . . . . . . . 218
   The University of Michigan SDS Wants It Their Way . . 218
   Alternatives to SDS Grow Stronger . . . . . . . . . . . . . . . . . 219
   SDS Member Benardine Dohrn Comes to East Lansing to
   Advocate — Sex Sells . . . . . . . . . . . . . . . . . . . . . . . . . . . . 220

Chapter 36: The Presidential Election of 1968 . . . . . . . . . . 222
   On To Chicago for the 1968 Democratic Convention . . 225
   Back In Detroit . . . . . . . . . . . . . . . . . . . . . . . . . . . . . . . . 231
   The Night the President Didn't Come To Dinner . . . . . 233
   The President Gives Hubert Some Maneuvering Room 235
   The Election Result of 1968 . . . . . . . . . . . . . . . . . . . . . . 236

Chapter 37: At the Kit-Kat Club . . . . . . . . . . . . . . . . . . . . . 237

Chapter 38: John Hannah Takes An Easier Gig . . . . . . . . . . 239
   Peace was maintained in East Lansing . . . . . . . . . . . . . . 243
   More Protest . . . . . . . . . . . . . . . . . . . . . . . . . . . . . . . . . . 245
   MSU Protest Gets Unruly . . . . . . . . . . . . . . . . . . . . . . . . 245
   The Peace Movement Expands and Progresses . . . . . . . 247
   East Lansing Stays Peaceful, Vee Stays Out of It . . . . . . . 247

Chapter 39: Riding the Horses . . . . . . . . . . . . . . . . . . . . . . . 254
   George Hall Wasn't Hustling At That Time . . . . . . . . . . 257
   Rick Gets His First Hint . . . . . . . . . . . . . . . . . . . . . . . . . 257
   The Fire Gets Too Hot . . . . . . . . . . . . . . . . . . . . . . . . . . 261
   Howard Sober, The Biggest Loser . . . . . . . . . . . . . . . . . . 263

Chapter 40: Old Enough to Fight, Old Enough to Vote....267
    Wesley Fishel Revises, Dissembles, Deludes. Who?....268
    The Guys At The Grill Sit Down With Wes Fishel.....269
    The Fall .........................................270

Chapter 41: George Hall Comes to East Lansing.........273
    The Bumboys Get a Hint..........................274
    Karen Gets A Package ............................275
    Ratface, A Very Bad Bedfellow....................276
    Denny Diamond, the Pied Piper Toots Away, and the Guys Follow............................................278
    Larry "Handles" Al..............................281
    Charlie's Last Trip With Vee .....................282
    Dude Mataya, A Four-Flusher?....................284
    Two Dogs Together Get Into A Lot More Trouble Than Two Dogs Separately ............................287
    Gambling, a Hard Way To Make An Easy Living?.....290

Chapter 42: The End Game ...........................291

Index .............................................302

Acknowledgements: ................................309

About the Author: ................................310

# Chapter 1

# AT THE UNION GRILL

The Student Union is a substantial three story beige brick and sandstone building in the middle of the oldest part of the Michigan State University campus on Circle Drive in East Lansing, Michigan. As you approached the west entrance of the building in the fall of 1961, all was quiet. The wind rustled through the tall trees on the boulevard nearby with soft restraint.

As you walked up the steps, you passed two green-oxidized bronze art-deco posts holding up two large globes to provide light during the evening hours. As you opened one of the two solid-oak double doors and ascended the gray-green terrazzo stairs into the spacious lobby, all was quiet and serene. It could have been the library. To the left is the entrance to the Union Grill; as you open the door there's something of a shock: Bam! A wall of noise, 500 loud conversations buzzing, cafeteria trays clattering, papers rustling The rhythms of the best music of the era moving the spirits of those present.

You'd walk past the athletes holding court at the "Round Table" near the entrance, further on back into the conversational heart of the grill: here are the East Lansing High School students, hanging out. Bob Vee is there, tall, self-consciously handsome, blonde hair piled high on the top of his well-shaped head. He's telling a story that makes everyone near him laugh, blue eyes merry with his enjoyment of the telling. Rick Fowler, big, muscular, slightly baby-faced, high-school football player and wrestler, casually dreaming of easy money, is talking to one of the MSU football players, trying to interest him in a wager. Bob Sherburn, "Sherb", slim, tousle-haired, alert, is talking to some of the high school girls. Larry Chappell, an ELHS sophomore, is talking to the same girls with a slow, southern drawl mixed with angelic looks. The girls listen, charmed. East Lansing math genius Dave Lawson, home from U of M, talks to Mike Munn, son of Athletic Director Biggie Munn, about getting involved in radical politics. Mike's sister Jane is near the Round Table and talks to the black football players with her ELHS classmate Karen Wallace.

Further away, apart from the athletes and the East Lansing students, is Professor Wesley Fishel: short, Van-Dyke-bearded, with a receding hairline. He discusses world events with students in a patient, informative, very articulate way. One of his students is Japanese; he shifts seamlessly in conversation between English and Japanese. He's one of the best, with dreams of influencing events in the world at the highest level.

Across Circle Drive from the Union is Cowles House, residence of MSU President John Hannah. He's there planning, always planning, to make the university bigger, make it better, adding colleges and departments; he reigns supreme. He's master of the university empire he has created in East Lansing. He wants to do more. He has the best of intentions. His sense of noblesse oblige pushes him to do more, to help perfect the world with his instrument, Michigan State University.

The spirits of those who were present at the school that day are high. The possibilities are great. The winds of post-World-War-II era optimism are at their back, swirling around and through them. This is a snapshot of America in the mid-twentieth century at its most confident.

George Hall is apart from all that. He's in Jackson Prison, just thinking about getting out.

# Chapter 2

## CHARLIE BARKE TELLS THE STORY

Charlie was born at Sparrow Hospital on Michigan Avenue in Lansing in October, 1944, delivered by Dorothea Dart, one of the first female physicians in the area. Charlie's mother Eleanor was something of a closet feminist. A textiles major at MSC, she graduated from the college in 1931, worked in Cooperative Extension for the college, then decided to stay home to raise a family. Charlie's father William was a self-taught tool and die maker who walked to work down Sheridan Street to Lansing Tool & Die, worked there long, long hours. Charlie grew up on Sheridan, quiet and tree-lined, in a sturdy, well-kept blue collar neighborhood where two or three cars would drive down it in the morning, two or three in the afternoon. It became Oakland Avenue in the late 50's, a one-way thoroughfare that ruined the neighborhood.

Charlie attended Fairview School, a new one. The school district was like the old woman who lived in a shoe and had so many children she didn't know what to do. Children were everywhere and Fairview was built on a plot of land that had contained World War II Victory Gardens a few years before. Lansing car manufacturing, the paychecks and the tax dollars they provided made Lansing grow fast, made it prosper.

At Fairview School, Charlie was in class with Bob VerPlanck, Bob Vee. Vee unknowingly stole the affections of Charlie's first girlfriend Nancy Blink. "He was so cute" she said. His parents made more money than most of the families whose children attended Fairview School, and they were soon out of there, moved to East Lansing, a step up. Charlie renewed his friendship with Bob Vee a few years later at the Union Grill. Vee made friends easily.

Charlie knew most of the people in this story, which is true.

BOB VERPLANCK "BOB VEE" SITTING IN THE
BOTTOM ROW, THIRD FROM THE RIGHT
LANSING FAIRVIEW ELEMENTARY SCHOOL, 6TH GRADE 1956

# Chapter 3

# IN THE BEGINNING

In the beginning Michigan Agricultural College had a modest start in rural Ingham County. The Michigan Legislature passed Act 130 in 1855 with an original award of 677 acres of "salt springs" land for the location of the College, as well as $40,000 to carry it through its first two years. Some of the land was swamp, which was drained—and they say government can't do anything right.

It was the first agricultural school in the nation, the prototype for the seventy-two land grant institutions under the Morrill Act. There was a reason for that. From the beginning, MACs first President, Joseph R. Williams pressed for a federal land grant that would support agricultural colleges like his own. He wrote letters to national leaders, personally lobbied members of Congress in Washington. He wrote much of the bill that Congressman Justin Morrill introduced in 1857, and much of the speech that Morrill used to introduce it. The act was vetoed by President Buchanan in 1859 to appease the South. Because Southern objections left along with Southern secession, it was signed into law by Abraham Lincoln in 1862.

As the prototype for the Morrill Act, the state of Michigan received its allotted amount of federal land to fund the future Michigan State University, a quarter of a million acres of land in an inverted "V" stretching from Manistee to Mackinac, to Saginaw Bay. Earmarked for the school and sold in the next century, the land produced a million dollar endowment, yielding 7 per cent interest. The Morrill Act assured the school its solvency in the long term, if not the short term.

The legislature was, and remains, tight-fisted. Their hope was that a scientifically run school and farm could support faculty, laboratories, library, and experiments while offering paid employment to all students. This was either an early exercise in privatization, or an early one in socialism, depending on your point of view. Their hopes were wildly optimistic. The college continued to struggle with the parsimony of the legislature, but endured and expanded with their federal land grant endowment. That would not change. President Hannah would be as ingenious as MAC President Williams at getting federal dollars. The little East Lansing college would become one of the biggest universities in geography and enrollment in the country. The Morrill Act would make it. John Hannah would make it big.

Classes began in 1857 with five faculty, sixty-three male students, and three buildings. One was the only dormitory, called Saints Rest. When its site was excavated a hundred and fifty years later, workers found the remains of a still, liquor bottles, and the remains of pipes. Even then, as in the 1960's, students did not always respect the rules. There was also a barn and a multi-purpose building called College Hall, which would eventually evolve into the Student Union. Rigorous classes in science, liberal arts, and practical training were mandatory. Three hours a day of manual labor were required to help build and maintain the new school.

The first president of the college was replaced because the legislature thought he wasn't practical enough. There were rumors that the legislature was going to turn the campus into a prison farm and grow sugar beets because of the president's lack of practicality. They didn't but the school did become more vocational. It became co-educational in 1870 with women taking the same courses as men. In 1896, women were given a more sheltered course of study called "Home Economics."

# Chapter 4

# DOESN'T KICK OR BITE

Lansing wasn't like East Lansing. Lansing was a town with a taste for cheeseburgers, not cheese soufflés. Early in the industrial age, it had great success. Ransom E. Olds was going to make it great indeed. It all began on River Street on the south edge of what is now downtown Lansing. The Olds family had a small two-story brick building there. It contained the Pliny Olds agricultural and marine steam engine works. His son R.E. Olds, immediately grasped the implications of Gottlieb Daimler's perfection of the gasoline-powered internal combustion engine in 1885. It would replace the horse. It would never be victim to boiler problems or to delays in "getting up" steam. R.E. may have had no idea that before the era was over that nearly two and a half billion cars and trucks would eventually be built with an internal combustion engine, but he knew Gottlieb Daimler, the founder of Daimler-Benz, was on to something.

R.E. first attached his father's gasoline-powered steam engine to the car and brought it out of the shed of the Olds family steam engine works early on a summer day in 1887. It had one cylinder and one horsepower. It didn't take to inclines or hills. It didn't have reverse. When *Scientific American* magazine came around to examine the machine as one of the early efforts at horseless carriages, R.E. said "it doesn't kick or bite."

R.E. Olds, like Henry Ford who later overshadowed him, was somewhere between paternalistic and progressive in his early days as a titan. He was superficially regarded as a tightwad, and was shrewd yet idealistic with his money. He opened his

CURVED DASH OLDS, 1902.
650 LBS, $650
MADE ON AN ASSEMBLY LINE — 10 YEARS AHEAD OF FORD

wallet and his bank account to make Lansing better. The notable exceptions were labor unions and people of color. When his brother Wallace, manager of the Olds engine company started by their father, sided with workers in a labor dispute, he fired him and purchased his stock. (He later brought Wallace back.)

The 1901 Olds was light, agile, comparatively inexpensive, and comparatively reliable. It weighed 650 pounds, cost $650, and had horsepower variously described as four and seven. It was "mass" produced on an assembly line that may have been Ransom Eli Olds' biggest contribution to the industry. He envisioned it after observing assembly line methods at a gun-making factory and in the making of railroad locomotives. After the introduction of the assembly line, his next great contribution to the industry, was the low cost and high production numbers of the curved dash Oldsmobile. They increased, increased some more, quadrupled, and peaked at 3,924 units in 1903. A young thin-faced employee of Edison Electric came up to observe the process. His name was Henry Ford. R.E. Olds popularized the small light automobile, affordable for people of moderate means. Mark Twain bought one, Hollywood actresses bought them.

The company prospered. The industry was full of incredibly smart, visionary people, mechanical geniuses inventing as they went along, where nobody had gone before. They were used to seeing the way, used to getting their way. After a 1901 fire destroyed the Olds factory in Detroit, Olds, who was making gas fired steam, gas fired internal combustion, and electrics, was forced to make a fundamental decision. What kind of power should their passenger cars have? The answer was not obvious; environmental concerns were not apparent. Electric was the most popular means of powering vehicles at the time. Steam was second. Internal combustion gasoline was third. He eliminated steam because of his experience with the lag time of "getting up steam." He eliminated electrics because of their weight, cost, and the limited range of their batteries. He said "Young [Thomas] Edison can't provide us with batteries that are any good."

Next, Olds had to decide where to build it. Then as now, with lack of sentimentality, especially for someone with Lansing roots, Olds started shopping among local governments in the Midwest and east coast for perks and incentives. Many communities were interested, from Pontiac, Michigan, to Newark, New Jersey. On the table as bargaining chips were enough cheap or free land for a factory, good rail connections, an adequate skilled and semi-skilled labor force, not filled with union agitators, and adequate parts suppliers close by. Lansing made him the best offer. Lansing won.

It was the smartest move the Chamber of Commerce types would ever make for the City of Lansing. Ransom and the city fathers agreed to the deal in all its particulars. Ransom Olds immediately moved back to supervise a factory that initially employed 400 and quickly grew to 1,200. The Oldsmobile continued to receive favorable publicity. National races and endurance runs were won. Oldsmobile prospered. Lansing prospered. By 1904 the Olds Motor Works became the leading American automobile manufacturer. Lansing became the nation's center of the industry.

*REDESIGNED 33 OLDS SOLD WELL, HELPED BRING LANSING OUT OF THE DEPRESSION SOONER, FASTER THAN THE STATE AND NATION.*

By the time of the market crash of 1929 leading to the Great Depression, R.E. had long since separated from the company that bore his name. He then established the Reo Motor Car Company, which in the Depression was on the edge of ruin. Oldsmobile, however, taken over by General Motors, was affected later by the Depression but recovered early. Oldsmobile's recovery was Lansing's recovery. Sales were fourth in the industry after Chevrolet, Ford, and Plymouth. In the pre-Depression year of 1929, sales (rounded) were 100,000. In the severest part of the Depression sales fell to 50,000 in 1932 with the company losing money in 1930, 1931, and 1932. A General Motors Institute student working at Olds said about the fall of 1932: "the plant was completely dead in the months before I came [in]. President Roosevelt had convinced the country that if we were ever going to get out of the Depression, everyone who had any money should start putting it to use. Over in Product Engineering they had some new handmade 1933 display models... I thought they were out of this world. Style-wise they couldn't be improved on." Sales went up 25% in 1933 from 1932, 100% from 1934 compared to 1933. General Motors announced a $2.5 million expansion for Lansing's Oldsmobile and said they would build a thousand cars a day.

# Chapter 5

# A Child is Born

On a starlit summer night in a cow-path off a narrow dirt road in a wheat field outside of Ottumwa, Iowa, the 1934 Ford sedan rocked gently in the summer night of that same year 1934. It was a soft and pleasant night. What was going on inside the car in the spacious back seat wasn't soft or pleasant. It was rape.

Gladys Ettaemelia Norris had met Frank Hall that afternoon at the local dry-goods store. He was a horse-trader just passing through. He found the slim teenager most attractive. Gladys found the man attractive even though he was older, she was also impressed that he had a nearly new 1934 Ford V-8. Frank was not tall. but he had a lean compact athletic build and an easy manner. They went to the movies that evening, then went to park. They went from mutual petting and groping to Frank tearing Gladys's clothes off. She was a virgin. She said "No". Frank had heard a lot of women say no when they meant yes. Gladys meant no. Frank didn't stop. He forced his way in. There was no pleasure for her, only pain. He took her home. She was angry. He was somewhat abashed. He asked if he could call her again. She said no. Several weeks later she changed her mind. She was pregnant.

The shotgun wedding took place without ceremony at the Justice of the Peace. Initially the idea of marriage was not that unpleasant to Frank Hall. It was very unpleasant to his raped bride. Frank had big plans. They'd move to Michigan where there was good land cheap and he'd pay for it by the profit he'd make buying and selling horses. Off to Michigan they went to Burlington Village, near Coldwater in southwest Michigan. At first things went reasonably well, but Frank's income was sporadic, and as the obviousness of her pregnancy increased, Gladys' temper and her drinking grew worse. Even before the baby was born, Frank was making plans to move back to Missouri.

On March 7, 1935, the baby boy was born who was neither wanted nor liked. His name was George Norris Hall.

# Chapter 6

# THE WAR AHEAD

John Hannah was not yet president of Michigan State College in the late 1930's, he was the secretary of the board of trustees, a position of power second only to then President Robert Shaw. It was a position he'd occupied since 1935, largely through his own conspicuously obvious abilities. It didn't hurt that he had married President Shaw's daughter Sarah. Hannah saw the same war on the horizon that FDR did, and in the same way. At stake was the survival of democracy and civilization as we knew it. But isolationists were real political stoppers. They made sure that FDR's freedom of maneuver internationally to stop Nazism and help future allies was severely limited. Not so with John Hannah. He played a much lower-level game on a much smaller board, with infinitely smaller consequences. The rules of the game in East Lansing, Michigan, were simpler. He had greater freedom of action. He made the rules. Later, when it came to political protests that he thought went over the line, he let the protesters make a couple of moves, then he stopped the game and removed the board—took all the protesters to jail.

What was at stake for Hannah was the building of a university. He built it by recruiting star academicians, at least one for every department. He built it by recruiting the best athletes in the country, oftentimes black football players which just wasn't done in numbers that amounted to anything except at MSU. He built it by involving MSU in World War II right from the beginning. He was neither an athlete nor a warrior, but he was vicariously enamored of both athletics and war.

## Isolationists before Pearl Harbor

Franklin Roosevelt, committed to the anti-fascist cause, but politically constrained, was duplicitous and deceptive, and stretched the application of neutrality laws. His critics thought he illegally stretched them, if he did not outright break them. His Machiavellian approach was dictated by a clear-eyed view of the world on the brink of destruction by Nazi tyranny. His political opponents, using the convictions of isolationism and the political cover it provided to attack him, were central to Roosevelt's thinking from the mid-thirties on.

The Republican Party made common cause with the Isolationists. Many, like Robert Taft were sincere in their Isolationism. Eventually Republicans became the bigger part of the movement, controlled the movement. Isolationism prevented the U.S. from helping Britain and the allies from 1936 on, though the fetters of the Neutrality Acts would ever so slowly and gradually loosen as European war started then escalated. None of the isolationists were bashful about their opinions. The country listened.

The isolationist most insidious and conspicuously troubling to FDR, was Joe Kennedy. He was patriarch of the Kennedy Clan which included daughters who didn't count in a male political world, and son Joe Jr., who he was grooming for president, as well as JFK, Bobby, and Teddy. Joe Sr. was charming, voluble, brilliant, rich, pathologically ambitious, amoral to the bottom of his soul. A cad and a thief with his mistress of the moment Gloria Swanson; he was a bootlegger and stock manipulator. He used his diplomatic pouch as British Ambassador to smuggle large quantities of Scotch to the U.S. When he learned that the Nazis were going to invade Czechoslovakia, he bought Czech bonds on the stock exchanges and sold them short.

In a neat bit of foreshadowing, the Chicago Convention of 1932 was every bit as significant for the Democrats as would be that of 1968, but in a much better way. Joe Kennedy moved his support from fellow Catholic Al Smith to put Roosevelt over the top, so FDR owed him. Plus Kennedy was one of the richest men in America. FDR and the Democratic Party could use his money. They used each other for years. FDR was better at it; Roosevelt appointed Joe Kennedy to be Ambassador to the Court of Saint James to get him out of the US. Once in London, Kennedy aligned himself with the appeasers who thought Russia and Communism were a greater threat than Hitler.

Many American industrialists, including many from Lansing and other parts of Michigan, agreed with Kennedy, though the latter group's concerns about communism remained dormant—for a time.

If FDR fired Kennedy, it was feared that as the 1940 elections approached, Kennedy would support Dewey and take Catholic votes with him, so Roosevelt called him home and promised to support Joe Jr. for governor of Massachusetts in 1942.

On the eve of the election, contrary to everything Joe believed, he supported Roosevelt in a nationally broadcast radio address. He said that Roosevelt was the candidate who would keep the country out of war even though he'd been saying the opposite for the last year. Three days after FDR's victory, Joe continued with his defeatist statements that were pro-Nazi, anti-Communist, and anti-Brit, so FDR fired him.

## War Preparation Continues, In The Country, In Michigan, In Lansing. Money Is An Issue

As the thirties shaded into 1940, and America's inevitable involvement in WWII edged closer, both sides denied reality. The Isolationists, including many Michigan industrialists, continued to reject our need to go to war. Roosevelt denied that he was getting us into war, but successive Congressional neutrality acts became more flexible as war started in Europe. The planning for war, clumsy and disorganized initially, slowly gathered momentum. First the economics of it had to make sense for those who would get us and the world ready.

Profit was also a concern for the industrialists. They did not like the British example of a steeply graduated income tax and a virtually 100% tax on excess profits. For many of the big businessmen, profit and patriotism would not be seen as antagonistic. There was a backlog of nearly a billion dollars in military contracts that were not being performed. It looked like a strike by capital. The industrialists were balking. Roosevelt, nervous about re-election, nervous about getting help to Britain, essentially caved and agreed to give them what they wanted. He was not the first or last President who was more concerned about winning a war than he was about financing it.

Early labor organizers were seen as subversive because they had the temerity to ask for more than they were given. This was not seen as the American way by the industrialists. The homogeneity of the Lansing work force, with its roots in Lansing was not fertile ground for labor organizers initially. In 1910 the population was overwhelmingly white, rural, native-born, 99% white, 1% black, a few blacks worked at Reo as janitors. By 1930 Lansing's population of 78,000 inhabitants was still 90% native born with 1.8% listed as Negro. With a public relations program started by R.E. Olds when he started Reo that proclaimed "We're One Big Family," it was partly sincere, partly self-serving, totally paternalistic. There was the Reo Clubhouse that showed free movies nights and weekends. A company band played there; there was a choral group, picnics in the summertime. There was also an avenue of upward mobility through apprenticeship programs, closed to blacks, and a small avenue to right wrongs thru a complaint department. In 1919, Carl Young, President of the Michigan Federation of Labor complained about blacklists and unfair treatment [of union organizers] in Lansing but he also supported: "An American labor movement for one country, one people, one class… [he denounced] one union, IWW,

Bolshevism, and kindred evils that are antagonistic to the organized American labor movement." Union organizing was not easy in the beginning in Lansing The Depression changed that. Detroit, Flint, and even Grand Rapids saw labor organization efforts organized with the contribution of communists; but not in Lansing; radicals, "Bolsheviks" had no audience ever. Labor union activists were still seen as subversive despite the fact that ninety-nine per cent of workers in Lansing had never heard of Karl Marx, and early labor union efforts were organized with input from progressives, but also with the involvement of the KKK.

During the Depression though, support for labor unions changed and increased. The labor unrest in Lansing in the spring and summer of 1937 was looked upon with a jaundiced eye by conservatives. On March 10th, 90 per cent of Reo workers, angered by wage reductions, layoffs, and the firing of fifteen men for unspecified causes, "sat down" ten minutes before closing time and refused to leave the factory until the men were rehired and the UAW-CIO was recognized as their sole bargaining agent. The strike lasted a month and was not settled until Democratic Governor Frank Murphy intervened. The company agreed to accept the union. Later that spring the UAW-CIO attempted to organize the Capitol City Wrecking Company by trying to persuade employees to not go to work. An injunction against them was obtained, and the overzealous Ingham County Sheriff Allan MacDonald attempted to arrest the strike organizers. Not finding them at home he arrested the wives, leaving the families young children alone in their homes. This started the labor holiday of June 7, 1937. By 9 a.m. crowds of workers flooded downtown, demanded that stores be closed. Numbering 2,000 they marched four abreast to city hall, and demanded that the women be released. The mayor refused. They then marched to the Capitol where Governor Murphy calmed them and secured the prisoners' release.

## East Lansing Stays Peaceful

The Labor Holiday strikers spilled into East Lansing, many MSC students, Art Brandstatter Sr.—football star and future Dean of the Police Administration School, future MSU-Group operative in Vietnam—was among them, thought that the union members were Socialists-Communists. Little did Art know that the UAW-CIO in Lansing was much-influenced by the right-wing populism of the KKK, not at all by Socialism and Communism. Several were thrown in the Red Cedar River. No one drowned. There is no evidence that any were injured. It was not the East Lansing way. Art could not have known that he and labor unions would agree about Communism and the Vietnam War twenty years later.

FDR protected and encouraged labor. Section 7(a) of the National Industrial Recovery Act provided for maximum hours and minimum wages in many industries. It also stipulated the right of workers to "organize and bargain collectively through representatives of their own choosing."

Many of Michigan's and Lansing's industrialists thought there was a socialist communist fifth column wrapped around FDR, subverting America. But any idea of a military effort against international Communism was swept under the rug by the strength of Isolationism and its leaders, including the Republican Party leadership. FDR's clear thinking on the immediate threat of Nazism was denied by the Isolationists.

# Chapter 7

# GEORGE HALL REMEMBERS PEARL HARBOR

George Hall was six years old on December 7, 1941. He remembered he was playing in the farmyard when his Mother called out to anyone within listening distance: "the Japanese have bombed Pearl Harbor in Hawaii." His Father was long gone, having moved back to Missouri after George's birth. The farm they lived on was on Warner Lake Road, a dirt road outside the village of Burlington in Calhoun County, Michigan, forty miles southwest of Jackson. It had no running water, no electricity, no indoor plumbing, but neither did anyone else's farm in the vicinity. They used the outdoors as a refrigerator in winter, and an icebox in the summer. George remembers gathering milkweed for the stuffing of life-preservers for the Navy. Early on his Mother wasn't drinking that much. She got a job at United Steel and Wire in Battle Creek that had a military contract. She made $.25 an hour. It was decent money. She commuted to the job on bald tires because of rationing. Soon after that they moved to a much nicer house and farm on Wheatfield Rd, which was paved. It had indoor plumbing and a fireplace. George had his own bedroom. After that things started to really deteriorate. His Mother and Grandfather started drinking more. George was beaten more.

# Chapter 8

## AFTER PEARL HARBOR, BACK IN LANSING

Back in Lansing, two days after Pearl Harbor, draft offices were mobbed by young men wanting to join the military. From the ages of eighteen to thirty-five, they were eligible. Younger men forged birth certificates, older men convinced authorities of their fitness. Some of the young had not yet begun shaving, some of the old had long been bald. High school seniors dropped out of school to join. Michigan State College by the end of the war had 2705 women and only 945 men left. Many of the men were returned injured veterans. Lansing's volunteers would serve honorably and well. The soldiers in WWII went for basic training all across the country. It would help unify section and class and race.

At the same time that there was an exodus of young men from Lansing, there was an influx of young men with draft deferments, most often with family dependents. Their deferments were deemed critical to the war effort. The workers came from the rolling farmland around Lansing and Ingham County. They came from the hills and hollows of Kentucky, and from the deep south. There were Irish, Arabs and African-Americans from the far South, Poles and Italians. And women.

Women came too, without college educations, 90% of the population, who had limited career avenues. They could be secretaries and typists, clerical workers, waitresses and housekeepers. Going to work at Oldsmobile as blue-collar workers, if they were single, gave them paychecks with time and a half for

*WOMEN — HELPING MAINTAIN THE ARSENAL OF DEMOCRACY IN WWII AT THE OLDS PLANTS IN LANSING, MICHIGAN.*

overtime. The checks were bigger than any had ever dreamed of and freed them of the economic need to find husbands. If married, their paychecks freed them from the tyranny of tight-fisted husbands. It would also be the beginning of two-family incomes and the prosperity that flowed from it. They would go to work in pants and floppy Olds-issued hats with hair-net bags in the back to keep their hair from getting tangled in the industrial machinery. Their small octagonal metal Olds badges with their identification numbers were pinned to the turned-up bills of the hats. They walked down the street in pants, smoking cigarettes. Radical at the time, their appearance shocked. Then it was tolerated. Then it was respected. The new hires, both men and women, were everywhere, doubling up in rooming houses, renting rooms in private houses, commuting from the farms with inadequate gas ration cards and bald tires because of rubber shortage.

Before war's end, 25% of Lansing's population, including state employees, were engaged in war production, the largest of any city in Michigan outside of Detroit. The percent would have been higher if state employees were not factored in. Twenty-four Lansing war plants held government contracts. Oldsmobile made light military vehicles and aircraft parts, crankshafts, rods, and cylinder liners for the Rolls-Royce V-12 Merlin engines that went into the Mustang P-51 fighter aircraft. Scores of smaller firms produced components on a subcontract basis. Reo manufactured 2 ½ ton trucks and heavier vehicles. By 1943 the Nash-Kelvinator plant alone employed 8,500 employees in the old Reo car plant that the government spent $80 million on to renovate. It made propellers for just about everything that flew, including B17's and B-24's, carrier-based aircraft, British Lancaster, York, and Mosquito bombers. The GM-owned Fisher Body made ailerons, rudders, and elevators for the B-29. Atlas, Federal, Lindell, Melling, drop forges made forgings, castings for just about all the war material that was needed.

## Chapter 9

## MEANWHILE, BACK IN THE SOUTH PACIFIC...

In French Indochina too, the Vietnamese died fighting the Axis and Fascism. They were our allies against the Japanese. We regarded it as a marriage of convenience. Our temporary relationships that American soldiers were to have with Vietnamese women when our Vietnamese War developed later was not that different than the relationship that our OSS had with the Vietnamese Communist Party. We thought it was temporary. They were not going to be jilted with impunity.

When the Japanese attacked Pearl Harbor, the Viets had been actively trying to rid their country of French colonists for over 75 years. After a mutiny of Viet soldiers, members of a nationalist non-communist movement were crushed in the Yen Bay garrison by the French in 1930, the field was left largely to the Indo-Chinese Communist Party, which Ho Chi Minh formed out of three feuding groups. The French easily suppressed them but did not destroy them. They stayed that way, weakened but still cohesive until WWII. Soon after the Nazi invasion of France and the French capitulation, the Japanese pressured the Vichy (pro-Nazi) French colonial administration in Vietnam into "right of transit" and control over French economic and military resources and installations. In return they continued to recognize French political and administrative sovereignty of Vietnam. The French security apparatus combined with the Japanese to suppress rebellion. The only nationalist movement left, the only guerrilla movement left, was the Vietnamese Communists. In 1943 General Guyen Giap began to lead large groups of fighters against Japanese military installations. By 1944 he had secured large parts of North Vietnam from the Japanese. The US, through the OSS supplied them with small arms and ammunition. In return they provided the US with intelligence about Japanese troop movements and helped rescue US pilots.

At war's end on September 2, 1945, Ho Chi Minh declared independence from the powerless figurehead Emperor Bao Dai, set up by the Japanese. Bao Dai cheerfully abdicated. The Potsdam Treaty stipulated that the Brits were to repatriate (oust) the Japanese in the southern half of the country, and the Chinese Kuomintang (non-Communist Chinese ) were to repatriate them in the northern half of the country. British General Douglas Gracey also ousted the Viet-Minh (Communists) from the south using temporarily rearmed Japanese troops to do it. This was not looked upon favorably by the Viet-Minh who believed they'd been double-crossed . Then the Brits left, the French attempted to reassert control. It was the beginning of the Franco-Vietnamese War, which lasted from 1946-1954. Early in 1944 FDR said that the French "had milked the region for a hundred years and that the people of Indo-China deserved better," but Roosevelt was dead before the war was over.

# Chapter 10

# THE ENCLAVE OF EAST LANSING

As one of the first suburbs, the managers and executives and owners of Lansing' factories found themselves moving to East Lansing and nestled in comfortably among the college faculty. The "executives" might subject themselves to the clamor and the clang, the buzzing and the humming, the grime of the shop floors in the factories that they owned or managed, but they did not want their wives and children too close to those factories.

East Lansing was an enclave, a place apart. For several generations after MSU was established, in 1855 and 1857, it was surrounded by a high wooden fence that literally and symbolically separated it from the rest of the community. East Lansing residents of the era, mostly faculty and staff, and professional and business people employed in Lansing liked it that way. Some fifty years later when annexation with Lansing was proposed, arguments pro and con were heated. MAC President Jonathon L. Snyder weighed in and supported independent incorporation for "sanitary reasons." The college was producing sewage that needed to be processed, and his arguments carried the day. (Those living in Brody Group later on, next to the smell of the sewage treatment plant, likely thought a better job could have been done). Finally, in 1907, East Lansing decided to incorporate and maintain its enclave status. Residents felt (and still feel) that it's on a higher plane, that it was progressive, a bastion of clean living and scientific investigation. From the beginning it was "dry"; no alcohol could be bought, sold, or consumed retail within the city limits. Also from the beginning, no people of color could live within the city limits. In actuality the city and its government were quite conservative. When it came to the alcohol, perhaps the people of the community presciently knew the minor mayhem that would come later when students and their own teenagers were given even more easy, and legal, access to alcohol fifty years later. No mayhem came from later integration.

Even before John Hannah became president and increased enrollment near ten-fold, MAC and the city were growing—with their kind of people. In 1921 MAC enrollment was 1,500, in 1926 it was 2,500. The City of East Lansing had also grown, estimated to be 3,600 in 1926 from half that ten years before. The Chamber of Commerce noted that "the city had become a preferred suburb of Lansing businessmen" and had "not a single factory within its confines—and not one is desired." The Chamber, which was about commerce, did not want their families to be in too close to that commerce. Teddy Roosevelt had talked in his 1907 MAC commencement speech about the goodness of manual labor. They were not a part of Lansing that labored with its hands. They were different. They were better. Lansing had actually been quite innovative about integrating factory and neighborhood. One example was the GM built Fisher Body plant at Verlinden and West Michigan on the west side, at the site of the old Durant automobile factory. (Much later, Vietnam war protesters held up signs where Wesley Fishel spoke labeled "bodies by Fishel.") The factory abutted a solid middle-class, working class neighborhood and both prospered for many years. The same was true earlier with the Reo factory and Clubhouse and the subdivisions that Ransom Olds built near them on the near south side. Olds also encouraged, perhaps insisted, that various classes of workers live in the same neighborhoods, superintendents, managers, foremen, line workers all living together, blurring class divisions, if not race divisions. It was a union of sorts, but much different than the East Lansing kind. Olds home remained within walking distance of the Reo factory. But as Reo faltered and GM's Oldsmobile prospered and production increased, factory organization became more impersonal, "The One Big Family" advocated by R.E. Olds diminished as WWII approached. There was still a certain amount of "oneness" that East Lansing was not part of. Cars allowed workers to drive to and from suburbs like East Lansing. The City of East Lansing remained factory free, negro free, alcohol free.

East Lansing, as one of the first suburbs, allowed those living in that suburb and working in the "factory" town of Lansing to separate themselves and their residence from their work—geographically, physically, psychologically, politically. This wouldn't do the factory towns any good, but in many ways it wouldn't do the East Lansing bourgeoisie any good either. The apartness of a suburb encouraged the separateness and superiority of East Lansing compared to Lansing. It gave East Lansing children, who were getting an excellent academic education, no education at all in practical economics about what made a national economy run and the role factories, including those that supported Lansing's car economy, played nationally and locally. They had no idea about the amount of taxes those factories paid, except when they got their own tax bills. It was a handsome endowment that East Lansing didn't have. They learned no Lansing sociology, had no experience, about people who thought differently than they did. The different thinking that was in the factory town of Lansing next door was not as gentle as it was in East Lansing.

The nightlife in dry East Lansing in the 1950s was not cosmopolitan, not exactly like Saigon was going to be for faculty involved in the Eisenhower administrations Vietnam efforts. Students had access to five or so bars. Coral Gables was situated past the eastern city limits, in Meridian Township, where everyone went to drink, dance, and eat pizza. Pizza is common now but was quite exotic then. Malcolm X worked at the Gables as a busboy in his teen years. In his autobiography, he mentions that no black people could walk the streets of East Lansing after dark. Paul Revere's Bar, a quarter mile further down the road, was where students and people of wider divergence went to do more serious drinking out of fluted revolutionary-era type Pilsner glasses. Monty's was another stretch down the road to the east. Dagwood's in Lansing Township to the west had good burgers, while Mac's, also in the Township on Michigan Avenue, had no redeeming or significant characteristics at all, except that the beer and liquor were cheap.

## Chapter 11

## RICK FOWLER IS BORN

On March 7, 1944, war baby Rick Fowler was born in Lansing. "He was a good boy," his Mother Christine said. "He was a big boy, a precocious boy, a happy boy." He grew faster than the other neighborhood children, bigger, stronger, more athletic in a town that prided itself on athletics. .In many ways he was also smarter. The family, Christine, John, Rick, and his younger brother by two years, lived at 214 Collingwood across from MSU's campus. Rick watched out for his younger brother. Collingwood was a main eastern entrance to the college campus. The MSC Student Union building was just three blocks away.

# Chapter 12

# JOHN HANNAH BUILDS MSU

Even before WWII was over, John Hannah had started building MSU both in the size of the campus and its mission. During WWII more than 10,000 US soldiers were given education to further their military training at MSU before going on to advanced training and service. MSU's involvement in international areas started well before WWII's end. It started innocently and idealistically, with the best of intentions. Like all brilliant leaders, he saw into the future, up to a point. John Alfred Hannah anticipated the Marshall Plan of 1948. The plan gave huge amounts of money, seventeen billion dollars, and technical assistance, to allied countries devastated by WWII. In a 1943 speech he expressed belief that MSU's future success as a university could be part of solving the world's problems by dealing with the political as well as the material:

> "After the war the devastated areas will have to be restored, great resources developed everywhere... challenges to our young men and women on a scale never before equaled... the greater challenge will not be material. The American democracy, the fundamental ideology for which we are fighting, must be a beacon of fairness and opportunity to common people everywhere, a pattern that the world will want to copy and make work for all the peoples of the world to their own immense advantage... the education of the men and women who can meet it will be the new task of our universities."

The international service plans of MSU begun in the middle forties to educate students to go off to other countries fit beautifully with the Marshall Plan of 1948, and President Truman's Point IV Plan of 1949 in which the technical-assistance-abroad program moved into high gear; amongst other places it also started with the Technical Cooperation Administration For Africa, the Middle East, and South Asia. It all fit with Hannah's plan to grow MSU from the very small agricultural school it was at its start.

Hannah launched one of the most ambitious building programs of any college in the nation. Many thought it too ambitious, that he was overdoing it. Borrowing funds at low depression rates, he and the Board erected dormitories, Williams Hall for women named after suffragette Sarah Langdon Williams, the first Presidents wife. Mason Hall for men, named after Stephens T. Mason, the first Michigan Governor. Later in the decade, FDR's PWA gave half the cost of any new building whose income could pay interest and principal on the university's half of the price. In short order Hannah presented blueprints for buildings housing music, health services, field-house, auditorium, and two more residence halls. Parents were happy with the new Health Center, though later students and parents had doubts about the quality of that too. Basketball and track drew crowds to Jenison Fieldhouse. The new dorms filled to capacity. Hannah made his payments on the bonds on time. He proved his critics wrong. That gamble was vindicated.

When John Alfred Hannah became president on July 1, 1941, MSC was still primarily an agricultural college with a regional reputation. He transformed it into an internationally recognized research institution As MSU economist and future acting President Walter Adams said: "He created a megaversity of national stature—an empire where the sun never set and the concrete never hardened." John Hannah created a vast university with a mission to give higher education to hundreds of thousands. He saw clearly that WWII veterans would want education. He responded to the need.

John Hannah's approach to getting federal dollars was shrewd, analytical, and relentless. He was an extraordinary reader of men. To get the federal money, he knew he would have to raise the quality of the University; to do that he would have to raise the quality of the faculty. In 1951 he hired Milton Muelder as Dean of Science and Arts, but used him as a director of research with the rank of vice president and gave him a great deal of latitude to build the faculty. Muelder's academic area was Bosnia-Herzegovina in the era surrounding WWI, or the balkanization of the Balkans. As an academic he studied strife and bloodlust. As an administrator, with Hannah's blessing he pursued the opposite at MSU. He helped the university grow bigger and better in an orderly way. When Hannah was trying to persuade him to take the job he said: "You're more valuable as an administrator than as a long hair."

Hannah's initial thinking about getting the money was to get it for agricultural research, as MSU up until that time was known as an agricultural school. After casting about for where the money was, he found that the National Science Foundation and the National Institute of Health had a lot of it. So did the Pentagon. Hannah was an Assistant Secretary of Defense at the same time he was President of MSU so he knew they had money. Faculty would have to be the ones to apply for it.

The first thing Muelder did for Hannah was to canvass the faculty to find its strength and weaknesses, and who was doing what research under what grants. The results were distressing. Most of the research was basic; very little was applied or advanced. There were almost no PhD's. Nobody was working on grants from the NIH or the NSF. Faculty would have to be built up before research grant money could be built up.

To do this required tact and imagination. The chair of the Engineering Department was a good example of the challenge

Hannah faced. He was an expert on furnaces but he didn't have a Ph.D. In Boris Pasternak's novel *Dr. Zhivago*, set amidst the suffering and near starvation of post-WWI, post-Russian revolutionary Moscow, the idealistic Zhivago has moved his family to an upper room in the family's spacious home so he would have only one room to heat. The wood stove was smoking and wouldn't work. Somebody suggested calling an engineer who lives nearby. Zhivago replies. "I don't need an engineer; I need somebody who knows furnaces." John Hannah had the opposite problem. Hannah needed an engineer, an expert research engineer, to bring in the money.

When the chair of engineering and others like him started retiring, Hannah, through Muelder, had to tread carefully. The faculty of the various departments didn't want to bring in anybody sharper than themselves, which was leading to steady deterioration. It was the same problem that the Greek social fraternity system had when a given chapter was going downhill at MSU or anywhere else. The existing active members were recruiting and accepting as pledges people like themselves that were making it decline. The solution was to "re-colonize" and have each fraternity or sorority at a school volunteer by lot, one or two pledges to reconstitute the deteriorating chapter. That's kind of the way Hannah and Muelder did it. They brought in a distinguished retired chair of engineering from the University of Illinois for a one-year appointment after coaxing the incumbent to retire. His task was to act diplomatically with the rest of the department, but most of all find a permanent chair and a good one to help build the department. A similar approach was taken in other departments.

In a period of eight to ten years Muelder recruited, with specific criteria, all over the country. He was very successful. One criterion was that the chairs had to "be able to get their satisfaction vicariously," that is they couldn't be a one man band. They had to delegate, they had to mentor and encourage the others in the department. Hannah's goal was to hire at least one nationally known researcher, an academic star, in all the hard sciences, and as many as possible in the rest of the schools. Muelder had wide latitude to hire. To establish availability, his first question was "How much do you want?" If they came up with a number, availability was established. Hannah was willing to pay. He hired Henry Blosser at a salary that was higher than his own and didn't care. He had higher concerns. Research money started to come in.

Sherwood Haynes was recruited in math, Julian Kately in computer science, J. Ballam in Physics, Walter Adams in Economics, his wife Pauline in American Thought and Language, Henry Blosser to build a cyclotron. Blosser made several trips to Washington to see the head of the Atomic Energy Commission, Glenn Seaborg, about research money. When it looked like they would be unsuccessful, Ballam from the Physics Department told Hannah they would have to be satisfied with less than satisfactory equipment, Hannah said: "If we can't get the research money, we'll build it ourselves. But Hannah got the money, $225,000. That was the good Hannah in action. He built the faculty to build the University to build the world. Michigan State University got bigger and better in those post WWII years.

# Chapter 13

# RICK

RICK FOWLER
EAST LANSING HIGH YEARBOOK 1962

Rick Fowler's parents were a couple of opposites His father John was a good man with a mathematical mind that Rick would inherit. He was as laid back as Christine was aggressive. He also drank too much. A plow-horse hitched to a racehorse. There was always that obstacle in their marriage. He was a salesman for General Electric where calculation and math skills were an important part of the job. John performed the job well and was happy with it. Christine wanted more, in many ways. John was ill-equipped to deal with the energy and wants of his wife and eldest son. Christine sold real estate for the Walter Neller Co. Christine was in marked contrast to her boss, Dick Neller Jr. He was as laid back as John Fowler. He just got out of her way and let her sell. Christine and Rick were contestants in a world that would leave John as a bystander.

Rick had many friends and had them over often. He attended Bailey School, a short walk away, with the sons and daughters of faculty members and others who lived in the interwoven close-knit East Lansing neighborhood. Like all neighborhoods, the post-war baby boom was in full swing. Kids were everywhere, and they were close, close together in their houses, close together in their play. Jim Hornberger, an excellent athlete himself, competed with Rick in many sports during high school, and was about half his size. He said he and his brother would leave in the morning and their mother would tell them "don't be late for dinner." The group included Jim and his brother, Rick, the Coomes brothers, Jim Miller, John Hauer, and several others. Jim said they had to get along because they only had one bat and one ball. If anyone with the bat or ball got mad, the game ended. They learned to work things out. Rick fit in well and was easy to get along with. He was nearly twice the height and weight of the others but did not throw his weight around. He was an excellent wrestler and football player.

Rick was an excellent student with a high IQ. He was a joiner not a loner. Even then he appeared to be everywhere, doing everything. He played the accordion and the clarinet, acted in school plays, had an excellent voice, sang in the choir. He interacted well with others and received excellent report cards.

But as he got older, he appeared to pay less attention to the limits his father attempted to impose, more attention to his mother who didn't impose any limits at all. Jim Klein, who grew up with Rick, talked about going over to Rick's house at the age of ten or eleven. Rick had a drum set with the works: snares, cymbals, bass drum. He had everything that could make noise. The drums could be heard through the whole neighborhood. Rick was playing them aggressively as he did everything. "The room started to vibrate from the racket," Jim said. Rick's father came into the room and in a very reasonable manner said "Rick, could you hold it down a little, maybe use the rubber pads? The neighbors can't be happy." Rick said, "I'm in here with my friends and you're interrupting. Don't come into my room again." Rick was nearly as big as his father at that time, and it was said with an edge, Jim said, with some threat to it. Rick's father did not enter the room again. Cymbals crashed, the bass drum thumped, the snare drum hissed, the neighbors went for their ear plugs.

It was not so much Rick that had bothered John, it was Christine. She pounded the drum that set a pace too great, a peace too little. He started drinking more.

A year or so later, one can imagine Rick's father sitting out on the front porch in his favorite chair having a beer. It was not his first or second or third or fourth or fifth. The boys were out somewhere. It was a summer evening and he was waiting for Christine to come home, as he often did. He looked out into the darkening Michigan sky. The horizon was mostly shades of gray with a narrow horizontal stratum stripe of pink, just enough to give hopes to optimists that the next day in mid-Michigan would not be as gray as the last. Suddenly he saw through the haze of his love and affection for Christine, saw the improbability, the impossibility of her ever reliably coming home.

He drank his beer down to the middle of the big swirling golden "S" on the black Stroh's label and sat it down. He went up to his room and packed his pressed paperboard suitcase, the one that had the imitation woven straw pattern with the narrow imitation dark leather around the edges. It was the one they used when he and Christine and the kids use to throw their things into the old Plymouth and drive up old Michigan 66 north to the lake for vacation. He packed even more completely and carefully than usual because he was not coming back. He never did, at least not to feign a conventional married life with Christine. It took them a long time to divorce.

His affection for her remained. His friendship with Christine remained for the rest of their lives.

It came to the central attention of Rick's adolescent mind, with the absence of his father, and frequent absence of his mother, just what is a bigshot? Was it flash, cash, swagger, chicks? And how did he become a bigshot? Without any adults around with any common sense, he must consult himself. Big? He was already big, but he could get bigger. He would get bigger and lifted weights to do it. Shot, shoot? He was shooting more ways than any of his buddies. Wrestling, football, basketball, card games at his house. His mastery of the games gave him some money, plus he had a paper route. Ten year later, Dave Godby, a local professional card player and bookie, exchanged a $500 bill for $500 worth of smaller bills. He said that "Rick was like little kid at Christmas. He wrapped the $500 bill around roll of tens and twenties." For Rick it was big money, flashy money, just like Vegas, just like in the movies. And the good-looking blonde? He hadn't even reached puberty yet, but as the casting director of his own movie, he knew Prudy Shelley, two years ahead of him at East Lansing High School, would fit. After aggressive and ceaseless courting she did. The swagger like in the movies? He could do that, and intimidate too.

In East Lansing, most people, most of the time, were not put off or threatened by Rick. They went to school with him. They played sports with him. He was one of them. They were also entertained often by his over-the-top behavior. They laughed with him, sometimes at him, but not to his face. At the same time they were respectful of his mental and athletic abilities. Because he was one of them, Rick's "act" didn't seem that out of the ordinary. The swagger they overlooked or discounted. Later, when he started believing in the act himself and took it on the road, people in other places started taking him way more seriously than the East Lansing kids, and were threatened by him.

With Rick's father gone he found even more freedom. At about that time, maybe before, he discovered games. First it was the simple ones: checkers, Parchisi, Monopoly, Stratego, pinball. He had to win. Then he discovered chess. He was hooked. He had discovered the framework in chess for the frame-work of life. There was time, space, and power. There would be other games and gambles that Rick could make more money on, but chess was always his favorite. His life would be about proving, mostly to himself, his power in the constricted space that he himself imposed on himself in East Lansing and Lansing—in the time he had available. He always felt that the time he had to demonstrate his mastery was short. He had to keep at it all the time.

Sometime after that, an old friend of Charlie's, Mark Waite, moved to East Lansing from Marquette in Michigan's upper peninsula. His father was a state police detective. Mark was just getting to know the East Lansing kids. Rick invited him over to play basketball. They were coming straight from junior high school, so Mark brought his basketball shoes. They played some horse and some one-on-one, rested for a while, and Rick made them a snack. By this time Mark had changed out of his basketball shoes and into his school shoes because he knew he'd be heading for home soon. He said his good-byes to Rick and his mother, and left for home, forgetting his basketball shoes. He called Rick the next morning and asked him to bring the shoes to school with him. Rick said they weren't there. A couple of weeks later Mark saw Rick walking down the hall wearing his basketball shoes.

Rick continued to grow, but not just in height like a lot of the kids. He grew big. He was strong and muscular, with a thin layer of baby fat on the surface of a strong, square jawed, pleasant looking face that made him look younger than he was. In many ways he was a baby. The gamblers and tough guys of Lansing and the outside world, lurking and observing East Lansing types like Rick, thought they were babies in many ways.

Rick was a heavyweight, the heaviest weight, in both junior high and high school wrestling. And he was good. But at East

Lansing High at the time, when guys would have fights or pick fights to prove who was the toughest, Rick was not part of that crowd. At Lansing Eastern High, fights after school at Mathew's ice cream store on Michigan Avenue were like the daily afternoon entertainment, unless you were the one doing the fighting. Rick was not a bully really, did not throw his weight around, but instead let his body language speak for him, It said, "Here I am. I am the toughest, or tough enough that I don't need to prove it." There needed to be a reason for Rick to get into a contest or a game. Initially it would be to prove that he was best. But by the time he reached high school, he had long since satisfied himself that he was the best, that he was the master. After that it was all for the money.

In his football playing high school days he once carried the sports section of the *Lansing State Journal* newspaper and quoted the sportswriter as saying: "Fowler penetrated the line like a young bull" to anyone who would listen to him read the story. But as time went on, he gravitated away from team sports like football. Increasingly he confined himself to sports like wrestling where he depended on himself.

Rick was friendly and gregarious. He enjoyed being around people, and had many friends. He started betting early, most likely for the bragging rights more than the money. One of the first bets was when he bet someone that he could carry John Hauer's bike to Alton Park and back to Bailey School without letting it touch the ground. It was an old 50's Schwinn with lights, a heavy battery to run the lights, streamers, the works. Made of heavy steel, lots of over-engineered steel, twice as heavy as it needed to be. To the other kids it had the weight of a Harley Davidson without the motor. The other kids couldn't carry it half a block. Rick carried it to the park and back, a distance of a mile. He won the bet.

Playing the games was also about mastery. Rick could be generous and buy people lunch from his paper route money, but about his mastery he was a miser. When he mastered the pinball machines and ran up fifteen or twenty free games, he would always tilt them out before he left. He never shared the free games. They were his winnings, the symbol of his mastery. Increasingly the bets were about money. Or as golfer Ben Hogan put it: "I've played games with friends, but I've never played a friendly game." Rick's "friends" would find that they weren't immune from the hustle. In later years they often became less friendly, or recognized the hustle and compensated by not attempting to become too good a friend with Rick, it would just be hurtful. Then there were those who were too dull or desperate for the friendship, or too desperate for the gamble, to figure out it wasn't about friendship at all. Rick would take more than one person like that and milk them for their bank accounts. Others could steel themselves against Rick's hustling tendencies and still maintain a friendship of sorts.

It was so much about the money that honor and pride and ethics, didn't much enter into it either. In the same way that he opposed fighting for the sake of fighting, he also opposed being honorable merely for the sake of doing the right thing—both behaviors were empty vessels. He was purely inner directed, purely into self, and the only thing that would make him act otherwise, and it would be all "act" was that he wasn't stupid, and would have highly developed social skills, saying and doing most of the right things most of the time, except when it came to money. The exception to his hustling would be his mother Christine, who would give everything she had to Rick anyway without being asked, and his future wife Prudy, and their son Ricky.

Rick won much more than he lost. An example was when he was wrestling Emerson Boles, the all-conference and all-state heavyweight wrestler from Sexton High, the high school in Lansing that had most of the black population. He'd been defeated twice previously by Boles, and was pinned both times. Boles was just bigger and faster, with better technique. Rick made a sizable bet with somebody that Boles wouldn't be able to pin him. In the match he literally ran around the ring away from Boles for the entire match so that Emerson could not get into a position to take him down for a pin. One of the referees reprimanded Rick. He faced Emerson off and they grappled for a few seconds; then Rick turned around and started running. The ref didn't know whether to laugh or be angry, or even to call the match. It the ref would have called the match, Rick would still won the bet because he wasn't pinned. If the ref would have known about the bet they wouldn't have laughed. Rick got his money.

In math class a year later, Rick back-talked his teacher, Miss Findley, after doing poorly on a pop quiz. He was outspoken and unrepentant. She kicked the wastepaper basket across the room where it ricocheted into a corner and bounced back toward her, a tin cornucopia of dreck, spilling its contents throughout the front of the classroom. This woke up Rick's classmates who were dozing off in the back of the class. They'd never seen Miss Findley like this before. She stomped and tromped back and forth across the orange peels, apple cores, empty potato chip bags and wadded up blue-books marked C+, kicking at them with anger. "You don't work. You don't study. You don't even try!" Miss Findley spoke with such passion because she did not have much of a life outside of East Lansing High, and she cared deeply about everything in it. She knew Rick had ability, yet he was her most smart-assed apostate. Rick was outwardly taken aback by Miss Findley's loss of self-control, but inwardly he took pleasure because of the attention. He also took note of the buttons of Miss Findley to push in the future, so he could again make her come out of her clockwork house and go cuckoo. Miss Findley was furious, but she was wrong. Rick would take some of the elementary things he'd learned in math class, and when his classmates were home watching Bonanza on TV, Rick would deal out poker hands face up and calculate the odds. Before poker books were written, he could write his own. He knew the odds of being dealt a pair, the odds of catching and winning with an under-pair, with maintaining a low pair against ace-king draws. When others with nothing else in their hands but a deck of cards might play solitaire, Rick would deal the cards and calculate odds, often late into the night.

In history class Rick paid enough attention to get by, and didn't know or care much about European or Asian history. He knew nothing about the history of chess and its Indian origins, but he read chess books and learned how to play the game very well. He played chess often at the Union, not with the bumboys who were hustling chess, but with the chess nerds. He'd lose to them and learn from them. Then he'd take that knowledge back to high school and play the chess nerds there—and beat them, for money. Pretty soon he was holding his own with all but the very best of the chess hustlers at the Union Grill.

At East Lansing High School, many of the kids were golden children of a golden era, children of parents of privilege. Discipline was lightly applied. Rick and Dave Fromer, a wrestling friend of Rick's from high school, were in the Union pool room one day. Rick saw the ELHS Assistant Principal Dorothy Lucas out of the corner of his eye. She saw him at the same time. "Dotty," Rick said, "why don't you pick up a cue and join us?" The Union Building was a north-south artery into campus from downtown across the street from the MSU campus. The halls were high traffic areas, especially when the weather was bad, which was a lot of the time. It was not known whether Mrs. Lucas had business on campus and was heading south through the building, or she was there on the lookout for class cutters like Fowler and Fromer. The ELHS administrators tried without success to keep the high school kids out of the Union without much success. Hank Bullough, the MSU player and coach, had also mentioned that Kramer and Carillot, future ELHS football coaches, also tried to keep the high school football players out of the Union, also without success. Mrs. Lucas wasn't amused by his remarks. She didn't join them for a game of pool. They were kicked out of school for several days.

# Chapter 14

## GEORGE HALL TAKES A DIVE

George Hall hitched a ride from Burlington to Union City, Michigan, that sunny summer morning in 1948. He was thirteen years old. Union City, a bigger village than Burlington was three miles further to the southwest, about forty miles from the Indiana state line. The land, good farmland for the most part, is flat and low. So low that the citizenry, before the Civil War, established a company to smelt iron from the bog and the kidney ore deposits found there and in the surrounding townships. It was the first furnace in Michigan to smelt iron from domestically gathered ore. The iron content was too low, however, and after a few years the company stopped the local mining and diverted its efforts to manufacturing plows and other agricultural equipment.

That summer was as prosperous a period as Union City had seen for some time. GIs, for the most part farm-boys, were home from World War II with money in their pockets and ideas in their heads. The commercial district in downtown Union City was flush with hardware stores and agricultural implement stores, dry-goods, bars and cafés that catered to them and the rest of the community.

On M-60 there are several blocks of prosperous, stately housing, including old Victorians with the dignity and stateliness of mansions. Some of the smaller houses with their shallow pitch roofs dated back before the Civil War. The east part of town is located on a modest bluff overlooking the St Joseph River. The tallest building in town is the United Methodist

Church on Ann St., its tall, unadorned lance of a steeple pointing skyward, high above the rest of the town.

West on Broad St, the main street through downtown, is the Union City Clarion Building, the only three-story building in town, on the left corner, and the sandy-colored glazed brick local bank on the right. The town hadn't changed since George came back to it after the war. Most of the buildings are turn-of-the-century two-story red brick, with what had been apartments above, mercantile below.

From the slight, gently sloping bluff toward the river, an old cylindrical steel water tower comes into view on the right, sharing the high sky space with the church, It stands sentinel over the St. Joe River, looking like a big robot anteater with proboscis in the ground. The St Joe makes a few gentle curves and turns as it passes through Union City; swirls and eddies and dimples mark the surface of the water. In 1948, the old iron bridge straddling the river had a high wide iron rail, pimpled with rivets, that stood above its floor. The triangles and gussets made the "I" beam steel trusses strong. It comfortably straddled the river to the lower land on the west bank. A couple of blocks down and a half block to the north was a tavern, converted from an old barn. It was called The Bucket. In local parlance it was called the Bloody Bucket. George would spend time there later on.

The bridge that spanned the water was not nearly as tall as the church steeple or the water tower, but George, small for his age, and standing on the bridge railing, found it tall enough, about five or six lengths of George. The river was about twenty-five or thirty feet below. It had rained heavily the night before, bringing the river to near flood stage, "On an average day the river was about five or six feet deep…. But it had rained heavily…." George could have broken his legs or worse. Much of the river still was shallow despite the rain He could see the mottled brown-green rocks on the river bottom below.

George had come in from the farm at Burlington, and the other kids were making fun of him. "Fraidy cat, fraidy cat," they chimed, "fraid to jump, fraid to jump." He would not be taunted or ridiculed. He jumped. As he left the edge of the bridge he smiled and became something else. The something else had no fear. He had conquered the leap. He had had left behind the fear. He also left behind the connectedness that he felt with the other kids. "I saw the fear that had been mine etched in their faces," he recalled years later. Through the clear summer air of the morning he passed with a rush toward the deep part of the river where the current ran swift and dug deep into the river bottom. When he collided with the river's surface in a splashing cascade of water, the river stung the backs of his legs and his rump. He went down to the bottom, his feet momentarily stuck in the mud of it. He stroked his way out and upward for air. He reached the surface and was free of it. He never thought of backing down from anything or anybody again. Much later on he would say, "How close to the devil and far from God is the man without fear."

Charlie Barke asked George if he had a step-father and if the step-father had any positive influence on him. He said "he had several," and "no they didn't have any positive influence." Charlie asked him if he tried to run away from the situation? He said "many times."

His mother was a good-looking woman who attracted men. She bedded them, used them and abused them. The sex wasn't enough. She drove them off. Her drinking got worse. George did not remember his father who did not stick around long, leaving the family shortly after George was born, gone back to Missouri. From the time he was six he was told, reminded, that he was a product of date rape. He did not feel loved by his Mother because he wasn't loved by his Mother.

He was small for his age and his mother and grandfather could still handle him. His mother held him down and his grandfather beat him with a length of garden hose. The beatings got worse as he got older, for little things, things he forgot to do, things that they thought he didn't do right. He never cried. "That would be giving in" he said.

When his mother was drunk, she gave him everything, to compensate George said, for not loving him. The things she bought him the family could ill afford. One of them was a Daisy rifle bb gun. The older he got, and the more he looked like his father, the more George was despised by his mother and grandfather for being both the 'father' and the son that ruined her life. The deprecating and the beating continued. One time his grandfather came into his room to beat him. He told him to stay away. His grandfather kept approaching. George shot him in the eye with his bb gun. "You're going to die in the electric chair" his grandfather said. George was ten years old.

The bright spot in his life was his grandmother. She gave him love, attention, biblical guidance. She told him "we're pals you and I, six, and sixty." She made him "ice cream" out of the snow flavored with milk from the families five cows that George milked, and flavored with vanilla and sugar. She made him Cambridge tea, hot water with a little milk in it, and had tea parties. She patched George's pants because money was scarce, but all the rest of the kids in the village had patched pants and families where money was scarce. He milked the cows, took them out to pasture, gave the barn cats each a squirt of milk, when he milked the cows. He went fishing in Warner Lake with a long cane pole and worms, caught rock-bass and huge blue-gills that he brought home and his grandmother pan-fried. They raised chickens and guinea hens for Sunday dinner and to sell. He had a good dog that chased cars, grandfather ran over him, not on purpose, but might have been drinking. George was lonely, but entertained himself. Much of his activity was inside his mind.

"I was getting beaten more often, I figured out that nobody was going to hurt me in a fight more than I was getting hurt at home so fighting and getting hurt didn't bother me. Some of the farm boys looked like they had been fed with HGH (growth hormone). They were tough kids and wanted to prove it. I got in my first fight and got beat, but I didn't back down. I started winning the fights."

He'd been working in the onion fields earlier in the spring, "topping out onions" for a dime a box. He'd worked hard and fast at it and made $6 a day. It was good money. He had money in his pockets. So one day he and Willie decided to go find his father. They pooled their money and off they went.

"Having been the navigator on many trips to Iowa and Nebraska with my mother and my grandmother, I knew how to set a route, so we just took off with a pocket map. I don't remember what we took with us, not much, maybe a change of clothes and a toothbrush, and our money of course."

And they found him. "I don't remember how we found him. I didn't have an address, just his name. I think he was in the phone book. My recollection is that I went to a police station, and they helped us locate him. In any event we made it, and we found him."

His father lived in a small upstairs apartment on Paseo Blvd., in Kansas City, Missouri, with a second wife and two small sons, George's half-brothers. There wasn't room for two extra kids, and, George recalls, probably not much money to feed them. "I remember his wife not being very happy with our arrival. I don't think my father was too pleased either."

Attempts to earn their keep didn't help any. "I have no idea what Willie and I planned to do. Planning wasn't high on our priority list. I remember we tried to get jobs. I wasn't overly successful, but I do remember setting pins in a bowling alley. Marshall's was the name of it I think. Willie got a job as an usher at the Midland Theater. We were hardly financially independent, and within a couple off weeks or so, my father put us on a bus back to Michigan. That was the last time I ever saw him." No love there either.

## Korea

On March 5, 1946 Winston Churchill, with Harry Truman at his side, gave his "Sinews of Peace" speech, more commonly identified as his "iron curtain" speech at Fulton Missouri where he received an honorary degree. "...A shadow has fallen upon the scene so lately lighted by the allied victory [of WWII]. From Stettin in the Baltic, to Trieste in the Adriatic, an iron curtain has descended across the continent... Communist fifth columns are established in complete unity and absolute obedience with the Communist center... There is nothing the Russians respect less than weakness. [The solution} is united sinews of peace [in the non-Communist western world.]

Harry Truman was listening. He established the Truman Doctrine that fought Communism wherever it appeared. There wasn't much acceptance of nuance, much acceptance that Communism sometimes was a lesser influence than nationalism or anti-colonialism. There wasn't much nuance in Korea.

For the defenders of the faith of the free world, President Harry Truman's Secretary of State Dean Acheson made a horrible mistake. In applying George Kennan's containment policy he had neglected to include South Korea in America's Asian defense perimeter. The American forces there were completely unprepared for an attack.

On June 25, 1950, nearly seven divisions of elite North Korean troops, many of whom had fought on the Communist side in the Chinese civil war, crossed the border at the 38th parallel into South Korea with the intention of conquering the entire South in three weeks . They had every appearance of succeeding. Harry Truman and his advisers quickly decided to draw the line.

It was the most bitter kind of war in which America and her allies fought, on horribly cold terrain, initially in summer uniforms. Then it was fought with superior hardware and technology against a numerically superior enemy that had its first

AT THE LANSING OLDSMOBILE PLANT, GENERAL DOUGLAS MACARTHUR IS SHOWN THE BAZOOKA FACILITY IN 1951 BY GM HEAD CHARLIE WILSON. (WILSON WAS LATER EISENHOWER'S SECRETARY OF DEFENSE SAYING: "WHAT WAS GOOD FOR THE COUNTRY WAS GOOD FOR GENERAL MOTORS AND VICE-VERSA.")

ranks armed. When the first human wave fell, the second ranks would pick up the weapons of the first and continue fighting, all in numbingly cold mountainous terrain.

At the brilliant landing at Inchon, General Douglas MacArthur had his greatest success. He was wrong about just about everything else that was to come. Commanding from the rear, in Tokyo, he ignored first-hand intelligence reports about massive Chinese involvement and troop build-up. He wanted to drive to the Yalu without the political supervision of Truman. He, along with worshipful staff underlings, thought he could do no wrong. He turned the war into a meat grinder where 70% casualties among US troops were common. The Truman administration characterized the conflict as a "police action" not a war. They were attacked by the far right for not winning, for losing China, and for not using nuclear weapons in both. The right's influence colored our politics and our military responses for a long time.

## George Hall, Trained To Kill By The US Government. Was He On His Way To Korea, Or Some Place Worse?

The US war with Korea was the situation as George Norris Hall, serial number RA 16-396-873, found it in December of 1951. He had joined the Army on December 4, 1951 with the expectation that he would be headed for Korea. He entered boot camp, basic training at Fort Leonard Wood, an army base, town, and area with limited charm. After he'd been given his army-issue haircut, he rubbed his head as all the recruits did, and found nothing up there; a symbolic shearing, shorn of hair and old ways. George smiled as he rubbed his smooth bald head and thought he was ready for the change, ready for the difference. He wasn't accomplishing anything in Burlington, Michigan, and he knew it.

His days in basic training started early and ended late. He was told what to do and did it well. He thrived on it as did his platoon, one of the best, in Co A of the 92nd AIBCCA (army infantry battalion, combat command active). He was good with a rifle and rated as a sharpshooter. He also completed a course in hand-to-hand, combat in which he excelled in spite of his small size. He enjoyed being physically active: he enjoyed the companionship. After boot camp was over he enjoyed the nearby bars and the women in them. He was approved for "leadership school," a prerequisite to OCS (officer candidate school). He'd been approved because of his good conduct and performance, but also because he'd scored well on the tests. That spring he was awaiting orders, likely to go to officer candidate school, possibly to use lethal force for Uncle Sam in Korea. It was not to be. In May of 1952 he was found out. He had forged his birth certificate. He was only sixteen years old. He was honorably discharged.

Within a month George Hall was back in Burlington, Michigan. He was with an old buddy Willie Marshall, and was driving an old car that used oil and needed some. Ed Smith's filling station was closed. They broke in, which didn't take much, took some used motor oil, some change that was in a cigar box, and a couple of candy bars. It was his first crime. Within a short time they were arrested. He was charged with and pled guilty to a felony and received two years of probation.

There was more trouble after that. The following year, 1953, he got into trouble for leaving Michigan and getting married without his probation officer's permission. They let him slide on that one, but within a few months, his wife was pregnant and had left him to return to her parents. He went up to Hastings to look for her and ended up getting into a fight at the Trio Café. He tore the place up pretty badly and just managed to get away before police came.

He heard there was a warrant out for me for malicious destruction of property, so he took off for Jamestown, New York, to look up one of his mother's old boyfriends. Jamestown didn't work out so he came back to Michigan to his grandparent's house near Burlington. Boredom won out and one night he walked into Burlington and ran into another old buddy, Esau Cole. (This is the same Esau Cole that used to throw George into fights as "bait" at the weekly movie shown on bed-sheets in the park at Burlington.) Esau was driving a fairly new Buick and was in an Army uniform. He asked George if he wanted to go to Marshall to look up some girls, George said sure. Marshall didn't like outsiders. Just inside the Marshall city limits, the police began to follow them, and Esau tromped on the gas. The car was stolen and Esau was AWOL from the Army. They crashed into a vineyard on the edge of town. Esau was hurt, but jumped out of the car and began running. George got away, but later when he tried to flag a car down to get a ride, it turned out to be a cop.

He was charged with fleeing and eluding or resisting a police officer or something like that and received 60 days in the county jail, after which my probation was revoked and I was sentenced to 2-15 years in prison.

"I did well on that first bit," George said, "ended up in a summer camp called Cassidy Lake, near Chelsea. I finished high school and was paroled, I think in May of 1955. I was a month away from being 20 years old and I had had enough of prison.

I got a job, got married again—my first wife had divorced me while I was in prison—but I had a penchant for picking winners. This one was a singer in country and western bar. We split quickly after she came home with hickeys on her neck. I was working every day and hitting the bars at night."

# Chapter 15

# BACK IN LANSING AS A BOOMTOWN

In Lansing and in Michigan in the early fifties, it was a time of guns and butter. The Lansing economy was attempting to supply the pent up demand for consumer goods resulting from the shortages of WWII, especially cars. At the same time there were substantial war contracts for the Korean War for Lansing's factories. Oldsmobile was busy selling record numbers of cars at the same time they were making compressors and turbines for the jet engine aircraft fighting in Korea. The "jet plant" on West Saginaw was 700,000 square feet in size and employed an additional 4,000 people making the turbine engines. It was the biggest plant GM had made until that time. Oldsmobile was given the sub-contract thru Buick that subcontracted with Pratt-Whitney. The turbines exceeded the quality of Pratt-Whitney's own and put out more boost. Lansing Oldsmobile's production of military hardware never exceeded 20% and they continued to prosper. But Reo had the military contract for 2 ½ ton trucks that extended into the Vietnam War era. They depended on it too much. Military production exceeded 70%. They also made lawn mowers, buses, and playground equipment, but it wasn't enough. When the Korean War was over, Reo began its death spiral. GM's trajectory went up, up, up. GM didn't need the sugar teat of military contracts, but the flavor would make GM like the future Vietnam War. They'd see it as a just anticommunist cause. The National Association of Manufacturers was fully supportive on the political lobbying front.

After the Korean War was over, MSU President John Hannah spoke at an Oldsmobile executive luncheon on November 23, 1954 to celebrate the production of the 50,000,000th General Motors automobile. Speaking to the increased output of Oldsmobile in time of peace he said:

> "And it speaks eloquently of what we can confidently expect by way of increased prosperity and employment if once we as a nation can rid ourselves of the threat of war, and be free once more to turn all of our talents and efforts to the production of peacetime goods exclusively, and get on with the unfinished American program of improving the living standards of our people..."

It wasn't to be.

RECORD SALES PRODUCING 100 CARS PER HOUR.
JOHN HANNAH SPOKE AT THE LUNCHEON CELEBRATING IT.

# Chapter 16
## EAST LANSING AND MSU

The small "downtown" of downtown East Lansing in 1955 and the college next door looked pretty much like a sleepy place in the middle nineteen-fifties, but that was deceptive. The business district was only about four blocks long. It was monochrome gray much of the year. It started east of the People's Church on the west end, went east past East Lansing State Bank, and extended just past Schnarr's Drugstore four blocks to the east on Grand River Avenue. In between were a Cunningham's Drugstore and Norm Kesel Florists across from the bank at Abbott Rd., down from the church. Other establishments included Linn's Camera, the pool hall, Ralph's Cafeteria, later Kewpees, VanderVoort's, a hardware store and a collection of men's and women's clothing stores. But across the street, John Hannah had been building.

Envisioning a bigger and better university, with a student population of 100,000 by 1970, Hannah undertook, in the early 1950s, the construction of the world's largest on-campus residential housing complex. He built one large residence hall, expanded enrollment to fill it, then used the tuition money to build another, and another, and another. He proudly proclaimed, on signs in front of newly constructed buildings like Olin Health Center, "This building is not built with state taxpayer money." State taxpayer money no, federal tax dollars yes. He built successful football and other athletic teams, realizing it was a very public and popular way to demonstrate success. He did it shrewdly and methodically as he did almost everything else. In the years spanning 1950-1965, the undergraduate population increased from 15,000 to 38,000 and the proportion of liberal arts and social science majors grew from 20 percent of the student body in 1960 to 54 percent in 1970. At the same time, federal government support of MSU expanded so that by 1960 it accounted for 69%t of the university's yearly budget appropriations. (Of the $22,369,000 in federal grants given to MSU in 1966, 18% came from AID to support overseas technical assistance programs, while the AEC, DOD, and NASA accounted for 11%.) There was no reluctance to take federal dollars, while at the same time publicizing that the buildings were not paid for with state tax money. Tuition Charlie's first term at MSU in 1964 was $79 a term for unlimited credits. To ensure that all people could attend college, John Hannah maintained a virtual open admissions policy stemming from the time of the GI Bill. Hannah worked to keep in-state tuition low. Students and parents were pleased.

John Hannah was not a simple man and does not reduce to simplicity easily. Stating the obvious, he was two kinds of men in one. His rush to "bigness," his rush to improve the world sometimes overshadowed the need to increase the quality of education. Quality of education was about more than increasing the quality of faculty. That lacking led to a tenuous "like" of the University, something less than love. When Hannah cast about for ever more money, federal money that he got for the MSUG Project that led us into Vietnam, neither side was entirely happy. John Hannah must have thought how ungrateful we all were. The students and faculty started seeing the autocratic and paternalistic cold warrior Hannah, not the kind, visionary and compassionate helpful educator. They saw themselves as numbers, in a very large and impersonal place. Hannah looked back at faculty with a somewhat jaundiced eye. As he told Milton Muelder: "Leave it to faculty and they'll run over you. You have to respect faculty, but not be captivated by faculty."

In 1955, President Hannah gave a preview of his thinking to educators and military personnel, in which he equated academic resources and human resources—the students—with any other resource.

> "Our colleges and universities must be regarded as bastions of our defense, as essential to the preservation of our country and our way of life as our supersonic bombers, nuclear powered submarines, and intercontinental ballistic missiles."

That statement summed up Hannah's thoughts that combined Marshall Plan-type internationalism with students as a university resource, his university resource, ready, and willing to serve in his military, just like in WWII. John Hannah wanted MSU students to be part of the world up to the last full measure.

## Chapter 17

## GEORGE HALL GOES BAD

"One evening in early 1955, I went to Two Johns Bar, a bar/restaurant on the outskirts of Battle Creek, and that's where Geraldine Horton entered my life. She was statuesque, an inch or two taller than me, and sexy times two. She was also fifteen years old and fresh out of Adrian Training School, none of which I knew when I picked her up.

"Gerry and I had a short fling. I took her to my apartment maybe three times, I'm not sure. We never went out on a date. It was strictly sex. She liked it and so did I. Then one day I went to her house to pick her up, and neither she nor her father were there. Her little sister let me in, and when I asked the sister to show me Gerry's room, she showed a bedroom with male clothes scattered all over the place. I asked her sister whose clothes they were, and she said her father's. It seems that Gerry's father and her shared the room. I left and didn't go back

"A short while after this incident, I was in another bar, and Gerry was there with her father. They were dancing rather intimately. It was none of my business. I wasn't in love with the girl, so I left.

"Then came my arrest one day when I reported to my parole officer. It seems another guy, Levi Goins, had attempted to rape Gerry. In the process of questioning her, the police asked her if she had had sexual intercourse before. She said yes, and gave them my name.

"I was charged with statutory rape, and I was not a happy camper. I didn't feel like I'd done anything wrong. After all these years, I still don't. But I did everything in my power to make things as bad as I could for myself. I faked an appendicitis attack, was taken to a Battle Creek Hospital, my appendix was removed, and as soon as I came out from under the ether, I got dressed and walked out of the hospital. Being the sophisticated brainiac that I was back then, of course, I went straight to my mother's house. By the time I got there the stitches were giving way and I was bleeding all over the place. I was in the bathtub trying to clean up when the police came. In retrospect, I'm pretty sure my mother called them. She was probably worried that I would kill myself.

"Anyway, when I recovered enough, I was taken back in front of the judge. Gerry's dad was there. They put me in a room with him, and he tried to talk me into pleading guilty, to make it easier on Gerry, was how I think he put it. I don't remember exactly the scenario, but I went after him. The police had to rescue him.

"I had a bench trial in front of Judge Steinbacker, was found guilty, of course, and when they brought me back for sentencing, I called the judge a swine. I have no idea why I chose 'swine' but that's what I called him. I know I was one angry young man. Steinbacker sentenced me to 8 to 20 years. Goins, by the way, got something like 3 to 10 (and the sex he had with Gerry wasn't consensual)."

## GEORGE HALL IN PRISON WAS NOT IN THE BELLY OF THE BEAST, INITIALLY

George calculated his shot carefully before hitting the ball through the first hoop with his croquet mallet. The croquet field was set up in the carefully manicured emerald green lawn surrounded by rose bushes in full bloom He was playing croquet with Rosie Heinz, the wife of Gerritt Heinz, the warden of Ionia State Prison. Rosie had taken to George after

George typed something up for her. George seemed to be able to type something up for everybody. He typed up parole officer reports, wrote parole violation field reports, "home to job reports," nearly everything for everybody dealing with parole. He had an "Outside Pass Without Custody," meaning he could leave the prison grounds almost at will, at reasonable times.

Then he met a girl named Terry Craft. He'd met her through her brother who he was in prison with. She wanted George to smuggle in a fifth of vodka to her brother, which he did. Her brother was caught with the vodka. Somebody snitched that it was George who brought it to him. His life in prison changed.

## No More Croquet

He was transferred to Jackson State Prison for "violation of trust" and was assigned to "Block 15"—solitary confinement, "the hole." Block 15 was about five feet by eight feet, dimly lit, with a slot in the door to receive food, a small sink, and a toilet. A mug with a razor was passed around two or three times a week. He was let out once a week to shower. He did not thrive.

He settled in for what to a twenty year old was "long time," twelve years. He developed a series of physical maladies related to his incarceration. He went through "anxiety neuroses. and was treated with Miltown and various other painkillers and tranquilizers. He was in and out of solitary at various times, for fighting, for smuggling tools out of the machine shop. George could protect himself, and he didn't use weapons though he was stabbed twice. George said, "One very big guy thought he was going to make a punk out of me, telling me all the things he was going to do to me sexually." George told him all the things he was going to do sexually to his mother. The guy charged. George hit him with the front of his hand in the throat where his neck met his chest. The guy dropped. George got more time in solitary.

The time did not go by quickly. He did not grow less angry. He had working stints in the prison laundry and the machine shop. He hustled gambling games, made money playing poker. He got, as he said "an education in dishonesty." Everyone had a scheme about easy money on the outside, from breaking into the many machine shops in the Detroit area and stealing their check protectors, to armed robbery.

"I met a male nurse in there that introduced me to Kant and Schopenhauer, after several weeks of reading I became an instant intellectual, an instant atheist. It didn't help my direction. When I was young I didn't go to church, but I prayed with my grandmother. I stopped all praying after that. Lack of religion didn't help me."

"I was paroled around Christmas of 1961 with a chip on my shoulder that would have provided enough lumber to build a small house. In 1955 I left prison with a firm resolve never to do wrong again. In 1961, I had every intention of getting my payback! And that's how it all began.

"The statutory rape was the major defining point in which way my life turned. Maybe I was destined to spend my life in prison, but I don't think, had Gerry not happened to me, I would have ever returned to prison. After I got out in 1961, that I was coming back was a sure bet."

## George Continues Down The Wrong Road

George was let out of prison five days before Christmas in 1961. He showed every sign of pursuing the dark pilgrimage that his black temper and blacker experiences seemed to dictate. He'd been toyed with by the judicial system. He would not be toyed with in the future by those he thought had treated him wrong. He'd seen things in prison, experienced things that no one should have to go through. The sub-culture that he'd become a part of, the socialization that he'd received, would not help him in the world outside the Michigan penitentiary system. His arrest record after that is four pages long.

## Chapter 18

## RAT-FACE LIKES HIS DRUGS

Charlie was 16 years old in 1960 when Kennedy was elected, had a paper route that covered most of the state buildings and offices in downtown Lansing. It was a good one. He had peddled his route and dropped the bound pile of papers in the lobby of the Mason Building with a resounding fwunk-thump sound. The noise echoed. Depending on how paranoid you were it either sounded like a car backfiring or a gunshot, or just a big bound stack of newspapers being dropped on the floor in a noisy way, from too high a height by an inconsiderate kid.

In addition to the Mason Building, Charlie's paper route included other buildings for state employees: the Hollister Building, the Tussing Building, as well as the Capitol and the Cass.

In the early 1950s during the Korean War, a draft-eligible young man thought that if he was convicted of arson he wouldn't be eligible for the draft. He succeeded too well. He started a fire in the Cass Building that burned for a week, and caused millions of dollars of damage, The taxpayers had to pay to repair the building, then for his imprisonment. The crown of several floors of the building was burned off. It never looked right again.

The Stevens T. Mason Building was standard cereal box modern, clad in sand-colored polished granite. It housed many of the bureaucracy's departments, from conservation to transportation. The lobby was a large expansive place, a little sterile, but not a bad place for a high school kid with some ingenuity to mess around. Also, a little discretion was needed because where Charlie put his papers down was close to the night watchmen's desk.

Charlie had time to explore after he delivered 150 or so of the then-afternoon *State Journal* papers. All he had to do at the Mason Building was collect the money that people left on top of the stack of papers that were left by the elevators. They were the ones left after finishing his deliveries in the other state buildings. He could wander around, come back and collect the money, then head home.

Arrangements were more casual then. It was before terrorism and bombings, and before the State Police were brought in to check the identification of everyone in the building. His dog Prince came with him. He was smart, appropriately friendly, politic, well liked, and he wagged his tail when he was talked to. Charlie had time on his hands while he waited for people to buy the papers. He first heard about drugs and other things in the Mason Building in 1960. He heard about them from "Ratface" Dave Smith. Ratface didn't really look like a rat. He had a kind of long narrowing face with big brown eyes that, upon first impression, would make the girls want to take him home and mother him. "He got the Rat-Face label because he acted so badly, transparently so, and everyone seemed to know it. He always seemed to be hanging around" Charlie said. Charlie was with him one afternoon and they were ramming around the neighborhood. It was a middle-class neighborhood on West Michigan Avenue, a few blocks from the state buildings. Ratface's mother worked in Governor George Romney's office at the Capitol. Charlie wasn't sure what his father did, but Ratface and his father didn't get along. He stopped at a trash barrel of a neighbor who lived several houses down. In the trash were a lot of little vials. Ratface said, "If we collect all the vials and get a few drops out of each one, there'll be enough for a shot." Charlie didn't say anything back to him except, "Yeah, I guess we could." But Charlie thought at the time, "Why?" Later, Ratface was convicted as a heroin addict and drug dealer, and became ingenious about getting medicinally pure pharmaceuticals like Oxycontin and Demerol from doctors. He got to know the guys that hung out at the Union Grill, and gave them and sold them drugs. Later he roomed with one of them, Bob Vee, a guy Charlie had known since grade school. "Vee was extraordinarily funny and talented and bright, but he didn't have enough sense to say no." Charlie said. Later on, when the drugs of Ratface and the other dealers were added to the stew of war concerns, gambling, sex and rock n roll, it taxed the Grill guys conception of their own youthful immortality, numbed out their lost optimism.

Later on that summer Charlie noticed that the money on his pile of papers was coming up short. This had never happened before. He couldn't believe that state employees were thieving a couple of dollars a day from some paper boy. The losses started happening almost every day, and they were really interfering with the profits of the route. "It made me crazy´ Charlie said. He was too restless and had too much nervous energy to sit and watch the papers when they really needed watching. One day, one of the old night watchmen said, "We got him." The "him" was Dave "Rat-face" Smith. He'd been stealing stuff from the convenience store operated by Minnie, who was blind. "Then they caught him stealing money from me. "I went looking for him found him, and pinned him up against the wall. You so-and-so. What do you think you're doing? Stealing my money? That's my *Journal* route, not yours. I'm doing all the work and you're getting all the money? You dirt-bag. Just wait" Rat-face didn't say anything. He was banned from coming into the Mason building anymore. Minnie called him a "rascal." That was an understatement.

# Chapter 19

## WHERE'S VIET NAM?

Charlie quit his paper route after sophomore year in high school in 1961. "It had been profitable, but I was afraid I would be confused with my paper-selling peers at the *Lansing State Journal's* downtown depot. The supervisor there was Bill Brown, "Brownie," short, Irish to the core, from New York, with an overpowering New York-Irish accent. He wore a fedora, pinned up in front in the 1940's newsman style, and a brown-green gabardine overcoat twelve months of the year. He drank way too much. No Damon Runyon character could have been more colorful. He was protected by Paul Martin, the publisher, who put up with the antics of Brownie and a lot of others. He was good-natured, jolly, but he had a temper. He liked me, called me Junior, liked my dog, really liked my mom. The redness in his face was a barometer of how mad he was, or how much he'd been drinking. He was taking a shower in the *Journal* locker room one day and I threw a pan of cold water on him behind his back. He chased me around the locker room screaming bloody murder. After running and laughing, mostly running, I put enough distance between the two of us to think about where the exit was and made it out the door. He couldn't follow me because he didn't have any clothes on. After my well-being was preserved I caught my breath and worried he'd have a heart attack. The next day both of us acted like nothing had happened. The *Lansing State Journal* seemed like a friendly place to me at the time. Didn't see it as a place of dim-bulb editors and trivia obsessed reporters or as a parrot for the Republican establishment of the era."

The other guys who sold papers down there were Charlie Caner and Peel, Scurvy Roy, and Potts. Charlie Caner, and Peel were both mentally handicapped; but Charlie Caner enjoyed politics and knew the name of every city councilman and county commissioner who ever was. Scurvy Roy had the nickname for a reason. Potts had a beer belly so impressively massive that, if he were female, he would look like he was carrying quadruplets. Charlie Barke was afraid he'd be lumped together with them, so he quit, even though $20 to $25 a week was good money back then, nearly enough to live on if he had not been well supported by his parents.

Charlie's neighbor Kenny Rajala helped get him the job with Western Union delivering telegrams. He was returning from his first run one Sunday morning in the summer of 1961:

Charlie said, "I was sixteen years old. The sun was mostly on my back but the air was cold enough for me to wear a light coat while riding a bike early in the day, even on a clear summer Sunday morning. I was on South Washington Avenue heading north. I rode past the Reo Plant on my right, past the Grand Trunk railroad depot that helped entice R.E. Olds to bring his factory back to Lansing. The wheels of my bike sounded out a steady drdrdrde on the red brick paving block on South Washington. I continued north past the sandy-colored, red brick trimmed R.E. Olds mansion on my left, past Governor Williams' house up Main Street, over on the right down River Street there used to be a shop of the Olds family business where R.E. tinkered on his first car many years before. Continuing north, I rode past J.C. Penney's on the corner of Kalamazoo and South Washington where I used to go with my mother to buy fabric for her sewing projects. My mother wrestled the bolts of cloth around expertly." To the seven-year-old at her side, they seemed big as airplane wings. "She looked for deals on fabric to make fancy cowboy shirts for me and slip covers for couches and chairs and anything else, animate or inanimate, that needed covering.

"I was in the 300 block south now, riding past the Woolworths where I used to read comics in the basement, past the Olds family's Hollister Building where I used to peddle papers, past Maurice's, the upscale women's store where my old girlfriend Sharon worked after high school. Maurice Tanenbaum, the owner of the store, was playing golf at Groesbeck Golf Course where I started caddying a year or so later. He quickly discovered that I knew nothing about caddying when he asked me to take him to the ball after a tee shot. I didn't have a clue where the ball was. He took me aside and said, 'You've got to follow the ball when it's hit and move your head and your eyes quickly to follow it.' He was kind, patient with me, didn't get mad at me, tipped me, taught me something.

"Continuing on, I rode past the corner of Allegan and Washington. A block up on Capitol was the Olds Tower, Lansing's only skyscraper, built of course by R.E. Olds. Several years before, I was young enough to have on short pants, seven or eight years old, though tall, and I was walking with my mother and holding her hand. A new '52 Ford convertible with the top down was stopped at the light, full of teenagers. They gave me a hard time about holding my mother's hand, jeering and guffawing. It takes forty-four muscles to frown, but only four to give someone the finger. I held my mom's hand with my left hand, and with my right hand gave them the finger. They almost fell out of the car laughing. My mother said, 'What are they laughing about?' I didn't tell her.

"Before turning left onto Michigan Avenue I looked right. Looking up to the second story in the middle of the block I saw the pool hall. Nothing going on there on Sunday morning. Only went in there once. Lot of guys in there looking for trouble. Down a block to the right was the Wentworth hotel where I used to fetch coffee for the manager of the Paramount News Shop near the corner of Michigan and Washington. He ordered his coffee with cream, no sugar, put in little half-pint glass bottles with circular paper disks for tops. The Wentworth had a second-story lounge-sun porch overhanging the sidewalk with lots of latticed panes of glass, overlooking the Avenue. The pols and the traveling salesmen used to hold forth there in their spare time. It was built with part of the reward money that Lansing's Lieutenant Luther Baker got for helping track down John Wilkes Booth after he'd assassinated Abraham Lincoln. His son, Luther H. Baker, became Mayor of East Lansing in the 1920s.

"I turned left on Michigan and parked my bike outside the Western Union Telegraph office. It was a one-story building dwarfed by the Lansing's new City Hall on the west and the bank of Lansing on the east. The Michigan Capitol was a block up at the end of East Michigan. The Olds Hotel was across the street. Only ten years before, it did not let black people stay there. R.E. was not liberal that way. Olds and Oldsmobile were everywhere, inside and outside the mind.

"I went inside the Western Union Office to get more telegrams to deliver. Western Union supplied a need. The clickity-click of its telegraph wires had long since replaced the hoof-beats of the Pony Express. First it was used for communicating over the wires pre-telephone. Then it was used for communicating the written word more quickly than mail. Shortly after that, it was the written word saying "send money." In the world pre-credit card and after, the company did and does a brisk business in providing both telegrams and money orders, cashed on site.

"I walked into the office and saw my buddy Kenny Rajala talking to the manager. The last words I heard the manager say were, 'Stay with them.' Kenny went out on his run. Later in the day I asked him, 'What was that about?' Kenny said he had to deliver a telegram to a black family on the west side. The telegram began, 'We regret to inform you…' No honor guard. Nobody from the military knocked on their door. No bedside manner. Just a kid from Western Union. 'Jesus,' Kenny said, 'I hope I don't have to do that again for a while.' Their son had been killed in Viet Nam. Kenny and I looked at each other: 'Where's Viet Nam?'"

# CHAPTER 20

# MSU'S FOREIGN POLICY

"It's like a row of dominoes. You knock over the first one, the rest fall very quickly."
—President Dwight D. Eisenhower, April 14, 1953

Working for Eisenhower, Secretary of State John Foster Dulles was trying to reclaim Southeast Asia and the world from what he thought looked like communist world conquest and domination. Eisenhower didn't send in the Marines. There had been a small mission there since 1950. He sent the CIA. He sent some bombers. He also sent MSU. Later on he'd urge JFK to send in the Marines.

Ngo Dinh Diem was installed as President of South Vietnam in July 1954 after serving as Bao Dai's prime minister. Bao Dai had been emperor, French puppet, Japanese puppet, French puppet again, then American puppet. But he'd outlived his usefulness. With Lansdale from the CIA pushing, along with the Dulles's and Fishel, Bao Dai was nudged willingly into retirement, again, and Diem was put forth to replace him as President. Almost his first official act was to have Washington send Wesley Fishel to advise him. Within a few weeks Fishel arrived in Saigon. A few weeks after that, with the artificial country on the very genuine verge of collapse, Diem asked Washington a second time for a technical aid package organized by MSU. This time Washington agreed.

There were four men from MSU initially sent on the inspection trip that followed. It included East Lansing's own

Arthur Brandstatter Sr., Dean of Police Science; James Denison, public relations specialist; Ed Widener, from political science; and Charles Killingsworth, an economist. They did their research on Vietnam on the way by reading newspaper clippings. Wesley Fishel was already there.

What they were reading wasn't good. Diem was technically in power, placed in his position by the US. He did have a small precarious base among middle-class Catholics and Saigon merchants. The French had established a deadline for pulling out and it was going to be quick. The Saigon police were controlled by a pirate sect, The Saigon mob controlled the police and had their own private army. The lowlands were controlled by private armies of religious sects including the Hao Ho, the army was starting to revolt against Diem, and the civil service was understaffed, unpaid and unmotivated. Two weeks later the four men returned to MSU and made recommendations for massive technical assistance in four areas, along the lines of a blueprint that Diem had designed at MSU while he was on the school payroll. The first was help in public administration. The second was in building a police structure and a national guard. The third was help in establishing a legislative body. The last was help in writing a constitution.

MSU's proposed contract for assistance broke down over technical issues, but in the early spring of 1955, John Hannah got a phone call. Later on, Fishel said that the phone call came from Vice-President Nixon; Hannah later denied that and said the phone call came from someone higher up than that, implying that it came from either John Foster Dulles, his brother Allen Dulles, head of the CIA, or Eisenhower himself. One can almost picture Hannah, an Eisenhower administration Assistant Secretary of Defense at the same time he was President of MSU, saluting into the phone and saying "Yes Sir." The request for the organization and the budget of the Michigan State University Group had been agreed to by the US government. It was the largest overseas technical assistance program that any university anywhere had ever been involved in. And it wasn't just technical, before the year was out, unmarked US Air Force planes flying out of Guam, started bombing Laos. Later on, Hannah was awarded the Presidential Order of Freedom with no intended irony.

The major parties at the Geneva Convention, including Russia, agreed to a partition at the 17th parallel to temporarily divide Viet Nam until elections could be held in 1956. Two temporary governments were set up, controlled by the Communists in the North, and anticommunists, substantially Catholic, in the South along with the French, and like thinking Vietnamese troops loyal to them. The U.S. did not sign the Geneva Accords. John Foster Dulles, Secretary of State, felt that it gave up too much to the Communists. Ike said that if elections were held then, Ho Chi Minh would win. The US signed a separate protocol saying we would not be bound by the agreements, but that we would not use force to oppose them. Paying lip service to that protocol helped bring MSU into the game. We had the best of intentions. We were going to use a lot of force. We were not going to allow elections. As Robert Scheer tells it:

> "The myths that they (US leaders, MSU, et al.) created, that they were "asked to step in by the Vietnamese people, that we were protecting "democracy" by blocking elections (stipulated by the Geneva Accords) remained long after Diem would be gone, And would continue to haunt white papers and succeeding Presidents speeches."

The US then moved unilaterally to replace Emperor Bao Dai, who was somewhat voluntarily ousted by the Vietnamese Communists and resurrected by the French as a figurehead. He was a flexible man who on his way out of power the first time, sold his rackets franchise to a friend in the Saigon Binh Xuyen mob that governed gambling, loan sharking and prostitution. He had no empire because he had no power. Bao Dai, the "night club" emperor, made most libertines look monkish, but he had perspective. When he was told that his favorite mistress was having relations with several French officers, he responded by saying "she is just plying her trade, I am the real whore." He had concubines tucked away in various palaces all over Saigon. He was put forth by the French as a short-term expedient to consolidate control and appeal to Viet nationalism. But the Vietnamese people knew he was only a French puppet and would not rally around him.

To the Viet Minh, the post-Geneva period was an extension of a nationalist war centered around independence and getting rid of the French colonizers. Now it was the Americans who replaced them. They wouldn't be gentle about it. To the US, Vietnam was a domino. If it fell to the communists, all Southeast Asia and more would go communist. To Dulles that could mean Japan, maybe even France, because she would be weakened by the financial strain of holding off the Viet Minh. We paid France for their financial costs while they were fighting. We were going to pay in blood as well as treasure in the near future.

### Wesley Fishel from MSU, Kingmaker

MSU Prof Fred Wickert worked under Wesley Fishel as part of the MSUG from 1955-1957. MSUG was the Michigan State University Group, an umbrella group that Eisenhower requested Hannah send to Vietnam. It would expand to more than two thousand people, filled with experts from throughout the United States. Wickert went to Viet Nam as a large-scale training expert to help construct the governmental bureaucracy of Ngo Dinh Diem. He taught personnel management and mass training classes to Vietnamese law school graduates who were slated to become provincial chiefs. According to Wickert, of the eighty-three students in his class, seventy-seven were assassinated by the communists in part either because they were perceived as outsiders, they were Catholics, and/or

WESLEY FISHEL

they replaced indigenous elected village chiefs who knew the people they were dealing with when Diem's appointees did not.

Wickert said Wesley Fishel was garrulous, charismatic, and a schmoozer. Other colleagues, besides Wickert, said his great gift was to charm and befriend people of power. He was a fluent speaker of Japanese and worked for Naval Intelligence in WWII. Joseph C. Morgan would say in a 1997 book, *The Vietnam Lobby: The American Friends off Vietnam*, published by the University of North Carolina Press, "Fishel worked for or with the CIA at the time he first encountered Diem in Japan." Morgan assumed that Fishel, as historian Garry Wills dubbed him, was one of the "Bogart professors," tough, liberal, activist, anti-communist.

After serving with distinction and physical and moral courage in the South-Pacific in WWII he became an operator. He also knew how to be a friend. He would have a friend. He would help make that friend president of South Vietnam. His friend would become the "third way," and Fishel would be a power behind the throne.

Fishel and his friend Ngo Dinh Diem were pint-sized, but had ten-gallon egos. They were made for each other. Separately they enjoyed modest accomplishments at best. Together for a time, they manipulated the most powerful country on earth, or thought they were, though it later became a question of who was manipulating whom on many levels between many players and countries and institutions. Fred Wickert said that Fishel had a "commanding presence in spite of having a fairly unimpressive physical appearance." A decade later, he came to understand that Fishel was not nearly as much "in command" as he thought he was. Neither was Diem.

Diem and Fishel met in Tokyo some time in 1950. Fishel had a PhD. from the University of Chicago and was an assistant professor at UCLA. Diem was in exile as a legitimate, courageous, but also imperious, nationalist. They were introduced by an old friend of Diem's, Japanese journalist Koyashi Komatsu, who had saved Diem from being shot by the Japanese when they had occupied Vietnam in WWII. Diem was the son of a military officer, destined by family position and training to serve in the mandarinate, the elite bureaucratic structure imposed on the Vietnamese by the Confucian Chinese during their thousand years of occupation of Vietnam. When the French followed the Chinese, early in the twentieth century, they bent the mandarinate to their purposes. Diem resigned from the government. With a sense of destiny he lobbied the French about independence, then the Japanese, and again the French, all unsuccessfully. He then lobbied the Americans with the help of Wesley Fishel. It was his most successful effort.

Fishel saw action in the South Pacific. In the aggressive US military island hopping that perplexed the Japanese, civilians as well as military, the Japanese were cornered. They were told by their leaders that the Americans would slaughter them all. Some jumped off cliffs; others sheltered themselves in caves, ready to destroy themselves and perhaps some US military as well. Fishel went into the caves and spoke Japanese to them at great personal risk. He talked them out. He saved their lives as well as the lives of our military. It would be his great humanitarian contribution. His successful WWII efforts against fascism gave him a can-do attitude. It was an attitude shared by his generation.

He took a position with MSU in the political science department in 1950. With Hannah's blessing he was going to operate for Diem. He was going to operate for MSU. He was also going to operate for himself. He thought he was going to operate for the good of our country. Fishel and Diem carried on an extensive correspondence starting from the end of WWII. They did each other favors. Fishel was going to bring Diem to MSU. He was going to make him "The One."

### Fishel Takes Diem Around

In 1953 MSU Professor Wesley Fishel convinced Diem to come to this country and MSU President John Hannah agreed to sponsor him. Diem spent the next three years in the US of A as a consultant to MSU's Government Research Bureau. It provided a paycheck. He also arranged for long-term residency. Diem was part of the Catholic elite in a country that was overwhelmingly Buddhist, which later became a big part of the problem. But while he was in this country he stayed for a time at the Maryknoll Seminaries in New York and New Jersey. His brother Bishop Can was an important contact to Catholics at Maryknoll. Maryknoll was under the jurisdiction of Cardinal Spellman, who soon became an important backer. Spellman, former Bishop of Boston, Arch-Bishop of New York, Military Bishop (of US Army), was given his Cardinal's hat by Eugenio Pacelli, Pope Pius XII, who made some very unholy alliances with Hitler and Mussolini. He was virulently anti-Communist, he appointed Cardinals who were the same. Spellman was anticommunist. Diem was anticommunist. As Spellman was quoted saying in the *New York Times* on August 31, 1954:

DIEM AND FISHEL AT MSU, 1953.

Americans must not be lulled into sleep by indifference nor be beguiled by the prospect of peaceful coexistence with Communists. How can there be peaceful coexistence between the two parties when one of them is continually clawing at the throat of the other. Do you peacefully coexist with men who would train the youth of their godless Red world?

During Diem's stay in this country, Fishel started introducing him to many influential Americans, many of them Catholic, who could help his cause. The people Diem was introduced to were politically sophisticated and liberal. Through Cardinal Spellman, Diem was introduced to Supreme Court Justice William O. Douglas. Douglas had been brought into the government by Joe Kennedy to work at the Security and Exchange Commission. He had traveled extensively in Viet Nam and wrote a book concluding that the French could not win against the communist Viet Minh. After some convincing, Douglas came to believe that Diem could be the third way that the US could back. He regarded him as "honest, independent, and [someone who] would stand firm against the French influence." At the same time he admitted that in a popularity contest Ho Chi Minh would still lead the field. Douglas then introduced Diem to Sen. Mike Mansfield, a former Asian affairs academic who was to become the Senate's leading expert on Viet Nam and an important architect in the formulation of US policy toward Vietnam in the John F. Kennedy Administration.

During this early period, 1951-54, Sen. John Kennedy and Mansfield became stern critics of the French role in Vietnam and enthusiastic supporters of an independent nationalist alternative that they would regard as the third way. Kennedy would be half right with the third way. The half that he got wrong would metastasize. They, for many years, through many blunders, would regard Ngo Dinh Diem as that alternative. The US and John Foster Dulles, after the French lost the Battle of Dien Bien Phu, needed somebody, quick. Anybody but the current occupant. Given what the State Department knew about the options, which was not much, Diem was the best of a bad lot. He became "The Answer," the "third way." He was not a French puppet or collaborationist; he was a nationalist as well as a dedicated anti-communist. He was a member of the Catholic elite, a very small elite, less than five percent. Ultimately the South Vietnamese, predominantly Buddhist, but with a melange of other religions, that included animists that believed the holy spirit dwelled in rocks, plants, and thunderstorms, ancestor worship and others, would not rally around him either. With U.S. support Diem was made Bao Dai's prime minister. Then Bao Dai again good naturedly allowed himself to be nudged aside, and Diem was named president in July 1954. Diem got MSU political science professor Wesley Fishel to South Vietnam in a hurry.

## Mr. Fishel Leaves East Lansing And Goes To Saigon. It's Not Sleepy

Saigon was already a bustling, teeming city of several million in 1955 that had grown more so with the influx of people north from the 17th parallel fleeing Communism after the Geneva Accords. One could imagine a *National Geographic* pictorial of the scene. Pretty girls were in elegant traditional women's dresses, the ao dai, a form-fitting tunic, that went from tight around the neck down to the ankles, and was split down there to nearly the waist, revealing pantaloons. All very sensual, very sexy. US troops mythologized the women, underestimated the men. (The US power structure, including those from MSU in VietNam, were going to do a lot of underestimating too.)

Others wore colorful flower-embroidered white tunics that went down below the knees of their identically covered pants. Peasants, male and female, wore dark–colored, loose pants and blouses and flattened conical hats—non la's. Children laughed while weaving their way around the obstacle courses of adult legs with practiced ease. Life was lived on the streets. Laundry hung on the lines out the windows of the apartments on second and third stories, criss-crossing the street high above. The bed-sheet flags flew, representing no nationality, no prior sacrifice, no symbol. There was no obvious call to die for a cause, just laundry, drying in the hot, humid, tropical Vietnamese sun. Everything essential to life in Saigon seemed to be carried in buckets or baskets counterbalancing each other on long poles on the shoulders of workers and peasants. The politics, though, were starting to become unbalanced. When the sun went down, everything changed

Outside Saigon, when night came, they were ready. The "they" were the nucleus, the structure of an independence-minded guerrilla army known as the Viet Minh that would carry no battle flags. They would fight and die, kill and be killed, to get the foreigners out. First there were ambushes, then sabotage, then full-scale attacks. They had already defeated the French and the Japanese invaders. The guerillas were not visible in the sun soaked streets of downtown Saigon, but they were there.

Fred Wickert, MSU professor and Michigan State University Group staffer in Viet Nam from 1955-1957 told Charlie about when he and his family first arrived in Saigon and were staying at a leading hotel:

> "Communist thugs came running through the Hotel Majestic, beating up anybody that looked European and could be French. There was a collection of fine wine in a storage area on a mezzanine floor. The communists smashed all the wine as a symbol of French occupation and decadence. The wine cascaded down the stairs and around our feet. Perle Mesta was there, along with all her baggage. She and her baggage were protected by the US Marines. We were left to fend for ourselves."

Down below, and away from the hotel, the ground was eclipsed by the humanity, the streets by the vehicles of humanity. The sidewalks, some of cobblestone, some of concrete, others of board and brick and dirt, could not be seen because they were full of people. The streets were filled with noise. There were a few autos, trucks, pedi-cabs and motorcycles, lots of bicycles and tri-shaws. As well, there was the noise of donkeys, pigs, goats and cows, the sing-song musical inflections of conversations and street-hawkers. The few cars were mostly pre- and post-war Renaults and Citroens, lots of 2CVs, and an occasional American sedan. Increasingly, but still not common, there would be the American-made limousines that carried the important to their appointments.

It was in such a chauffeur-driven automobile that Wesley Fishel rode to his meeting with President Ngo Dinh Diem. Earlier in 1955, he would not have to have been driven there because he was living at the Gia Long Palace on Cong Ly Street with Diem. But as Diem became superficially more secure, his need for Fishel's advice lessened. The April 1966 *Ramparts* article describes the scene: "The limousine, bearing license plate No. 1 from the government motor pool roared down the long driveway of the French villa, picked up speed and screeched along the road toward the palace where the President was waiting for breakfast." The peasants who scrambled out of the way may have wondered what he was about. Wesley Fishel from MSU knew what he was about. He was going to make Vietnam and the world safe from Communism, He was also going to make himself.

**MSU FACULTY LIVE WELL IN SAIGON**

Wesley Fishel from MSU, as proconsul, lived well in Saigon back in 1955 before the war got going full bore. So did his lieutenants including Brandstatter, Denison, Widener, Scigliano, and scores of others. For most of the professors, Saigon was the closest thing to the high life they had ever known. Academicians, who generally appeared to live the ascetic life, at least on the surface, were able to get in touch with their inner epicurean. Academicians and their families, perhaps at first a little awkward, fell into the ways of the former French colonists. They moved into the spacious villas in the French section, rent free. Premium liquor was available at the commissary for $2 a bottle, and servants were $20 a month. Beer was a nickel. Those less concerned with propriety who had contact with the Saigon street found women available on a short-term basis for a dollar. Longer-term relationships were available for the price of a lie and a promise to be broken.

The professors, with various "hardship" and "incentive" clauses, made close to double their normal salaries in Vietnam. A professor earning $9,000 a year for teaching class in East Lansing got $16,500 for "advising" in Vietnam—tax free. A good roast beef dinner in the student Union cafeteria was $1.20. A new car cost $1,900 in the US, a new house $3,000. The average wage was $3,851 a year.

The Viet Nam adventure also helped careers. Despite the lack of substantial scholarly research during MSUG in the fifties, two-thirds of the MSU faculty who went to Saigon got promotions either during their stay there or soon after their return. Fishel, who had little published work, and who was absent from the classroom for a year at a time, was promoted to full professor in 1957. The MSUG professors were, of course, sincere about their mission for the most part, whether they should have been or not. They had the best of intentions. There was skepticism, low level initially, in some quarters. But at least one critic became an enthusiast after a leisurely junket to Saigon on behalf of the project.

## NOT ALL OF MSU'S, AND THE USA'S EFFORTS WERE INVOLVED WITH POLICING. THEY DIDN'T ALL LIVE LIKE ARISTOCRACY. THEY WEREN'T ALL "YES" MEN

Fred Wickert talks of the time in 1955, he and MSUG anthropologist Gerald Hickey were in the central highlands interviewing tribal chiefs:

> An eight foot long cobra came after us and attacked. He fortunately mistook the warmth of the tire on our Jeep for the warmth of a human body, and attacked that instead. We stayed in huts on stilts, which kept away the tigers, but it didn't keep away the river rats. They were very sexually active, on top of us and around us, and squealed with delight. It was terrible.

The resettlement of large numbers of people fleeing the North was a double-edged situation. By 1957 Diem's resettlement goals switched from the lowlands to the highlands where tribes like the Montagnards were located. The highlands were almost a place apart. The French had sectioned off the area and it was sparsely settled except for the tribes. The French used it for producing coffee, rubber, and tea. Its cooler breezy climate was well suited to recreation and vacations from the hot and humid cities. Diem and his supporters regarded the Montagnards and the rest of the tribes as semi-nomadic, wasteful in agriculture, and without a "land tenure" system. That is they didn't buy and sell land. This meant that their concerns did not have to be taken into account. They were all regarded as ethnic minorities who were an obstacle to that great god Progress. The best way to assimilate them was to integrate them with those people coming in from the North.

The MSU Group found that Diem's approach was wrongheaded. "After being sprinkled with chicken blood by the tribal elders, the Montagnards were accepting and courteous hosts, and spoke candidly about their views on the encroaching French-speaking Catholic Viets from the North," said Wickert. The tribesmen viewed the settlers as invaders. Diem said the tribes were nomadic and wasteful. MSUG found them to be neither. They had settled agriculture and allowed fields to be fallow and to replenish. They also were found to have a land distribution system that needed to be taken into account. The resettling Viets were "squatting" on land the tribes had already cleared for planting. The Viets also called the mountaineers "moi" which means savage, and "they all thought that they were mandarins."

Resettling the highlands was all a part of Diem's open bias toward Catholic Vietnamese in all parts of the country, not just the highlands. It had a legitimate humanitarian side, in that it was enabling the Catholics to flee from the North, but it was also practical. The international Catholic Church hierarchy, the Northern Viets fleeing Communism, all were part of Diem's base of support. He had encouraged Northerners to come south by the hundreds of thousands. They received much more financial and material assistance than the Buddhists and Protestants. The Montagnards, and other non-Catholics in need of government responsiveness were pushed aside.

The civil service and military hierarchies were disproportionately Catholic in a country overwhelmingly Buddhist. Catholic financial relief aid was providing substantial help to the Catholic refugees, little to the Buddhist refugees. They were contributing some thirty-five million dollars. Because they were putting some money into the pot, they wanted to control the whole pot. Msgr. Joe Harnett, working for Cardinal Spellman, wanted to put aid in the hands of village priests. The MSUG argued that it would increase favoritism and that the priests had no time or administrative ability to dispense the aid. They put it all in a report.

The MSUG report was not well received. Control of aid and resettlement issues in the highlands were all discussed. Wolf Ladjinsky, a US agricultural expert from the New Deal, at that time a vague job description, perhaps with a CIA connection, wanted the report shelved. Wesley Fishel, to his credit, distributed it. The settlement problem was not helped when Diem, finding the report disturbing, went in 1957 to the highlands at Ban Me Thout to investigate and someone tried to assassinate him. MSUG's Wickert and Hickey knew resettlement policies would continue to have problems as a result. The Montagnards and others were urged forward in their independence sentiment by Communist propaganda.

By 1958, US policy makers considered Diem's interests, Vietnam's interests, and our interests, to be the same. Nothing was done about MSUG recommendations. Diem continued to make decisions that would lead to his downfall. A year or so later, Assistant MSUG head Bob Scigliano published an article advocating more freedom to express "opposition viewpoints." He also acknowledged that the threat of communist attack necessitated "certain restrictions of political liberty." His co-author Robert Hendy lobbied for the creation of "short range, high input aid programs for brightening the daily lives of South Vietnamese families." The balanced article angered Diem. His response was. "It reflects an ignorance of how we do things here." That article, and the increasing persistence of others, would lead to Diem's cancelling of the contract of MSUG.

DR. HANNAH ARRIVES AT AN LOC RESETTLEMENT
CAMP IN VIET NAM, 1956.

In the MSUG's final report on resettlement, they heartily patted themselves on the back, saying that the resettlement program was a success, which it in part was, in that 900,000 North Vietnamese, mostly Catholics, were successfully re-settled and housed. But it came at a great postponed cost. It alienated non-Catholics and other tribal people in addition to the Montagnards. It continued to widen the cracks in Diem's small and wobbly base.

## An Embarrassment of Riches For MSU

MSU's role in Vietnam was manifold. Between 1954 and 1962, the years MSU was involved, the US poured nearly $1.5 billion into South Vietnam to pay for its state building programs. MSU got a big share, $25 million in profits, for its role in providing everything from armaments to establishing a new secret police (VBI ) to replace the old French secret police, the Sureté, for Diem. The armaments came from the Defense Dept., and were left over from those the US gave the French in WWII. From May 1955 to June 1962, the MSU Advisory group employed over two thousand people. MSU was paid from the Foreign Operations Division, later Agency for International Development (AID—John Hannah later became Director), for the design and establishment of all parts of the South Vietnamese bureaucratic structure. All designed to save the world from Communism that would start domino fashion in Viet Nam and consume South-East Asia and stop who knows where.

John Foster Dulles was pretty much singing out of the same hymn book as the McCarthy wing of the Republican Party. China had been "lost." If we didn't step up for the French, Dulles feared that France would be so weakened it could go Communist. Greece was fighting a civil war to stop communism. And in Southeast Asia, it wouldn't stop at the water's edge; Japan too could go communist. But US military support of anti-communist forces would be in violation of the Geneva accords so Eisenhower needed to employ an alternative approach. He'd bring in "advisors" in the form of MSUG. Then Ike would recommend to JFK that he do what Ike had done only in limited fashion, expand our forces in Vietnam.

From 1954 almost through the duration, the United States was making the payroll for the South Vietnamese army. In 1955 the US said it wasn't giving out any more checks unless the Army cooperated with Diem. From that time on, Diem used the Army to crush the sects that controlled the police and elements of the Sureté. It was up to Brandstatter, the team player to rebuild the new police force. Brandstatter and the rest did this as effectively as possible. In one of his first trips to the country, rumors were afoot of an impending coup against Diem. Brandstatter personally inspected the palace guard to make sure that they had enough guns to meet the threat. The new police force would provide the base to help secure Diem a consensus government of minimal consensus. Unfortunately, it would be gained by taking dissenters to jail among other things.

Arthur Brandstatter Sr.

That new bureaucracy was increasingly used to clamp down on rival politicians and dissenters. Though the rumble of military machinery was not commonly heard on the streets of Saigon in the middle-fifties, the knock on the door in the middle of the night was. Ngo Dinh Diem's political opponents were being been taken away, often tortured, frequently raped. They were the lucky ones. Diem had given orders to his provincial chiefs to execute those who were even suspected of being Viet Minh.

## MSU Faculty Supervisors Close Their Minds And Their Eyes And "Soldier On"

In MSUG reports before the last, there appeared to be a conscious effort within the MSUG Project to prepare reports that were at least palatable to Wesley Fishel, and ultimately to John Hannah. Milton Taylor, an economics professor who was sent to Nam as a tax advisor, said that his reports were often rewritten by the project head. When he questioned the practice, he was told that there were "higher considerations" at stake. Later when Taylor returned home he was called on the carpet by Hannah. Hannah reportedly scolded him for his comments because they "helped cost MSU a large amount of money," and "frankly, Professor Taylor, you're not worth it." Other universities and institutions apparently were poaching on the same meaty contracts that MSUG had.

For the faculty on the scene, overlooking Diem's "excesses" became more and more difficult. By 1956, Diem had jailed more than 20,000 of his people, both Communists and non-Communists. Adrian Jaffe of the MSU English department, an early supporter and later critic of the university's Vietnam adventure, recalls some vivid street scenes in which, each morning, men, and more often than not women and children, were hauled out of the jail across from his office at the University of Saigon, handcuffed, thrown into a van, and driven away to an island camp, not quite a concentration camp, known as "Devils Island a la Diem." Taylor wrote that: "There is little difference seen between Diem's autocratic regime and Communism. There is little will to defend the government." Professors in the project, because of their intimacy with the Vietnamese security apparatus, knew this was happening, Jaffe said, but they said and did nothing.

At the same time in the late fifties, Fishel praised Diem with words that would have made future LBJ press secretary Jack Valenti blush. When Johnson was president and Valenti was in the room while he was talking to other people in meetings, he would rest his feet on Valenti's lap as if he was a hassock. Valenti, effusive in describing LBJ, said that he "slept better every night knowing that Lyndon Johnson was my President." Later when Charlie was a reporter out west, and Valenti was head of the Motion Picture Producers Association, he was no longer a sycophant. He was the big boss, a big jerk. Charlie talked to him about getting credentialed to see MPPA movies after he left Variety, and though he did take Charlie's phone call, "he treated me pretty much like crap. Didn't give me the credentials. Suck up, shit down, a pretty common political approach."

Later, Valenti would be the conduit for more than $50,000 in privately raised funds to give to Fishel for the Friends of Viet Nam pro-war speakers' bureau. Fishel's grad students said that over time he became disillusioned with Diem, enough to break with him. But he never lost faith in the cause. Besides, there were other people in power who he could charm. He attributed problems in Vietnam to the corruption of the system, the corruption that power causes, the nepotism that enabled so many of Diem's relatives and underlings to be part of the government, especially his brother and sister-in-law, the Nhus. They were not as well intentioned as Diem supposedly was.

The Diem regime was helped in their "efficiency" in controlling dissent by Wesley Fishel and Arthur Brandstatter. Brandstatter, the Dean of MSU's School of Police Administration was given riot guns, ammunition, tear gas, jeeps, handcuffs, and radios, left over from war material that we were going to give the French after WWII. It was originally scheduled to be distributed to municipalities for police work. It was felt that the South Vietnamese national guard, and the Vietnamese Bureau of Investigation, which replaced the old French Sureté, needed it more. Their secret police were trained by Brandstatter and it was his baby. He gave the military hardware to them. The VBI was regarded as less corrupt than the municipal police forces, which early on was in the hands of big city mobs and various religious sects. But giving VBI the guns and other military weaponry was obviously political. It had to do with the unstated MSUG mission, Brandstatter's mission, which looked with a blind eye on the consequences of giving the weaponry to an organization that was actively involved in more than police work. A big part of MSUG was about being a cover to get around the Geneva Accords. It was also about giving control, both consciously and unconsciously, to Diem's brother Nhu, and Madame. They controlled the thirteen national security agencies that "encouraged" loyalty to Diem, and suppressed dissent. We weren't supposed to be using force according to the Geneva Convention.

This was not the nostalgic "political solution" Wesley Fishel said twenty years later that he had so much favored "in the beginning." This was the beginning, and any realistic political solution was not on the table.

The 3000 strong VBI was officially tasked with responsibility in customs, immigration, revenue, and major criminal offenses. They had greater authority than local police. But as it had under French control, the VBI increasingly concerned itself with political control. They had a vast network of undercover agents. They used extreme methods which violated civil rights. MSU was also providing cover for the CIA in Vietnam and back on campus in East Lansing.

MSU student Steve Badrich was dating East Lansing's Maggie Hackett at the time; Maggie had a house on Evergreen that was a gathering place for anti-war activists. Badrich, along with Joel Schokloven, and David Hooker wrote song lyrics dedicated to Wesley Fishel to the tune of Johnny Rivers' "Secret Agent Man":

> Sitting in his office one day,
> Saigon planning tables the next day,
> Wesley always gets his way,
> He's backed by the CIA,
> Odds are he'll be anywhere tomorrow.
> Super-Fishel man, Super-Fishel man,
> Where Wesley takes his field trips,
> Not even Bond would go,
> Saigon's first regime was his creation,
> We wondered where he went that spring vacation,
> Because in the public eye,
> He's a teacher not a spy,
> A servant of the truth, and not the nation,
> Super-Fishel man, Super-Fishel man,
> We haven't lost a teacher,
> We've gained an agent man

The issue that would divide the MSU faculty, then the university, before the Viet Nam War divided the country, was providing faculty status for the Central Intelligence Agency, the CIA. The Michigan State University Group, MSUG, was increasingly used as a CIA front and stalking horse for the CIA, the State Dept., and the US military. It wouldn't know what it was getting into. Or maybe it would.

This was not the East Lansing, the sleepy East Lansing that its inhabitants thought it was. East Lansing and MSU were a town and a school with an institution-wide inferiority complex when compared to their neighbor to the southeast, the University of Michigan and all the rest of the higher status universities. MSU more or less accepted its status, except when it came to breakout football teams of the era. But the secret was revealed for the parvenu college. Its place in ascendency was being secured by substantial academic pandering and the money that came with the sale.

### See No Evil, Hear No Evil

Despite the denials of President Hannah and Fishel, CIA men were hidden within the ranks of Michigan State University professors. They were listed as members of the MSU project staff, MSUG, and were formally appointed by the University Board of Trustees. Several were given academic rank and were paid by MSUG. The CIA agents' instructions were to engage in counter-espionage and counterintelligence. Their cover was with the police administration division of the MSUG governed by Arthur Brandstatter. It appeared on the official organization chart of the MSU Project as "VBI INTERNAL SECURITY SECTION." This five-man team was the largest section within the police administration division of the MSU operation. The police administration division in turn was by far the largest of the four divisions of the MSUG. It was all a device to get around the Geneva Accords

*DEAN OF POLICE ADMINISTRATION, ARTHUR BRANSTATTER, SR., WITH SOUTH VIETNAMESE PRESIDENT DIEM, 1956.*

## IF IT WALKS LIKE A DUCK, AND TALKS LIKE A DUCK

VBI was MSU shorthand for "Vietnamese Bureau of Investigation," the new name the professors, including Brandstatter, had given the old French secret police in Vietnam, the Sureté. The head of the "Internal Security Section" of the VBI was Raymond Babineau who was in Saigon from the outset of the MSUG. The other four men hired later by MSU and listed on its staff chart as "Police Administration Specialists—Douglas Beed, William Jones, Daniel Smith, and Arthur Stein—gave their previous employment as either "investigator" or "records specialist" in the Dept. of the Army.

Despite the protests and denials of Hannah and Fishel, the CIA men were identified by two former MSUG officials, Stanley Sheinbaum and Professor Robert Scigliano, an MSU political science professor who was assistant MSUG chief from 1957-1959. Later, in the seventies, when Charlie was going to grad school in California, he took classes from Bob Scigliano. They talked about the good old days at MSU, and though they talked around the subject, Charlie never did out and out ask him why he left MSU, but his impression was that he'd been either forced out or encouraged to leave by Hannah. He'd published a paper about Diem's suppression of opposition political parties that angered Diem enough that Diem mentioned Scigliano to Hannah when Hannah visited the country. Scigliano told Charlie that he had agreed with MSU's and US goals in Vietnam, but he came to have no use for Diem and his increasingly dictatorial regime or MSU's CIA cover-up work, and later published a paper confirming that MSU provided cover for the CIA. That independence of thought couldn't have done his career at MSU any good. He left to teach at the State University of New York, then Cal State L.A., then became an academic nomad.

Though Fishel didn't disagree with Scigliano and Sheinbaum about Diem's need for reforms, he said later about them "I know of no country in the world where these 'kiss and tell' memoirs are well accepted by the people hit… It is bad manners and unethical to attack or publicly criticize people you are supposed to help while you are working for them." Fishel didn't stay loyal to Diem, but he always did stay loyal to the US anticommunist cause, and didn't understand people like Scigliano and Sheinbaum, both also anticommunist, that thought US policymakers and Diem had crossed the line.

When Sheinbaum, as part of his duties as campus coordinator, hired Smith and Jones, he recalled that he was proceeding to investigate the background of the applicants before accepting them, when he was told it wouldn't be necessary. The message came from Ralph Smuckler, a former MSUG head, and later Dean of International Programs in the expansive International Building that MSUG profits from the federal government paid for.

## Nobody in Here but Us Chickens

Scigliano said he became acquainted with the men during his first meeting with the police advisory group with Brandstatter in Saigon. He said that Babineau, whom he knew from the organizational chart as head of the VBI Internal Security, was introduced as CIA. The other CIA agents were also introduced. Babineau made a short speech in which he expressed hope that the professors and his people would get along well. Scigliano recalls Babineau saying, "We hope that we don't get in your way."

## Parlez-Vous Francais?

The entire unit went on a "hear no CIA, see no CIA basis," There was an unspoken rule that the CIA was not to be mentioned. The CIA came into the project headquarters early in the morning, stayed for about an hour, then left. They all drove their own cars and spoke French more fluently than anyone on the MSUG. They became the first people in the spy business to join the tweedy ranks. "Some of the CIA guys attained faculty status at MSU, some as lecturers, some as assistant professors, depending on their salaries. I know, because I remember signing the papers that gave them faculty rank," Sheinbaum said.

## I Broke Up With You First

The CIA stayed under the MSU bed until 1959, Scigliano and Fox state in their book that "the United States Operations Mission [that paid for everything in the MSUG] also absorbed at this time (1959) the CIA unit that had been operating within MSUG. MSU threw the CIA out, or so they said. It was unethical, but it was also untidy. It was axiomatic that academicians, trained to talk about what they know, would talk about what they knew, even if what they knew was supposed to be secret. In 1955, in academic circles, it was a rivulet of gossip. By 1959 it had become a steady stream, embarrassing and offending the academic community, even though it was not much known outside of it. Hannah tried to turn off the faucet, without success, and with widening repercussions.

MSUG operatives and MSU professors Adrian Jaffe and Arthur Taylor were for the MSU mission before they were against it. What they saw in Saigon as a part of MSUG turned them into critics, somewhat muted at first. What they said was not muted to Diem. The contract between Diem and Michigan State said that members of MSUG could not use materials gathered on the job "against the security or interests of Vietnam." Diem was also not happy that MSU was curtailing their police work after being urged by him and the US mission to expand it. Greater involvement would almost surely involve professors in the shooting of howitzers and drilling troops in the jungle, which, of course, President John F. Kennedy would have the CIA and the Green Berets doing in short order.

Despite Diem's complaints, MSU believed that its contract would be renewed in 1962.

Hannah sent Alfred Seelye, dean of the Business College, to smooth things out by telling Diem that the university was prepared to weed out any trouble makers and that they would "write scholarly scientific studies and not sensational journalistic articles." Diem was adamant that the agreement with MSU be terminated. Besides, the "secrets" were no longer secret. The Geneva Accords were being flagrantly ignored. Without a deal, Seelye returned to East Lansing and, with straight-faced hubris, announced that the contract would not be renewed to protect academic freedom and integrity. That would be the business dean's minor contribution to the coming cynicism of a generation. The air was full of lies that spring about MSU's involvement with MSUG.

Though many of those involved in the MSUG project abdicated their intellectual and moral responsibility as critics, some did not. The MSU community was the first to know, and some did their best, like Scigliano, Jaffe, Taylor and several others, despite officialdom's attempt to mute their dissent, to sound the alarm. The ones who did not, of the Brandstatter stripe, were the true believers. With pure and unwavering, if deeply flawed, idealism, they believed that the fight against communism overvalued all problems. The dissenters did not have an easy time of it.

President John Hannah didn't help. He was angry that dissenting professors did not go along with the program. He suggested that there was an "apparatus at work on campus that is a tool for international communism," and was worried that MSU would become another Berkeley. He established a special unit within the campus police to keep tabs on student and faculty political activity that was thought to be subversive or communist. It was to be known as the "Red Squad." It would only have tragi-comic consequences in the community, but would be symbolic of the developing tensions and divisions. There would be enough real tragedies and divisions to come, inside and outside the bubble of East Lansing.

# Chapter 21

# BACK AT THE UNION, WAY BACK

As early as 1905, campus leaders had called for a social and community center for students, faculty, and friends. Not until after World War I did the MSU alumni finally start a subscription drive to build a new Student Union. The announcement to build the Union was made in 1921. A nearby band played the national anthem at a nearby retreat to commemorate the war dead, and the ending of "the war to end all wars," World War I.

The building project for the Union Building started, stopped, and started again. Excavation was done by hand by students, faculty, and other interested participants. The enthusiasm that this effort created allowed the cash-strapped project to excite and interest new donors, who enabled progress on the building to move forward. The resulting publicity came to the attention of the legislature, with sympathy for the always cash-strapped college they allocated $300,000 for the project.

On the south, main entrance, porch side of the Collegiate Gothic Building, over the entrance hangs an Art Deco relief that heroically portrays the mythological figure Prometheus who brought fire and creativity to mankind. Light illuminates music, drama, sculpture, research, engineering, and agriculture. Later on, for all their sociability, the bumboys didn't do much to bring more light to any of those areas,

The cornerstone was laid in 1924 and was substantially completed in the twenties, but it was not really finished until Works Progress Administration (WPA) funds were made available during the Depression. After World War II, when returning vets started attending college in record numbers under the GI Bill, the Union was temporarily turned into a residence hall for them. An east wing, a bowling alley, and a billiard room were added at that time. This was the Union as Charlie found it in high school in 1961–62.

## THE GRILL — THE BUMBOYS

Charlie said he didn't know who came up with the term "bumboys," but they were a loose assemblage of young men or boys who hung out at the Grill and attended school, giving school light attention. Many of the bumboys had talent. They were often hustlers and con-men, dedicated to never working a 9-5 job. They fell into different generations and hierachies, which influenced their world outlooks. The older generation of "bumboys," the originals, came to MSU from the east—Boston, Jersey, Brooklyn—for a reason. Some were there just because they could pay less for out-of-state-tuition at Michigan State than they could pay for tuition in New York and the east at mostly private schools. Others were there on non-football, athletic scholarships.

Denny Diamond was part of that group. Denny was into no good stuff. "Dennis J. Diamond, Riverdale, New York" as he would courtly introduce himself. Good looking, well-dressed, garrulous, only mildly overbearing, and charming. He wore the finest quality mohair suits, stolen, and later drove a Mercedes 300SL gull-wing, likely stolen. He was not nearly as charming as he thought he was. But he was high spirited. Nearly everyone seemed to be high spirited. Everyone thought he was funny. At the time, Denny was probably into stuff that could only be imagined. He would come into town years later, whacked out on drugs and haunt everybody. But at the time he was famous for having parties, and owned a duplex on Grand River, east of Hagadorn near MSU's eastern edge, where he held the parties. He also installed a one-way mirror in the bathroom of the adjoining apartment which he rented out to coeds so that he could watch them dress and undress. This is something the Housing Inspection Dept., established years later, would never have approved.

Some of the bumboys on athletic scholarships were Ron Schwarz, swimming, the leader of that crowd, and "Tosh" Toshimura, a Japanese-American from Hawaii; also swimming. There were hockey players Dick "The Head" Wall and Irv Brodsky, from Brooklyn. Brodsky, who was Jewish, made a living on summer break selling bibles on the country by-ways to Christian farm wives. Bill Lafferty made a living buying and selling oriental rugs and antiques after he sold bibles with Brodsky. They identified themselves as seminarians to their church contacts where they were selling bibles.

Mary Lou Gillengerten's arms were demurely wrapped around her tucked-up knees as she smiled radiantly while she sat on the diving board in her one-piece bathing suit at the new Men's Intramural Building pool. It was her picture on the cover of pamphlets that MSU used to lure high schoolers to MSU. That picture was probably responsible for bringing more lusting teenage guys to MSU than all the talk about facilities, and all the scholarships offered to National Merit Scholars. She had attended EL High. So had Fred Norfleet. Fred was crazy about her but that affection was not to be returned. Fred was a bumboy but he was also a devout and sincere Christian when a lot of the bumboys were not devout about anything but gambling, and were not known for sincerity either. Fred led by example, and would urge people to be better to each other. Unfortunately he had mental problems, stemming from, the rumor went, his grandparents' belief that his father had poisoned his mother to death. Fred had a tendency to be committed to a mental institution in the winter when the snow started to come down. He passed out LP records of Handel's *Messiah* in homage to the approaching Christmas. Fred was known as Freddie No Trump.

There were no choirboys at the Grill, but someone who might have benefitted from Fred's lessons was Willard Wood "Woody" White II. Woody was the devilish part of the brotherly duo of saintly Marshall Clay White and himself. Woody looked like a choirboy. Later, in fact, he would get religion and become a monk of sorts—for a while. Marshall, his younger brother by two years, literally turned blue in the winter time, a condition attributed to juvenile diabetes, not to his blue blood. He also turned color in his fury toward some of Woody's actions. Marshall looked like a little Greek god, and was honest and straightforward. Woody was less so.

Woody's father Willard was the comptroller of Lundberg Screw Products, one of the original satellite companies capitalized by R.E. Olds at the beginning. Woody's mother Mary was a little daft, but she could give a pit bull lessons in holding on. When Woody and Marshall got close to draft age, Mary, a card-carrying Republican, called up Governor Bill Milliken and said. "Until we mine Haiphong Harbor, I'm not supporting any war in Vietnam."

Willard's brother, and Woody and Marshall's uncle, was Al White, a prominent developer, almost the only developer in East Lansing at the time. Al was part of the upper-crust gay community, didn't flaunt it, didn't conceal it. After World War II, he developed Whitehills Estates, by purchasing a parcel of land on both sides of M-78, from north of the high school all the way to Lake Lansing Road a mile or so north, and bounded by Abbott on the west and Alton on the east. He financed it at least in part with funds from Frank Jury of Jury-Rowe furniture, who was a friend. The rumor was that the parcel he sold to build the East Lansing Post Office alone paid for most of the total acreage.

Whitehills, both old, south of M-78, and new, north of M-78, were where the upper-middle class and the new rich lived in East Lansing through the fifties, sixties, and seventies. Whitehills was regarded as a step up in status from the pre-WWII housing that existed in East Lansing at the time, which was very nice in and of itself. What used to be East Lansing voting precinct 15, north of M-78 in Whitehills, was one of the two most Republican precincts in the metro Lansing area. Al would later develop Whitehills Lakes to the east and north, where the houses looked to be the size of the dormitories on MSU's Circle Drive and made the old houses of Whitehills look like huts. Whitehills residents, and the residents of suburbs like them, would be in agreement with everything that John Hannah did about protest in East Lansing. They'd be the bedrock of his support. If they'd known about MSU's involvement in Viet Nam in the fifties, which they likely didn't, they would have approved of that, too. John Hannah was a political animal and a smart one. He would initially not get too far out in front of his followers.

Woody White later become a very solicitous nephew of Al White much later in Al's waning years, and received an inheritance for his efforts. Sometime during those years of the mid-sixties, Woody took brother Marshall's black 1958 Impala Convertible and used it to steal someone's TV. He then went to the old Lucon Theatre across from campus on Grand River, got in an argument with an old EL teacher he didn't like, and pushed him through a glass door, injuring him. Then he broke into Duke's Shell Station on the corner of Harrison and Michigan Avenue. This was all in one night. A one-man crime wave. Vee would imitate and mock Woody's father, limply liberal, with a mildly rebuking voice: "Woody, you shouldn't have done that; you just shouldn't have," "To my knowledge, nothing ever happened to Woody for any of it," Charlie said. Woody later served as a medic in the U.S. Army and came back alive. It helped turn his life around.

Another older Grill bumboy was Freddie Hamilton, known as Freddie One-Trump, to distinguish him from Fred Norfleet (No Trump). Fred was the son of Carson Hamilton, an English professor who was Charlie's writing Prof. Charlie said, "When

I had him for a class the rumor was that if you wrote anything about the Vietnam War that he didn't approve of, or if you wrote anything about counter-culture activities that you did approve of, you couldn't get an A on your papers or in the class. He was an older gentleman, must have been close to retirement, must have been disappointed in his son's aversion to the 9-5 life. But he liked me, and I reciprocated by not writing about the war or anything related, and I got an A in the class. I needed the 'A's to compensate for the C's and D's I got in my other classes. A sort of beatnik-hippy girl in the class who I thought wrote wonderfully, wrote about the war negatively and got a B."

Anyway, Freddie No-Trump, who was about 25 or 26 at the time, Charlie said he was called that because he was not that good at hearts or poker, but the guys said that it was for his ability to make difficult bids in bridge, difficult to do if you didn't know what you were doing with the game, which Freddy did. It was rumored that he had some legal problems with inappropriate behavior with his underage step-daughter. The guys at the Grill thought that was funny, like everything else. Freddy was no beauty, which, combined with a ferret-like appearance, little money, and less grooming, led some to believe that he did not have much "trump." What did they know. He went on to become one of the hundred highest-ranked bridge players in the world, partnered with Charles Goren, became a member of the Bridge Hall of Fame. Later on he moved to Las Vegas and hired himself out as a partner in duplicate bridge tourney for the honor points he would garner and share with the partner. One year he placed second in his quest for the McKinney Trophy which was awarded to the world player that acquired the most honor points. His brother became a ranked chess player. What a lot of the bumboys had in common is that many of them had great mental and athletic talent but never had nine-to-five jobs. Some of the kids who hung out at the Grill were from Towar Gardens.

Towar Gardens was on the north side of Lake Lansing Rd., across the street from Al White's development on the south side of the road. It wasn't that bad by the standards of the east side of Lansing but Al White thought so little of Towar Gardens that he built a ten foot wall along the north edge of Whitehills so the residents didn't have to look at Towar across the street. They could look at the wall instead. Then, almost as an afterthought, he gave everybody on the periphery who lived in Towar money for paint, and in some cases even painted their houses, just to spruce things up a little, and, of course, not drag down the property values of Whitehills across the street.

Being from Towar Gardens didn't keep everyone from achieving social acceptability.

Larry Chappell was a Towar Gardens kid who was as socially acceptable at the Union as he was at East Lansing High where all the girls were crazy about him. He was good looking. He was affable. Larry's family were from the hills of Missouri. They were honest, hardworking people but Towar Gardens carried the stereotype of being on the wrong side of the tracks. Towar was described by East Lansing resident Karen Wallace as "a shit-hole with dirt roads," but she was proper East Lansing and was from the correct side of the tracks. The residents consisted of a few black people, quite a few Mexican Americans, and a lot of white people of modest means who kept their property up and themselves and their kids out of trouble, But the community was separated from East Lansing by more than Al White's wall. They were separated by rigid economic segregation as well. Even though Towar and the new Whitehills subdivision were across the street from each other, they each had their own grade schools. Whitehills kids had Whitelhills Elementary, Towar kids went to Donley Elementary. Though the grade schools were class-segregated, the middle school and the high school were not.

Off Larry went to middle school and high school with the bourgeoisie. He was a hit. He had slow talking southern

LARRY CHAPPELL  BILL CHALIMAN "CHAL"
EAST LANSING HIGH YEARBOOK 1964  LANSING EASTERN HIGH YEARBOOK 1962

friendliness and charm, good athletic abilities, and the body of a weight lifter even though he wasn't one. He also had enough toughness that he seldom had to prove it. Chal, Charlie's friend saw him fight once. "he had Ali quickness, hit hard, got in about twenty punches to the guy's mid-section in about two seconds. The guy closed up like a book, then keeled over." Larry crossed the class boundary with ease, not that it was that hard to cross, because the children of East Lansing, confident and open, were at least outwardly not that snobbish, and Larry fit in easily. "Larry was a couple of years younger than we were,"Charlie said, "but didn't look it." He was a kid whom everyone liked, especially the girls. He went steady with Linda Knapp in high school, then went unsteadily with many, many others. Later, testimonials of their affection would grace the walls of the women's restrooms in Paul Revere's, Beggars Banquet, and other bars in East Lansing when the town was no longer dry. Bill Chaliman, Chal, a friend from Eastern High, roomed with Larry later on in those years. Larry was talking matter of factly about his prowess with women. Chal knew women liked Larry, they were always coming around inquiring for him. Chal had doubts that he was that good. Larry said "name a woman that you can think of and I'll have her in bed." Chal went down a mental list of the women he knew and came up with the one he thought was the least likely to go to bed with Larry, and gave Larry her phone number. Larry dialed her up and started a conversation in his friendly, slow talking, drawling way: "Hi, my name is Larry Chappell, I'm a friend of Bill Chaliman's, In five minutes they were talking like they were best friends."What are you doing? Wondered if I could come over and we could talk." Over he went, they talked, had a couple of beers, talked some more. Around nine-thirty the girl said: "It's about my bedtime. You can join me if you want."

Larry started hanging out at the Union and started picking up life lesson-cues from the bumboys. They wouldn't do him any good. He never got into trouble, never did any thieving, but the lessons of his parents became dimmer, and the allure of the hustle became greater.

He worked at Oldsmobile for a while, but that only interfered with his involvement with the bar scene and the girls. He worked as a delivery man for Sohn Linen for quite some time as well.

In 1964 Larry had enough going for himself that at that time he didn't need anything that Rick had to offer in the way of gambling hustles. He was doing okay for himself. He wasn't that close to Rick or he wouldn't have hit him over the head with a tree limb on Charlie's behalf when Charlie got in a fight with Rick after high school. But as 1964 turned into 1965, then 1966, things started to change. He had a draft problem. He had a drinking problem. He acquired a wife who bore him a child. The draft and the wife and the child went away. The drinking problem stayed. He would fight it for the remainder of his life. Later on, he would be the one who brought the girls to the parties.

What was curious about some of the bumboy crowd, and some of the others, was that they referred to themselves as the "The Crew." Charlie knew it wasn't the crew where you rowed the skinny little boats that looked like big water-going centipedes. He didn't think a lot about it. It wasn't until decades later and he'd done some reading in the area, and also on the mob that he finally figured out what they were talking about and modeling themselves after. They wanted to be gangsters. Right in the halls of academe. A stone's throw from Beaumont Tower where "pinned" girls were serenaded and the carillons chimed.

Charlie got acquainted with the Union Grill scene eight years after Wesley Fishel and Diem started maneuvering. He was a senior in high school in 1961. He was pretty much accepted into a new loose clique, where he remained throughout high school, that wasn't interested in getting into trouble. He began to see and enjoy life a lot more, and stayed on more of an even keel. "The time I spent at the Grill at MSU's Student Union was very cool," Charlie said "Wesley Fishel was spending time there too, but I would not have known him if I had seen him."

The Circle Drive entrance to the Student Union was technically the front entrance. It had a half-flight of stairs winding up on each side of a patio where students could enjoy the warmth of a much appreciated sun after a long Michigan winter. It also seemed to "front" everywhere. A substantial entrance on Grand River, the main avenue through town, for whatever reason was locked to the outside but there were also entrances on the east side adjacent to the then-named Home Economics Building where Charlie's mother had taken classes some thirty years before. Since most women at the time were either "home ec" majors or education majors, a fair number of them hung out at the Grill between classes along with the bumboys, the athletes, the East Lansing High kids, and the Lansing commuter students. The entrance that Charlie and the guys he knew used was the west entrance on Abbott because it was the closest entrance if they were coming from the west, which they were, and if they were lucky they could find a parking space. An expansive lobby up a half-flight looked out on the right on an expansive lounge. Across from the lounge on the east side of the main north-south corridor was a Women's Only lounge with Pewabic tile as a wainscoat. Next to that was a phoning area containing twenty or so pay phones where students could call parents long distance, or girlfriends. Most often it was girlfriends. Unanswered phones rang late into the night from operators trying to collect additional quarters from the students for conversations that had extended long past the three dollars they had initially deposited. The telephone callers were long gone.

On the north end of the lobby was the Grill. In the basement there was the cafeteria and the pool hall. Beneath that was a bowling alley. Up above were two floors containing "ballrooms" and other meeting rooms. Pro and anti-war groups gathered there in later years.

"In 1961, some of us Eastern High guys started hanging out at the Union Grill. We all either remembered Bob Vee from Pattengill Junior High, or got to know him soon after we arrived." They also got to know the music. "The music we heard at the Grill was way ahead of what we were used to hearing," Charlie said. "Guys like Ray Charles just weren't heard that much." It was mostly black music. At the time, music was conservative and segregated. White kids listened to white music, black kids to black music. Lansing's WILS played mostly top-20 stuff that didn't do much rocking and rolling, maybe at night; Jerry Lee Lewis was played some. Jerry Lee was somewhat radical in his own right, and also disreputable because his first wife was his first-cousin, thirteen years old. There was a clear channel station out of Gallatin, Tennessee, named after Thomas Jefferson's Treasury Secretary, the Swiss-born Albert Gallatin who reduced the national debt and lowered taxes at the same time. Back in the early sixties nobody knew or cared who Gallatin was, but they cared about the station sponsored by Randy's Record Mart that played all cool black music. "Ray Charles was socially unacceptable to start with for racial reasons, but the Uhhhhh and the Ahhhh in "What'd I Say" and his other recordings were seen as "jungle rhythms" and as pelvic thrusts in the middle of the sex act. The wondrous piano and organ riffs and rhythms and melodies and velvet gravel of Ray's voice were forgotten. This was before the sexual revolution that would make Ray's moaning between the piano playing seem tame by comparison. He went on to become respectable and mainstream and make Burger King commercials.

By the time Charlie had started spending time at "The Grill," MSU's involvement in Vietnam with Michigan State University Group, MSUG, was over. The effort that involved thousands of people and hundreds of millions of dollars, that created then propped up the Diem regime, was over. But the Viet Nam War and US involvement in it was escalating. The fallout from the MSUG effort had not yet begun.

Art Brandstatter Sr. had been one of the first men on the scene for John Hannah's MSUG in Vietnam. Charlie knew his son Bob, the best of Arthur's five sons. Both Bob and brother John Brandstatter attended Lansing Community College with Charlie. Art Sr. served Hannah and the US government loyally in Vietnam. A big jovial man in his mid-fifties, Brandstatter had played talent scout for the MSUG police operation, among other things. The MSUG operation had been so big that even MSU's heralded Police Administration school wasn't big enough. He'd recruited specially trained cops from all over the country, fingerprint experts, small arms experts, intelligence experts from the Detroit Police force, the New York police force, the FBI, and even the Dept. of Defense. All had MSU faculty status. The professors were activists in international relations and policing, the CIA and the cops were professors. They were all on the MSU payroll, all paid for by the feds. Things were starting to get weird.

## Chapter 22

## GEORGE HALL MOSTLY STAYS OUT OF TROUBLE

George Hall's move to Lansing for a new start was going fairly well. He'd committed some frauds and robberies and had just been released from Jackson Prison. His start in Lansing was fairly auspicious. He bounced around some. After working at Industrial Die he worked at Olds, then worked as a business machine salesman. He also started gambling more, did some bookmaking aided by front money from prosperous bookmaker Ike Johns. Only when drinking and or coming down from Dexedrine highs did he have trouble with the police. He mostly stayed out of trouble… in Lansing.

George presented a good appearance. He was clean-cut, slightly baby-faced, with well-barbered wavy hair. He always wore a sport coat and could have been mistaken for a graduate student in the early sixties. He also had an air of extreme alertness, aided by a penchant for Dexedrine, which he called L.A. Turnarounds because, George said, "You could drive to L.A. and halfway back before you came down." He carried a briefcase but, unlike a graduate student, in his briefcase was a gun, not textbooks. Paradoxically and stranger still, it was a realistic plastic toy gun. It meant that, at this stage of George's life, he didn't want to hurt anybody. In George's mind, it made more sense than it does in ours, because George had no fear. He was more than willing to fight if provoked, pretty much anybody, no matter how big, so the plastic gun was designed to warn people away from him if need be.

There were two kinds of testosterone-fueled tough guys in the broader Lansing-East Lansing community at that time. The first was a small group who would fight about anything at any time and carry an argument or a fight as far as it would go, even if it included knives or guns or death. The other group was just about everybody else, including tough guys who really didn't want to hurt anybody badly, and could accept being beaten in a fight; and athletes who, as hyper-competitive as they were, understood that all the games count one, and that there was always another game on the morrow. The bumboys fell into the last group. The first group included men who were sent early to prisons and graveyards. George Hall was part of the first group. With great conviction and no impulse control when drinking, no confrontation or problem was too small to maximize. The rage of spending six years in an eight foot by five foot cell when he hadn't done anything wrong would not go away. He would not be silenced. He would not be smothered. He demanded justice and satisfaction in all things.

# Chapter 23

# RICK FOWLER, BETTER THAN BUBBA?

"Rick's World," Rick's movie, had a fantasy aspect to it that might have seemed strange and farcical to an observer. Rick's brain, inside and outside, was jumbled up with a combination of reality, fantasy, and romantic waltz with himself. He was the most amazing and reverential of men to himself. It was a vision more powerful than any of the drugs that Vee and the others were taking. He'd been that way since he was a young boy. Winning a bet, winning a contest, was even more pleasurable than sex to Rick, plus he liked the money, but it was mostly about winning, putting it over on somebody.

To give his world some reality, Rick studied and practiced. He had a technical approach to just about everything, as well as cards. He was a very good arm wrestler. He could beat everyone at East Lansing High, and moved on to the athletes in the Grill, for money, of course. It was always about the money. He engaged in strengthening exercises. He lifted weights. But a lot of the guys lifted weights. The MSU athletes lifted weights, were bigger and stronger, and spent more time at it. They had a professional approach. How to beat them? He decided it was all in the wrists. They might be able to bench press several hundred pounds, lift the back of a car a foot in the air, and make the crowds roar on Saturday afternoons, but there was nothing in the conditioning and weight rooms that spent any time with wrists. Rick did. He beat football players Ed Budde and Jim Behrman, beat Skip McHolley. And best of all, and the most ego-inflating, he beat football star Bubba Smith. Beat Bubba!

And it was for $10, twice! How good was that? His muscles didn't get any bigger, but his head and his swagger did.

Rick's ego didn't need inflating. He was already totally impressed with himself, which led to still more interior fantasy with or without exterior confirmation. It was 1964 when he was beating Bubba. He was only two years out of high school, barely twenty years old—beating one of the best athletes in the land at a physical contest, no matter that it mostly involved muscles of the wrist, no thinking or judgment.

Charlie's Eastern High friend Bill Chaliman trimmed trees for the City of Lansing in the summertime along with a lot of former area high school football players and wrestlers. Chal was on a different crew than Charlie was. One of the guys on the crew was a guy named Gordy Reese, a quiet unassuming guy, a gentle man. He also was as big as a house and a champion Big 10 weight lifter. Chal, whether out of mischief, or just wanting to see a good match, suggested an arm-wrestling contest. Gordy immediately agreed, as did Rick. There was quite a turnout.

Rick had bet a fair amount of money on himself, about $100. A hundred dollars was a good week's wage and would buy a good used car. There were a lot of side bets. The place for the contest was a cement table outside the south side of the new Men's Intramural Building Pool where Mary Lou Gillengerten had so famously had her picture taken perched on the diving board a few years before. It was next door to the football stadium, south across the banks of the Red Cedar about a quarter mile from the Student Union.

Forty or fifty people gathered around to watch, about half Grill rats and half very big, muscular guys, friends of Gordy Reese, fellow weight lifters. There wasn't much talk; they just got down to business, their muscular right arms planted on the table saluting each other, then gripping each other's hands. The signal to begin was given. For a moment, nothing happened. It was like a freeze-frame photograph, everything and everyone stock still. Then muscles started to tremble and shake, veins on the foreheads of Reese and Fowler started pulsating. Beads of sweat dripped off their foreheads and spotted the top of the cement table. They leaned into each other. Still nothing happened. Then, slowly, like a mighty tree starting to fall in the forest after a chain saw had cut its last link with the sky, Rick's arm started, ever so slowly, to go backward. Could it be so? He'd never lost. Backward another half inch, then another Then his sweaty wrist started to slip slowly away from Gordy's grip. First it slipped an inch, then the slip accelerated. Reese was left only with fingers, like a bad handshake. Then he was left with nothing. He was gripping only air. Rick was cheating. Reese said, "You can't do that." They tried it again. Rick slipped his wrist out again. "Okay, Rick," Gordy said, getting up from the table, understood that Rick wasn't going to play fair and that it was senseless to continue. He gave Rick a cold look. It looked like he was thinking about beating Rick's ass. Gordy's friends gathered around him like they liked the idea.

Rick was all alone. He had friends there, but they weren't the kind of friends who would back him up in a fight. Rick was losing a lot of face, but he wouldn't lose his money. He once again proved that it was all in the wrist; in this case it was about letting his wrist get bent over backward so his opponent had nothing to grip and nothing to pin. He didn't get pinned, so he technically didn't get beat and technically he didn't have to pay. It was the high school wrestling match against Emerson Boles all over again. It wasn't a technical defeat. It was a "corn-beef" of significant proportions, flim-flam or cheating, either conspicuous or inconspicuous. Gordy and his buddies murmured to each other but they didn't do anything. They were athletes. They were civilized. Rick looked abashed, humbled, but he wasn't. He didn't give Gordy any money. Rick thought he was wonderful. He could care less about the "face." With Rick it was all about the money. He'd made a good read, a good call, kept his money.

# Chapter 24

## FIRST BEER, THEN MSU

In the fall of 1961, Charlie, still in high school, was standing in the chill outside The Beer Depot, a beer and liquor store on the corner of Kalamazoo and Detroit Street on the border of Urbandale. Clinton liked the sound of "Detroit Street" because it sounded tough like Detroit. On the other side of the Kalamazoo Street Bridge, a half mile to the east, was the Michigan State University campus, the college known to all as MSU. It was a long way from Urbandale metaphorically speaking. The State Capitol was up Michigan Avenue two and a half miles west. The beer store was shiny turquoise concrete block. The smell inside was a combination of old wood floors, stale candy, stale beer, and cigarette smoke, mixed up with the icy fall air. Charlie always liked that smell. A neon Pfeiffer Beer cartoon fifer was in the window, tootling away and promising transport to anyone who drank Pfeiffer beer and got a buzz on. Off they'd go to some better place with a vague regimental bond, where the pleasantness of the buzz and the unit cohesion of the drinkers transcended all.

They, along with Clinton's buddy Dave, were trying to get someone to buy them some beer. They were on their way to a party in Urbandale, a friendly place, no pretensions, no grandeur, not much level or plumb with housing or people, who were mostly black, and older. Urbandale was a ghetto before we knew what the word meant. It was also invisible—to the citizenry, to the police, and to housing code inspectors. The citizenry didn't see it because it was tucked into a curve of the Red Cedar River, and you wouldn't and couldn't drive through it to get from here to there. Nor was it the kind of place you'd go sightseeing on Sunday afternoons. Lansing City police didn't patrol it because it wasn't part of the city; it was part of the township.

The shacks and houses and even the people seemed to lean against one another as if for mutual support. The predominant building materials of the poorer houses were tar paper and corrugated cardboard. Miss Jones lived in such a tumble-down house.

They drove to the home of Miss Jones, then knocked on the door inside her little lean-to front porch. Part of a curtain was drawn diagonally across a pane of window revealing the skeptical and curious eye of Miss Jones. She opened the door and invited us in. She was a black woman of indeterminate age, not young. Her mouth and lower lip were defective so that she could not contain her saliva in her mouth. She drooled and spoke somewhat unclearly, wiping off her drool with a handkerchief. Dave understood her perfectly. "Dr. Bear," her significant other, tended to her like she was the Queen of Sheba. She liked Dave and Dave made small talk and flirted with her. Dave was older, well built, muscular, and handsome despite a mean look that was not totally concealed by smooth talk. Charlie was pretty much adolescent scrawny. Clinton was adolescent pudgy.

Dave finally got to the point, which was, "Would Dr. Bear go get us some beer?" Miss Jones, speaking for him, said, "Anything for you, Dave. They all got into Clinton's car with Doc and drove back to the Depot, which was just down the street and around the corner. They gave him four dollars for a case of Stroh's and in a couple of minutes Dr. Bear was back. He gave them the change. They gave him a six pack and dropped him off back at Miss Jones'.

They arrived late to the party. Cars lined both sides of the road, like giant, serpent-like, post-apocalyptic metallic hedges that delineated the street on a very dark night. The lines of cars began fifty yards before they got to the house, a sign of a good party. They entered the house by the front door and saw a hundred people, mostly black, in a room meant for twenty. A sea of bombed humanity weaved back and forth to the music, A stratum of cigarette smoke hung head high over the rooms with the crowns of the narrow brim homburgs that some of the guys were wearing sticking up above the layer of smoke and bobbing up and down like corks. It was difficult to see, but Charlie recognized one face belonging to Louis Andrews, a tall lean dapper African-American, mad at everything. "He'd been kicked out of Sexton, the west-side high school, and was going to Eastern with us," Charlie said. "I made a mental note the first time I saw him to stay far away from him."

If they'd had followed Charlie's plan, they would have just gone around the crowd of dancers and straight into the kitchen where the keg was, but Dave had to go through the crowd and make smooth small talk with everyone. Charlie was unavoidably being brought into the proximity of Louis Andrews. "He was slow dancing with a beautiful mulatto girl," Charlie said. Dave came up to them, rubbed her butt and smiled at her. Louis pulled out a chrome-plated pistol, swung it in an arc past Charlie's nose, shoved it under Dave's chin, and cocked it. The dancing stopped. The music stopped. Dave started talking like he was surprised and embarrassed for Louis for violating Emily Post etiquette in social situations like that. Louis just looked at him. Dave kept on talking. Charlie said he was surprised that Louis didn't shoot him; Charlie left, in a hurry. He never even had a chance to have a beer.

Outside, it was cold and starting to rain. He walked north up to Kalamazoo Street. Dagwood's Tavern was on the corner of Kalamazoo and Clippert. He went in to get out of the rain. He was shaking, not from the cold but from having a gun pointed in his direction. The bar was full. People munching on their cheeseburgers, topped with thick slices of onion, fried mushrooms on the side, washed down with beer. They looked peaceful, like they belonged there, not wanting to hurt anybody, not afraid of being hurt. Charlie dried out, calmed down a little bit, but still had so much nervous energy that he felt like walking, felt like pondering some life changes. Didn't want to be part of Clinton's and Dave's death wishes.

He walked east on Kalamazoo toward Michigan State's campus a half mile east. When he got on campus, things seemed cleaner and safer than they were in Urbandale, even in the dark and the fog and the rain. On his right, lined up in rank and row, were steel half-can-like humps, the quonset huts that once housed married World War II veterans after the war. . .

He passed Jenison Fieldhouse, where basketball, indoor track, gymnastics, and wrestling teams competed. It was all quiet, mausoleum-like with the lights out and the crowds gone. He passed Demonstration Hall, which housed ROTC as well as the ice rink where varsity hockey was played. Charlie and friends from the neighborhood used to skate there on Saturday and Sunday afternoons to live Hammond organ music. The organ played the songs of the day in spirited fashion but took the sharp edges off the songs in a churchy sort of way. Carol Heiss trained there for the Olympics and endured the harsh criticism of her coach, a French-Canadian who Charlie thought was mean, but Charlie didn't know much about being trained. The East Lansing High girls like Toni Tryon, the unobtainables, taught the younger kids their figures. Charlie idolized her from afar.

He stopped at the statue of Sparty, the MSU mascot. He was spare and magnificent, and glistened in the rain, holding his helmet, ever vigilant, like only a statue can. He was a symbol of manly discipline and endurance like the Spartans at Thermopylae who held the pass against a hugely larger Persian Army. The MSU Spartans as underdogs had to try harder, do more with less, overcome their inferior status as a land grant agricultural school. In their battle for dollars from federal grants MSU won the battle.

Charlie thought that finding a new peer group might be a good idea. He crossed Circle Drive and walked past Cowles

House where President Hannah lived. The lights were all on. He kept going, up to the Union Building. It was closed and dark and locked. If it had been open, he wouldn't have known many people anyhow, maybe Bob VerPlanck, Bob Vee. He walked home up Michigan Avenue. The Capitol, dim in the distance looked like a sodden wedding cake

## BOB VEE

"All the good men I know are dead, and I'm not feeling well myself" was the inscription in Vee's yearbook, from East Lansing High, Class of 1962. Starting in the Grill, Bob Verplanck, Vee, became good friends with many back in 1961. (He also became very good friends with Prudy Shelley, who was going to marry Rick Fowler; and Karen Wallace who was going to marry Dave Lawson.) Vee, as everyone called him, was tall, blonde, blue eyed, humorous with a light touch, and very bright. Charlie had gone to school with him several years before at Fairview Elementary in Lansing. "In a deerskin coat with fringe across the chest and down the sleeves, he made the girls' hearts do whatever it was that girls' hearts did back in fifth and sixth grade. I don't think he had any enemies," Charlie said. The only people he ever angered, mostly adults, were those who years later became offended by the sight of him destroying himself. That and the fact that he had way less sense than the rest about drugs and alcohol, no sense of mortality at all.

Bob Vee's mother was Madeline VerPlanck, nee Snedeker, but she was popularly known as Martha Dixon, hostess of the local TV cooking show, *The Copper Kettle*. As a cooking show hostess and careerist, she was way ahead of her time. His father, Russell VerPlanck, was the manager of Lansing's Civic Center. The two of them made more money than most of the families whose kids went to Fairview School. In 1957 they moved to Audubon Avenue in East Lansing where their backyard abutted Glencairn School.

BOB VERPLANCK "BOB VEE"
EAST LANSING HIGH YEARBOOK 1962

Vee was athletic, but was severely asthmatic so did not play high school sports. When Charlie saw him again at the Union Grill, he was friendly in an off-hand sarcastic kind of way, and they talked like it was almost yesterday that they'd gone to Fairview School together. He hardly remembered Nancy Blink. He didn't remember her affection for him at all. Instead, he spoke of his affection for a girl named Gloria Peña. She was from Venezuela and was attending East Lansing High. She moved back to Venezuela when they were sophomores. She had been spoken for in marriage at the age of ten.

"He didn't seem to be looking at life with the same yearning and desperation that we were. And why was that? Was he as fatalistic as his yearbook suggested. I don't think quite. Mostly I think it was because he didn't have much use for the success stories as they were played out in East Lansing, Michigan, though he never said so in those terms." Charlie said.

Starting in junior high school, maybe even earlier, Vee's mother was having an ill-concealed, affair with Hal Gross, who was the owner of WJIM-TV, WJIM-Radio, and more business entities than could be counted. Gross was reputed to have secured his license in part because of his Democratic Party connections in the early fifties. He was no bleeding heart, and in fact he made others bleed—for their money. It was said that he might be the one person who could get blood out of a turnip. Much later, the sale of WJIM was forced politically because of ad "clipping" and political editorializing, all against FCC regulations. Various succeeding corporations who owned the station represented themselves as white knights, but were discovered to be just as venal as Hal Gross. A WJIM employee who had a responsible position there over many years once told Charlie after the station had been flipped a couple of times: "It just shows you that Hal Gross was not the only son-of-a-bitch in the TV business." Later on in the protest era, Gross' news department did not cover housing protests, anti-war protests, on campus or anywhere else. For anyone who got their local news from local TV, the protest didn't exist.

Anyway, Hal's WJIM was one of the few TV stations—and the only CBS network affiliate— outside Detroit in the state of Michigan. He would vie with Lyndon Johnson's affiliate in Austin, Texas, for the lockup in a market. The awarding of a license to ride on the people's airwaves was politically determined for Gross, just like it was for Lyndon Johnson. For Gross, not as well connected as Lyndon Johnson, it was not a sure bet. It came in. Even Gross, with a sure and insightful instinct about business, was doubtful enough about the success of his license, or at any rate said he was, that he designed the "Country-house," the station's business offices on East Saginaw, in a "U" shape around a swimming pool. If the station failed, he could turn the business offices into a motel. He would not fail.

The TV license would be a license to print money. The station became one of the most profitable, if not the most profitable, of any TV station with a similar-sized market in the country. The offices in the "Country-house" set the industry standard for a suburbanite-type tasteful luxury in the era of the fifties.

Inside the glass-enclosed entryway and to the right was a big room that could serve as a conference room and a dining room, and not so surprisingly, also had a very expensively appointed bright and shiny copper-clad kitchen where Martha Dixon cooked and televised *The Copper Kettle*. Though Hal and Martha had obviously cooked something up, the heat was at a moderate and steady temperature. Hal was never to divorce his wife, and Martha was not to divorce Russ until Vee was out of high school.

Martha loved strongly, loved well, loved with focus. First she loved her half-brother and two sisters who she dropped out of school in the sixth grade to raise in the absence of her own mother who was out carousing. Then she loved her husband, the handsome, eligible Russell, the most eligible man in Jackson, Michigan. He owned a bar there and was nearly at the end game as an alcoholic, "was waltzing on a regular basis with the pink elephants" Vee said, when Martha was able to get Russ to stop drinking. She loved her first-born prodigal son Bob (Vee ) "Idolized him" Vee's brother Tom said. She also loved her baby boy Tom. She mentored and nurtured many a newscaster and sportscaster at WJIM. By the time Vee was in junior high school, Martha had moved on from Russ and fallen for Hal. Vee never forgave her. He still respected her, and he feared her somewhat, but he did not forgive her for betraying Russ. He loved his father, but showed him no deference and had no fear of him like most of us did with our fathers. He did not call him Dad or Pops like we called our fathers, he called him Russ. They were more like peers. Perhaps Bob had sympathy mixed in with a little contempt for the cuckold. He would not be nurtured by Martha or anybody else. He would not be put in a position to be in love and be betrayed.

121

At any rate, Vee never screamed, never got angry in any way that was threatening. He had a sharp tongue with an edge and sometimes used it, but seldom with real meanness. When he did lose his temper, it was always under the influence of something. He did what he did best, which was to demonstrate his talent, at humor and wit, at pool and poker, at everything but school, which he wasn't bad at either.

The great Bob Vee. The Golden Boy. He knew he was good looking. He knew he was charismatic and had the ability to get people to do what he wanted them to do. But all his life, he was unwitting, unaware, and unconscious of himself as a leader, even though a leader he was. He didn't lead for self-gain, for aggrandizement, or for any noble or ignoble purpose. Mostly he led to the next party. "His definition of a party changed from ours in the years ahead," Charlie said. "Ours was the quest to find the holy grail of a party where there would be a big crowd, the crowd would be connected to the common pulse of the music and move to the rhythms of it and would be scanned for the 'It' girl somewhere in the room."

The time he spent with the highly political Dave Lawson only confirmed his suspicions about the vanity and illusion of material success. Dave was a couple of years older, graduated from EL High in 1960, and attended the University of Michigan as a math major, but he always seemed to be around. Vee, later on, spent a lot of time with Rick Fowler's wife Prudy.

Vee's goal would be to take bits and pieces of the counter-cultural life and try and make something of them. They were puzzle pieces of the Age of Aquarius and Dionysius, the anti-war movement, the drug culture, the rejection of 9 to 5, the rejection of white-collars as clean. He would try and cobble together a life that didn't involve a lot of moral compromises and did involve physically active productive work. It also involved taking large amounts of drugs and alcohol. He almost made it. He got a lot of his ideas from radical Dave Lawson, sincere, kind, and smart.

Vee was a lot of fun, always funny in the most trying circumstances, and during those early years of the sixties was the perfect person to help Charlie gain entry into the goings on of East Lansing and the Grill. He of course, would also not have known who Wesley Fishel was either, when Fishel spent time at the Grill between the times he took up residency in Saigon.

## Sports

It wasn't always easy to talk sports. It was a time-honored tradition that when one of the guys went to pick up another of the guys, small talk would be made with the parent who invited them in. One night, Vee was over at Charlie's house on Sheridan St in Lansing, waiting for him to get ready. The great lingua franca in East Lansing was sports talk. Charlie's father was older than the rest of the guys' fathers, a little remote, tired, and worn down from overwork, and a little deaf.

"How're you doing, Mr. Barke?" Vee asked.
Silence.
Charlie's father was behind his paper reading.
"HOW'RE YOU DOING, MR. BARKE?" Vee asked again, more loudly.
"Well good," Charlie's Dad said, as he put down the paper to talk. "I expect I'll live."
"How do you think the Spartans are doing?"
"Who?"
"You know, the Spartans, MSU's football team."
"Well, I hear they're supposed to be pretty good," Charlie's Dad said.
Vee thought he'd try a different sport. "What do you think about round-ball this winter?"
"What ball?"
"You know, basketball."
"Well, I just don't know…"

Basketball had barely been invented when Charlie's dad was growing up. Actually, if Vee had tried boxing, Charlie's dad could have given Vee an education on the Louis-Schmeling fight of thirty years before. He watched the Wednesday night fights sponsored by Gillette, where the boxing ring bell went "Ding" and the sing-song jingle started out "Be smart, and be on the ball" and closed with "Gillette Blue Blades we mean." But Vee didn't go there and he also didn't play pool with Charlie Barke's father, who as unlikely as Vee might have thought it, could have given Vee a run for his money. Forever after, when nothing much was going on, Vee would say, "We could always go talk sports with Barke's old man."

Sports were just about everything to the guys, by any Webster's definition both archaic or current: "a chance to make merry, divert, amuse, cheer"; "to expend money in gambling, wager, bet"; "to expend wastefully or carelessly (as in riotous living)" "to spend lavishly and ostentatiously" "amuse by light and playful activity. To speak and act jestingly without consideration;" "game or contest in which skill or physical prowess is used and on which money is staked." They were "into" sports. They were sports. It was sports virtually 24-7, when not distracted by drinking or women. The bumboys were not at all distracted by school.

Football coach and MSU player Hank Bullough said John Hannah told him not to recruit guys from the east coast. "They're too much trouble." Hannah told Hank. "They're like you Charlie, left-wingers, trouble-makers." The guys from the East that hung out at the Grill, the non-football players, may have been trouble but it wasn't because they were left-wingers, they were totally apolitical. Many were athletic as well. Schwartz, Tosh, and Barratt had swimming or golf scholarships. Bob Ciaffoni was a particularly honorable and good guy who moved to Vegas, placed second in a big poker tournament, and won $250,000 (it would be equivalent to $1,000,000 now), then wrote a couple of books on Texas Hold'em poker.

# Chapter 25

## DIEM COMES BACK TO TOWN

NGO DINH DIEM RETURNS TO MSU (WHERE HE BEGAN HIS RISE TO POWER), FOR WHAT WAS SUPPOSED TO BE A "VICTORY LAP" IN 1957. HE HAD HANNAH'S BLESSING.

In a period of optimism about Diem in 1957, Diem returned to where he first got help in his quest for the presidency of South Vietnam. His first stop was in Washington. Ike said to Diem, "Your patriotism is of the highest order… an inspiration to all the world." Diem said to Ike: "Your faith in my country has produced the miracle of Vietnam." He then returned to MSU to receive an honorary degree. Michigan Governor G. Mennen Williams declared "Ngo Dinh Diem Day." He was greeted at Lansing's airport by John Hannah, Wesley Fishel, Lansing business and government leaders, and state and university officials. Diem was at the head of a long procession of new Oldsmobiles led by a police escort, also driving new Oldsmobiles, that took President Diem back to campus where he got his start. He addressed an audience of 4,000, all interested in his remarks about keeping Southeast Asia safe from communism. The man who introduced him was uber-press agent and cheerleader-in-chief Wesley Fishel. Godfather John Hannah watched from the wings approvingly. Hannah said at the time: "Although it [South Vietnam] is not yet a perfect Jeffersonian democracy, it has established the foundations of a democratic government."

After Diem's remarks, Governor G. Mennen "Soapy" Williams presented Diem with one of his trademark green and white bowties. He said he hoped it would "bring Diem luck in his future political efforts as it had for him." Diem responded by saying, "I don't know if what works (as good luck) in your country will work in mine. Three weeks ago I was fortunate to escape assassination." In the coming years, the military and political situation deteriorated, assassination attempts continued.

In a 1961 memo to Diem from Wesley Fishel that Fishel said he passed on to national security advisor McGeorge Bundy, and other Kennedy staffers, Fishel said:

> "There is a profound deterioration, politically, socially, and psychologically (in Vietnam)… Militarily, the recent influx of thousands of American officers and men

is starting to make a distinct change... turning what was a minus into plus. (But) I find it hard to believe that (long term) the Chinese and Viet Cong will allow the challenge to go unmet... I don't mean an invasion out of the North, but a heavily intensified terror campaign that may spread to the cities with the intent of panicking the populace and weakening Diem more.

Unless Vietnam experiences a major and favorable psychological shock within the next few months, I doubt whether they will be able to survive because the regime has failed to mobilize the hearts and minds of the people."

# Chapter 26

# JFK GETS US IN DEEPER

Charlie Barke had a *Lansing State Journal* paper route in the state office buildings that included the Capitol Building. JFK came to town to campaign. "He talked about a missile gap [in which the Russians supposedly had more ICBM missiles than the US]," Charlie said. "I listened to him while I was peddling my papers. The talk about a 'missile gap' wasn't accurate. But Kennedy 'out-Nixoned' Nixon in the demagoging department and he won."

He exhibited all the Kennedy talent, all the Kennedy grace, He was a war hero with a beautiful cultured wife and a staff of the best and the brightest, mostly from the Ivy League, especially Harvard. They would be doers and shakers, wouldn't be bound by the normal political limits, the normal limits of political reality. Speaker of the House Sam Rayburn said about them, "Some of those guys should have had to run for county Sheriff." Lyndon Johnson as Vice-President said "those Harvard's know as much about politics as an old maid does about fucking." (Later as President LBJ would get taken in by the Harvard's about foreign relations and politics too.) Clark Clifford, an advisor to many Presidents, observed them from the beginning and said "Oh boy, they think they're going to change politics, change government—like a road sign that says, 'Brilliance Ahead.' Three months later, I saw the roof fall in."

Six months after Charlie listened to Kennedy's campaign speech, in his inaugural address he said, "We shall pay any price, bear any burden… support any friend, oppose any foe…

to assure the survival and success of liberty." From the moment JFK uttered the last syllable of the last word of his oath of office and the loudspeakers echoed his words out over the National Mall, he came to own a difficult geopolitical situation passed on to him from the Eisenhower Administration. It was an attempt by the US to remove Fidel Castro from power.

The CIA was going to use Cuban exiles to invade Cuba. At the same time Kennedy was taking his oath, the Alabama National Guard was training Cuban exiles in Guatemala. Kennedy had met with Eisenhower the day before. Ike urged him to push on with existing plans. Kennedy did. He would be true to our bi-partisan foreign policy and true to his words in the inaugural. His involvement, known as the Bay of Pigs fiasco marred the Kennedy presidency and affected his decisions about Vietnam.

With bad intelligence about a Spanish culture about which they knew little, the CIA provided the president with more bad intelligence. The reconnaissance was worse. The attacking exiles were supposed to have an escape route to the mountains in case of failure. They were dropped off in a swamp with no escape route. The military and the CIA said Castro forces would not be able to get to the remote area in less than twenty-four hours. They were there in four, with armed Cuban peasants for back-up. The result was a looming disaster. All that could save the men was action by the U.S. military in the form of aircraft to strafe the oncoming Cuban troops. Kennedy didn't do it. He pulled the plug.

John Kennedy, a courageous man, pulled the plug, didn't provide the air cover, abandoned other courageous men in their fight against Castro. He took a beating in the press. He took a beating from the right wing. JFK the war hero, and the equally courageous Bobby Kennedy were not used to being accused of lacking courage. His critics tormented him psychologically. They restricted his ability to maneuver in foreign relations, including his options in Vietnam. His reputation for courage, his manhood, had to be maintained. He shared the optimism of his WWII generation, his sense of class and Kennedy dynastic entitlement that had always given him his own way. It included the questionable service of the men around him that loved him. One of his many long term mistresses, given a job in the White House, observed those around him like McNamara and said: "They loved him too much, they loved him even more than the women did. He wanted to be tough, they wanted to be tough, wanted to please him. It was always you're fine, everything is going well, everything is going to be all right when everything was not going to be all right." As Harry Truman said, he'd have been better off with a dog.

## Somebody's Lying

Fishel kept a picture of Diem on his office desk inscribed "Thank you my friend, for all you have done for Vietnam, I will not forget." That did not necessarily mean that Fishel would regard himself as best friend forever with Diem. Fishel said that he told Diem in 1962 that unless fundamental reforms were made within eighteen months, the regime would collapse.

Fishel said in the fall of 1963: "I knew that people were planning a coup, and I had a pretty good idea of who the individuals were. But I didn't know until afterward that we had played an active role with the plotters."

But the *New York Times*, in an April 16, 1977, article about what happened to Diem in November of 1963 had a different take: "Fishel had reportedly become increasingly dismayed by Mr. Diem's repressive regime and was serving as a high level State Department adviser in Washington in the crucial week before the coup that would overthrow Diem."

Pete Gent had a much more harsh and ugly version about how Fishel's friendship with Diem had deteriorated. In describing those days many years later, Pete Gent MSU basketball star, Dallas Cowboys star wide-out, and author of *North*

*Dallas Forty*, described himself as a hillbilly from small-town Michigan. He said he didn't have the time to socialize and go to school at the same time, so the "socializing had to go, or really never get started in the first place." He was an honor student and was a little more aware of what was going on in the world than most. He'd heard of Vietnam, though he didn't know exactly where it was. He described himself then as pretty much apolitical; but he knew that Diem was the country's president. Pete was a member of Excalibur, the MSU honorary fraternity, though he said that "at the time, I didn't know what Excalibur meant, didn't know what the sword in the stone was." He was at a meeting of Excalibur in the fall of 1963, in the private meeting room at East Lansing's Coral Gables Restaurant. He remembers future Michigan governor "Jamie Blanchard being at the meeting." Also at the meeting was Wesley Fishel. "Fishel was very drunk, Gent said. "He told us he was working with the CIA and they were going to kill Diem." Then Pete said, "Fishel told me that he'd been talking to the Kennedys and they were going to get him a gun to kill Diem, that he'd be dead before the week was out. I knew the first part of Wesley Fishel's statement was bullshit. But I've been forever curious about the last part."

## A Buddhist Monk Burns In Saigon

On June 11, 1963, Thich Quang Duc, a Buddhist monk, doused himself with gasoline and lit himself on fire in protest of the Diem regime's political repression. The eighty-five per cent of the South Vietnamese population who were Buddhist were not being allowed to practice their religion by the five per cent of Catholics who were the ruling minority. They were taken to jail for showing their flag and any other overt practice of their religion.

Thich Quang Duc left a letter behind, the gist of which was: "All Buddhists and lay people should unite and strive for the preservation of the Buddhist religion to protect it against a repressive political regime." His plan was to show the world the injustices of the Diem regime. It worked. Pictures of the self-immolation were shown around the world. Madame Nhu, Diem's sister-in-law "had the looks of an elite courtesan and the soul of a Nazi bully." Wesley Fishel said the beautiful and charming Madame was "brilliant, vivacious, bitchy, and brutal in a Borgia-like fashion as ever…, and had alienated substantial segments of the population." Her husband was head of the thirteen police agencies that oppressed the Buddhists among others. She called the immolations "barbecues" and said "let them continue."

Political leaders in Washington saw the picture, too, and read Madame Nhu's remarks. It helped push events toward the end for Diem. Fragilely constructed and maintained by the US, the regime had always teetered over the abyss. Now many in Washington were ready to let him fall. They had found only tepid enthusiasm among South Vietnamese generals for initiating a coup.

## The Coup against Diem

President John F. Kennedy was torn. He was getting contradictory counsel from all sides. He told the State Department to tell Diem to back off from the Buddhists and that portions of aid money would be withheld if he continued. He encouraged some to explore the possibilities of a coup, dissuaded others, told still others to tell Diem that he would have to separate from his brother Nhu, which was like telling the President he had to separate from Bobby.

Wesley Fishel's anti-communism trumped friendship. He no longer thought Diem could succeed. He no longer had the privileged position and access he used to have. He was never one to underestimate his own comprehension of events. He had turned on Diem to further anti-communism and also to further Wesley Fishel. He had other people in high places to ingratiate himself with.

The rumors of a coup against Diem were all true. If they were circulating at a pizza restaurant in East Lansing (in the Excalibur Room at Coral Gables), they were certainly circulating in Saigon. The smell of blood was in the air that first day in November, all Saints Day. In the French-influenced city of Saigon it was La Fete des Morts, the Day of the Dead, November second.

Captain Ho Tan Quyen was a senior naval officer loyal to Diem. At noon he was picked up by his deputy to go to a restaurant to celebrate his birthday. On the drive through the suburbs the deputy shot and killed him. It was the first of more assassinations to come that weekend. It would be the end of Diem and his regime.

Ngo Dinh Diem had always been a US creation, a US pawn, the value of which differed depending on which component of the US foreign policy bureaucracy was playing him. Some historians feel that the US tolerated his assassination because he was engaging in back channel negotiations with North Vietnam for a coalition government. General Maxwell Taylor, chairman of the Joint Chiefs of Staff, was against the coup because the Joint Chiefs felt there was nobody any better to replace him. Henry Cabot Lodge was for the coup. Former US Senator Cabot Lodge, Nixon's running mate in 1960, was appointed by Kennedy to be US Ambassador to Vietnam. Kennedy had defeated him for his Massachusetts senate seat in 1952 but he was still important to Kennedy for the Republican support he gave to Kennedy's bi-partisan Vietnam policy. There was a saying that Lowells spoke only to Cabots, Cabots spoke only to Lodges, Lodges spoke only to God. Because God was apparently not available for conversation, Lodge spoke to Kennedy. He told him Diem was an "inefficient Hitler" and pressed for the coup. McNamara and the CIA were against it, not for any moral reasons, but because they also had concerns about who would replace him. Lodge would say years later: "The United States can get along with corrupt dictators who manage to stay out of the newspapers. But an inefficient Hitlerism, the leaders of which make fantastic claims to the press, is the hardest thing for the US Government to support." Professor Wesley Fishel from MSU and MSU public relations man James Denison, along with James Lansdale of the CIA and Robert McNamara, Secretary of Defense, were four of the many who had made "fantastic claims to the press" about the virtues and the progress being made in South Viet Nam by Diem. But that had all changed, as either ambitious sycophant or independent thinker, Fishel changed his mind and got on the right side of prevailing US establishment opinion about Diem

Kennedy vacillated. He was infuriated that he was losing control of the situation. Roger Hilsman, assistant secretary of state for Far Eastern Affairs, was for the coup and tried to convince the president that "the die was cast." The Joint Chiefs looked on from the sidelines and said, "It's developing like an Asian Bay of Pigs."

Soon after the killing of Tan Quyen, the dissident generals ordered their troops to seize the police and naval headquarters, radio stations, and post office. The palace, where Wes Fishel had been a long-term house guest in years past was also surrounded. They asked Diem to give up but he refused. They attacked the palace at midnight. Diem escaped to the suburbs. He tried to call President Kennedy through the US State Department but didn't get through. He asked for State Department help and got a noncommittal answer. He called General Don and told him he was willing to surrender if he would be given proper respect for his rank and position. General Don was a lifelong colleague of Diem's and was not bloodthirsty. There was talk about flying Diem to exile in Europe. Diem called the CIA's Lucien Doyle to see about getting a plane to take him there. Diem was told it would take twenty-four hours to get a plane. A lot can happen to a disliked leader in a helpless position over twenty-four hours. Diem and his brother Nhu were shot and killed while manacled in the back of an armored personnel carrier by Nguyen Van Nhung. The hated Nhu had his throat cut as well. (Madame Nhu was in the US surrounded by bodyguards and escaped assassination.) Nhung was an aid of the ARVN's (Army of South Vietnam) Duong Van Minh, or Big Minh, who would replace Diem. One of the Joint Chiefs said, "except for being weak, dumb, and lazy, he was the perfect candidate." In serial fashion, nine others would replace Minh, both slightly more, and substantially less, savory and competent.

General Maxwell Taylor described the Kennedys watching of unfolding events as "like they were watching a football game." Kennedy later told Under Secretary of State George Ball, "We fucked that up."

The Kennedy administration was most concerned with plausible deniability.

Wesley Fishel's gig as counselor to President Diem in Vietnam was over. Fishel would move on to counsel President Lyndon Johnson on Viet Nam.

### Waist Deep In The Big Muddy

In the summer of 1963, before JFK's assassination, Kennedy had proposed sending Vice-President Lyndon Johnson on a fact-finding trip to Vietnam. Johnson was aware of the troubles and assassination rumors surrounding Diem, but he was not a man with great physical courage. He was reluctant to go. "Don't worry, Lyndon," JFK said. "If something happens we'll throw you the biggest funeral Austin has ever seen." He came back subscribing to the rosy, can-do scenarios advanced by Secretary of Defense Robert McNamara.

Early in his congressional career, Johnson had been a Roosevelt man, but Texas was one of the earliest Southern states to react against the Roosevelt agenda. Communism was a concern. Johnson took careful note that Truman was blamed for "losing China." He became a man of the senate, knew its rules, written and unwritten, became the most powerful US Senator in the nation's history. After JFK's assassination, early in 1964, Johnson had a problem. He had ascended to the presidency as a result of national tragedy, not as a result of election. The grace and beauty and style of the Kennedys were not shared by Lyndon Johnson. The love the Eastern establishment had for Kennedy did not necessarily transfer to a syrupy, Southern drawling, arm-twisting man who was a graduate of South-West Texas State Teachers College at San Marcos. His task was enormous. His political brilliance was equal to it; calm the country, calm the markets, dampen conspiracy theories about the Russians being behind JFK's death, keep JFK's staff on the reservation, prevent his long time enemy Robert Kennedy from running against him in 1964, then step out of John F. Kennedy's shadow and become president in his own right. He did it.

JFK and LBJ were both political elites in their own way. Their backgrounds could not have been more different. JFK got his start when his father Joe made a deal with Boston's former mayor and then Congressman James Michael Curley. Curley was in jail, had been reelected from jail, and was still a congressman. The deal was that Curley would back out of his congressional seat and support JFK for it in the next election. Joe would give financial support to Curley in a future Boston mayoral bid. Kennedy and Curley agreed and JFK was elected to Congress. Joe would go on to engineer and pay for more of JFK's success, which, of course, could not have happened without the son's huge talents.

Johnson got his looks, and his size, his big ears and big jaw, his energy and his ambition, from his mother's family, the Buntins, through the Baines. He didn't get any money from anywhere in the family. The land and the economy both produced parched and sparse amounts. His father and maternal grandfather had held the area seat in the Texas legislature and were dedicated populist in the William Jennings Bryan mold, fought "the interests"—including the likes of Joe

Kennedys—and lost, and the family was reduced to poverty because of it, sticking to principle. Johnson never forgot about his experiences. He had to substitute himself for a mule on a road gang grader, had to do "nigger work." It gave him empathy for the "nigger," the poor, the neglected. Joe Kennedy was a principled isolationist, but there is no known example of him ever sacrificing any of his money for principle. LBJ's father sacrificed everything but his good name. LBJ was determined not to fail, not to have to work in the fields, not end up like his father. He got to Congress pretty much on his own. He always thought that he had to work a lot harder to get his senate seat than JFK, and later Bobby, had to.

# Chapter 27

# THE UNION GRILL AFTER 1961

"Life" [by the Contours], playing on the jukebox in the Grill:

> What's tough?
> Life
> What's life?
> A magazine.
> How much does it cost?
> It costs 20 cents.
> I've only got a nickel.
> Whoa, oh well, that's tough..."

The song seemed to be talking about the pilgrimage we were on in quest of experience and education, as well as the general shortage of money to take the trip. But later on the song got real and gave us a sign:

> "And then I got a call from Uncle Sam
> (well I went in town to see the draft board man)
> I thought if I told him of all my luck
> But he just said
> Whoa, oh well that's tough."

Those who were in the room at the time paid little attention to the first stanza; they were grooving on the melody. They were oblivious completely to the second stanza that sang about the draft, a sign of things to come.

The Union Grill was hopping to the music of the juke box, which dominated the background sounds of all the talking,

talking, talking of a full to overflowing Grill. The whole scene of all these sophisticates was very cool to a kid like Charlie, who didn't understand until much later that most of the students were there for a reason—to get an education. It was a temporary union of very different kinds of people: a handful of blue-collar high school kids like him, what seemed like half of the very middle class East Lansing High school kids, a fair number of commuter kids from all over Lansing, studying or killing time. The students from the east, New York and New Jersey, seemed to supply all the latest coolest music and all the hippest styles for everybody else. All mixed with some of the best white college athletes in the country, and absolutely the very best black athletes in the country because the south wouldn't play them.

The players in the Union billiard room could be gentlemen and they could be jerks. Not all were bumboys. Some were bums who used their intelligence in practical applications. Others weren't bums at all. "China" was an elderly, courtly gentleman who always dressed impeccably in suit and tie. He did not gamble; he held court. The MSU billiard room was one of the few places in town that had three-cushion billiards and snooker tables. Charlie's first impression was "Where are the pockets?" Then he saw how the game was played and how complicated and difficult it was. China would play anybody, and would instruct and mentor many. When he shot, there would be a clickety-click and the paths of the balls would be almost preordained. Like magic the correct angles were divined and pursued, their stopping points calculated and realized, to be struck by another ball, also previously calculated. It was eerily good and talented. Rick Fowler played with him and was respectful, unlike how he often acted toward others. He learned and got better.

The juke box played the best pop and rock and Motown and jazz and folk, directed by the easterners. Coach Hank Bullough said Hannah told Bullough that he thought that the eastern universities' biggest failing was that they didn't have low cost education for their own students and that they ended up at MSU.

There was a big "round-table" just inside the door that seated maybe twelve to fifteen people. The athletes were the Knights who sat at The Roundtable. The squires were everyone else. The damsels were the MSU coeds and the East Lansing High girls. Star athletes included Bubba Smith, Clinton Jones, George "Mickey" Webster, Ed Budde, and Wayne Fontes, all players who figured in MSU's great football teams of the sixties coached by Duffy Daugherty, bound for the Rose Bowl and the pros.

The important guy that Charlie didn't know had a balding large head, and a nose that was nearly the same size. His chest and his ego, were as big as the star athletes sitting nearby. Also like the athletes, he had a devoted retinue of followers, among them a lot of young women. He held court, except he didn't bed his female acolytes. He was a father figure to them, and taught them in a particularly effective non-patronizing way. His name was Professor Wesley Fishel, banty-rooster Wesley Fishel. Most of his students said that he was the best teacher they'd ever had. They did not know him as a founder of the Diem regime and an architect of American involvement in the Vietnam War.

Though Fishel did much of his teaching at James Madison College and had his office on the third floor of Case Hall, he did not hang out there or take part in organized activities with the other teachers. No doubt many of them were jealous. He was intellectually superior to most of the other teachers, certainly a better teacher, and he had seen a lot more of the world than most of them. But the height of his teaching achievements, where he really towered over his peers, was in his political connectedness. He was counselor to presidents. He knew all the political leaders in Southeast Asia including Japan, and spoke fluent Japanese to them. The speakers he brought to class had their hands on the levers of power. When Wes Fishel was an operator in Viet Nam and Asia he did well. As a teacher on campus, he was one of the best.

## Athletes At The Grill, Beginning With Biggie

Sports were what made the Grill so fascinating for the bumboys. They were sports, into sports, and the best sportsmen in the country were sitting at the Roundtable in the Union Grill talking about sports. To them, life couldn't get much better than that. except that the athletes who were at the Grill, mostly black, some white, were thoroughly professional about their lives. They would in fact become professional athletes seen on Sunday and, while they always had time for the girls at the Grill, they had no time to indulge in the drinking and gambling and other "sporting" behavior of the bumboys. They were also affected by the war. Black and white athletes mostly came down on different sides of the issue. Some of the white athletes heckled and threw cold water on Jane Munn, Biggie's daughter, (without knowing who she was) when she held vigil outside Cowles House, Hannah's residence, to protest the war. Former MSU football player and Sociology Prof. Carl Taylor and others, thought it was done "with the tolerance if not the approval of the Administration."

"Biggie Munn, legendary MSU football coach and Athletic Director, didn't like his daughter "hanging around the Grill with the black football players," said Mike Munn, Biggie's son and Jane's brother. But he probably wouldn't have liked her hanging out with the white football players either. After all, Biggie had been one of the first "fast big men," a football star himself at Minnesota, and knew about football players and girls. Biggie was bereft and befuddled about who Jane was hanging out with and why. His list of "didn't likes" about what she was up to was a lot longer than his list of "likes." It included white football players as well as her political views and her political friends.

Duffy also told the black football players to stay away from the white women, but as if by natural law, the women—black and white—were "coming in through the windows," as Bubba Smith said. The players may have had to clear out the love letters left in their doors like they were junk mail, but they "didn't

141

MIKE MUNN
EAST LANSING HIGH YEARBOOK 1960

JANE MUNN
EAST LANSING HIGH YEARBOOK 1962

flaunt it around the coaches, maybe around the Grill, but not around the coaches. The coaches knew about it, didn't like it, but gave the players that much slack," recalled Taylor.

Biggie and John Hannah were on the same page. They were the ones who brought the black athletes to MSU, together. The closest John Hannah, ever came to a football was the ovoid egg, or perhaps the chicken, whichever came first. He picked many lieutenants from the ranks of football. Biggie was one of John Hannah's lieutenants, along with many others. They were "team players." Bringing black players to MSU was morally the right thing to do, they believed. It was also good for the university. It was all agreed on. Biggie confined himself to football. Art Brandstatter, and a host of other administrators and faculty would concern themselves with Vietnam and "playing team ball" regarding it.

According to Mike Munn, Biggie got his start working as an assistant coach for Fritz Crisler at the University of Michigan.

"Fritz didn't want Biggie to come to Michigan State so he told Biggie that when he retired, he'd make sure that Biggie replaced him. Biggie compared notes with another assistant coach and discovered that Fritz had made the same promise to him. He and the other coach made a pact that they would both take the first head coaching job that was offered to them. Biggie went to Syracuse; then the next year John Hannah brought Biggie back to the state of Michigan and to MSU."

With Biggie, he picked wisely and well. He encouraged and supported Biggie's efforts to recruit black football players wherever they might be. MSU had credibility throughout the nationwide black community because of its history of recruiting black players and treating them well. With head coach Duffy Daugherty, MSU brought black players up from the segregated South in far greater numbers than any other university in the country.

Biggie supported them in word and deed. As Mike Munn tells it: "They were playing somewhere in the South, Texas, I think, sometime in the forties or early fifties. They were just getting off the bus and were heading for their hotel rooms. The hotel management said the black players couldn't stay there. Biggie called somebody up and said, "We play together, we stay together. If we don't stay together, we don't play.' It got worked out and they played." Did they ever. They played, and won, and won some more, sixteen All-Americans, national titles, Big 10 Titles, four Rose Bowl appearances between 1953 and 1965.

To John Hannah, when Bubba and Mickey Webster and Clinton Jones were sitting at "The Round Table" in the Union Grill in the mid-sixties, along with the other athletes, it must have been part of a pleasant dream about what integration could be and the way a football program could go, Star basketball player and future Dallas Cowboys wide-out Pete Gent said, "I really loved the guy (Hannah). He showed me every courtesy." Pete said he used to go see him in his office and ask for advice. Pete was everything Hannah could ask for as a scholar-athlete. Later, after his Dallas days, Pete said Hannah offered to get him a job as an Asst. Prof teaching English. Though that was before Gent's long hair and long anti-establishment views and other problems developed. He'd graduated and moved on before war protest started.

The end of the pleasant dream for Hannah, shading into nightmare came later on when the black athletes and other black students came up from Detroit and Flint with their Afros and their attitudes, especially their anti-war attitudes. They didn't bring the "act" and the manners and the old-time religion of their parents and grandparents with them like the first black players who came up from the Jim Crow era South. Again Carl Taylor:

"Their Saint, their God, was Malcolm X, they brought Jesse Jackson as their preacher. They respected Martin Luther King, but he was too moderate. When Martin Luther King went to Los Angeles to try and stop the rioting in Watts, someone shouted out, 'We don't want your dream, Martin; we want a job.' Jesse was different. Jesse wore dashikis; he had a big Afro; he talked about Black Power. It brought the hippies and the counterculture, the white anti-war radicals together with the black students." A union of the peace movement and the civil rights movement developed at MSU and the nation.

The Munn siblings, and Dave Lawson, all from East Lansing, were part of that antiwar/civil rights union that began the nightmare for Hannah and ended Biggie Munn's quiescent era. They also spent a lot of time partying with Vee. As white athletes attacked anti-war protesters, including Jane Munn, black athletes and white radicals defended and protected them.

Mike Munn said that Biggie and John Hannah had a close, confident relationship, unlike MSU Presidents DiBiaggio and McPherson with later football coaches. Hannah wanted to make MSU bigger and better. He regarded winning athletic teams as fitting into the description. The questions of who had the power and who had the popularity were not of concern to him. His ego and vanity were not invested in that issue He was secure enough, had perspective enough, to not worry about whether an iconic football coach was more popular than the president of a university, which, of course an iconic football coach was. Besides, Hannah had a university to build and run, a world to rescue, a cold war to fight.

"At the time he [Hannah] and Biggie both fought hard to get MSU into the Big Ten, going toe to toe against U of M that didn't want them in," Mike Munn said. But when Alonzo Stagg took the University of Chicago out of the league, that left a spot open for MSU and they made it on December 12, 1948. They were co-national champions in 1951, but couldn't play conference games or in the Rose Bowl because of already arranged scheduling. They went to the Rose Bowl in 1954, and set the stage for more black players and more football success. Biggie, far-sighted and an organizational genius at football, set the stage for the sixties and Duffy Daugherty.

The players loved Duffy, and Duffy loved the players. Quick with a joke, a quote for every occasion, accessible, available, Duffy seemed to be able to delegate, actively intensely coach, and enjoy himself, all at the same time And he was fielding the best teams in the country during many of those years. Duffy coached for nineteen years and had four National Championships, two Big Ten titles, four second place titles, 33 All-Americans, and seven national top ten rankings.

He coached the best players who hung out at the Grill during the best years.

The black athletes had been talked to plainly about how to act at college. The advice came from two different directions, with both saying essentially the same thing. From their family, often a nuclear family dominated by a grandparent, the black athletes heard, "You've been blessed by God with this opportunity, an opportunity that could take you to places you, we, have only dreamed about. Places that would have been impossible for our people to go just a few short years ago. You've got to be way better than the white boys. Don't mess it up." The coaches said the same thing with less philosophizing, and with all the sensitivity of Marine Corps drill instructors: "Screw up just once, and you're out of here."

That harshness wasn't really necessary. Again as Prof. Carl Taylor tells it:

> The guys from the South knew Jim Crow, knew how to "act." It was fertile ground for athletes who came up from the South. East Lansing was a college town, but not a big city, so it had fewer distractions. Also, the black guys were not total naïfs. They knew a hustle when they saw one; if they hadn't done any, and more than a few had, they certainly had friends and relatives that had. They knew enough to stay away from the U Grill hustles.
>
> Aside from the good life and the freedom they'd never had before, away from the strictures of family and church and the pre-civil rights era South, with all the glory, and the women, they were also confronted with what seemed to be a never-ending phalanx of police that seemed to notice them. A more conspicuous presence than was the case in their home towns as long as they understood their position.
>
> A whole lot of police: campus police, East Lansing police, Michigan State Police, the Ingham County Sheriff's Department, Lansing Township Police. Carl and the football players were not the only ones to notice. It was hard not to notice. That was just the way Hannah with his criminal justice academic programs, and Jack Patriarche, the East Lansing city manager with Charlie Pegg as his police chief, wanted it.

The admonitions of family and coaches, the presence of police everywhere, but most especially their own determination, took them in a different direction than the bumboys and the grill rats. When asked why the athletes at the Grill didn't get into trouble, Coach Hank Bullough said: "They didn't have the money to gamble; they didn't have the time. They had practice, and in those days, coaches could make practice as long as they wanted, or as many days or weeks as they wanted in the spring." He also disagreed with Carl Taylor. and thought that many of the athletes were "kind of naive." Pete Gent had an outlook similar to Hank Bullough: "I was green as grass [the kind the cows eat]; I had to go to practice, I had to keep my grades up for my scholarship. I didn't have time to hang around the Union Grill a lot."

There was a lot of good-natured social interaction in the Grill, at the "Roundtable," but there was an invisible wall between them. They did not party together or hustle.

"The athletes came to the Grill because they knew somebody," said Bullough. "The price of food was cheap, they lived nearby, and they had classes nearby at Berkey Hall. They were not there at night like the gamblers and the rest of those fools."

They did not gamble in any meaningful way; card games were for fun, not money. Being knights of the Roundtable had its prerogatives: easier if not easy classes, easier if not easy jobs in the summertime. But still they often had only a minimally necessary amount of money in their pockets. There was never so much as a rumor of gambling on their part. With a rumor mill obsessed with football, that could be unreliable and exaggerated, any athlete who ever so much as thought of placing a bet on a sporting contest, would have found his name in the next day's newspaper headlines. Meanwhile, the bumboys were betting hundreds, thousands of dollars every week, often with money they didn't have. Two different worlds that didn't really interact except for social pleasantries.

Why did America and MSU love football so much along with the bumboys? Charlie asked Hank Bullough that question.

He looked at Charlie as if Charlie didn't know the answer, there was no sense of him trying to explain it. Charlie persisted; he said it was competitive. The implication was that merit ruled. He acted like that was all that needed to be said and wanted to move on to a different topic of conversation. But he added, "It's not like politics. The rules are the same for everybody. Plus it's a man's game. Men make the rules. It's not like soccer with all those soccer moms running around."

It was a man's game and the women liked the men in it. Time had to be made for them by the athletes. Football players were royalty, or at least nobility. They were Knights of the Round Table. The bumboys, the fans, everyone else were at best squires. In chivalrous times each football player would have been the champion of a fair lady in the royal box at the tournaments. But there were a lot of fair ladies and only so many champions. The football players were in short supply. And the ladies weren't wearing chastity belts, girdles maybe, which may have postponed the moment, but not chastity belts. Life with the ladies and all the other experiences at a big Midwestern university was pretty much a new experience for the white players, but it was totally new for the black players from the Jim Crow South.

The specialness of the football players was all reinforced at the Grill by the bumboys, many of whom were athletic themselves. They didn't quite fawn, weren't quite in the jock sniffer category, but they were genuinely appreciative, intelligently aware of everything the football players did on Saturday afternoons.

Outside the Union, Bubba's new Buick Riviera with "Bubba" in small script on the upper part of the door, was parked semi-permanently in a 10-minute parking zone. Bubba, in back of the line, was a force of nature, taking players as big as he was, as muscular, as strong, and knocking them on their backs, then going for the ball runner and getting him, quickly, unerringly, with little or no yardage gained. Webster, the artist, had swallow-like agility and speed and grace and hawk-like instincts for the capture of the prey. He would swoop out of nowhere, bang into the ball carrier, and take him down. When I asked Roberta Yaffe, the first female sports reporter for the *State News*, about Webster's play, she couldn't concentrate on the question. All she could say was "he was beautiful, astonishingly beautiful." The great teams of that era were much about defense. MSU never gave up the big play; nobody could sustain a drive. Hank Bullough said:

"Against a lot of those ranked teams we played in those years, they'd have 40-50 negative rushing yards at the half, plus we had Juday and Jones and a lot of other good guys on offense. If the opponents got the ball on the 20, they could forget about it. If they had a short field it was possible."

Even then State's goal line stands made it improbable. Biggie, and Duffy after him, assumed, expected, demanded. and got a win. To the players, every win reinforced the need to stay out of trouble, stay away from the hustles, for all the bright and shining possibilities that the era held.

There were a couple of minor exceptions to the athletes' betting. They were harmless. They were macho. They involved Rick Fowler.

## More "Cornbeefing" [Scams]

There was thieving for money, but there was also thieving of things relating to the university. After all, the bum-boys were going to college, part of their universe, and the universe was there to scam. The scam was called corn-beefing, or cornbeef, or beef for short. Some of the "beefs" going on were just rumored; others were real. The tests were no secret; 20% of the university had the tests to First Aid and History of the Motion Picture. Pity the person who had to fight the curve without having the test beforehand. Jack Keating had all the tests for all of the chemistry courses thru keys obtained from the Chemistry Department offices. He didn't share them so there's probably no danger of a whole generation of Dow Chemical engineers only having the knowledge of the first chemistry class they had in eleventh grade. No person in need of medical attention should have to be treated by someone who took "First Aid" at MSU with the final exam in their back pocket. Another of the guys had someone in the Administration Building who automatically okayed all his student loans, then he ran up the bills, and declared bankruptcy.

One of the rumored scams was to wire a car so that either the brake lights temporarily didn't work, or there were no taillights. Then the owner of the car would pull in front of a car driven by a little old lady and hit the brakes, then be struck in turn by the old lady. The driver would stagger out of the car complaining of neck pain and inquire about the extent of her insurance coverage.

Tom Mulligan had a partner in crime [unnamed] that Garry Barratt, a natural athlete and scratch golfer himself, said that he was the most gifted athlete he'd ever been around, and that included the varsity athletes at the Grill. The guy was a scratch golfer, fast swimmer, excellent diver, and excellent billiard player. He was also a thief. Mulligan, amiable and unfocused, except for with women, was the son of a successful and wealthy surgeon who was the Mayor of Mt. Clemens, Michigan. There were rumors that Mulligan and his buddy visited rural high schools around the state for quite a long period of time, broke into the offices, and stole the IBM Selectric typewriters, back when the IBMs had the value if not the portability that an expensive laptop computer has today. Charlie assumed it was true, because Mulligan asked him if he wanted to buy an IBM Selectric. Cheap.

# Chapter 28

# ASSASSINATION OF PRESIDENT JOHN F. KENNEDY

Politics had brought JFK to Texas that third week in November of 1963. He was getting ready for the 1964 elections and he expected it to be tough. On November 21st in Houston, his campaign had organized a massive, successful rally at the Houston Coliseum. Flags waved; the friendly crowd roared.

The next morning in Dallas the general atmosphere was different. There were still friendly crowds, ten to fifteen deep along the entire motorcade route. But also in the crowds were people passing out handbills titled "Wanted For Treason—JFK." The president's picture was on it, looking like a mug shot. When the president woke up in his hotel room that morning he opened up the *Dallas Morning News* and looked at a full page ad bordered in black like a mourning announcement that made similar charges such as giving up sovereignty to the communist controlled United Nations, betraying the forces of a Free Cuba, and approving the Nuclear Test Ban Treaty. The president turned to Jackie and said "You know we're heading into nut country today."

He'd been through problems, in war, and with his own precarious health, and overcame them. He had been close to death several times and was still alive. He had no fear of assassination.

On the sixth floor of the Texas Schoolbook Depository was a man who was going to kill him for reasons that remain mostly conjecture. JFK's death contributed to the death of our generation's optimism. It made it easier to protest the flaws and hypocrisies of the American Dream, easier for the Grill guys to embrace and pursue their nihilism. It also made it easier to protest the conventional wisdom of a widening war in Southeast Asia. All the hopes and dreams, the quest for a better life in a better world, that were evoked in a New Frontier were lost. LBJ picked up the torch and moved the country with his domestic legislative victories that did so much for the black and the poor of our country. He also picked up the torch of Kennedy's efforts in Vietnam.

In early 1964 Lyndon Johnson's political approach quickly evolved. Make nice to the Kennedy supporters and pass the Kennedy legislation. He did this and then some, while doing his best to not talk about the Vietnam War. He said: "Everybody was worried about war, men were worried about heart attacks, women were worried about cancer of the tit." Why talk about war? Talking about it he said "was like having a one-eyed mother-in-law with her eye in the middle of her forehead. You didn't bring her into the living room if you could help it."

As the summer of 1964 approached, Goldwater made things easier. He was regarded as an asset, not so much because he advocated nuclear war in Vietnam, but because he talked about it all the time, quoted the Joint Chiefs of Staff who said that the war was being lost but couldn't talk about it. They were willing to advocate the use of nuclear weapons.

**The Gulf of Tonkin Resolution**

Johnson had not become the unparalleled power of the Senate by going it alone. He held sway over two branches of government. In late July of 1964, he was presented with an opportunity to legitimize our expanded involvement in Vietnam by involving the US Senate. It was known as the Gulf of Tonkin incident. He portrayed it as an aggressive act of war by the North Vietnamese and allowed the US to portray itself as the victim, then declare and wage a "defensive" war.

The details were murky. On July 30, 1964, two South Vietnamese patrol boats based in Da Nang had started on a raid of two North Vietnamese naval bases, which took place the next day. At the same time the American destroyer *Maddox* was embarked on a covert operation titled 34A. Congress, and certainly the American people, were not informed of the nature of the *Maddox* mission, which was, using sophisticated equipment, to get North Vietnamese and Chinese radar installations to turn on their equipment so that they could be charted for possible later destruction. As it started on its mission, it passed returning South Vietnamese patrol boats that had attacked the North Vietnamese bases. The North Vietnamese regarded the *Maddox* as being a collaborator in the naval base attacks and attacked it with three PT boats. One was destroyed. On August 6, the *Maddox* approached the coast again and it was attacked again. Secretary of Defense McNamara claimed we were thirty miles from the coast, when in fact we were much closer.

Johnson wanted a resolution so that he could respond in "a limited way." He said, "I'm not going in unless the Congress goes with me." He brought in members of the US House, twenty or so at a time. Ray Clevenger, a freshman congressman from Michigan's UP at the time, now living in Ann Arbor, said "Johnson went around the room and asked each of the twenty present "Do you have any problem with my conduct of the war?" Nobody said anything. He brought the rest in twenty at a time. None said anything. Congressional support was assured. By 5 p.m. on August 5, 1964 the first planes were leaving the aircraft carriers *Ticonderoga* and *Constellation*. They hit PT-boat bases and an oil depot at Vinh. It ended the charade of advisors and deniable covert operations, all the activities the MSUG was involved in. We were going in, all the while claiming it was going to be a limited response. Goldwater was the extremist.

Senator William Fulbright was picked by Johnson to get the Tonkin Resolution through the Senate because he owed Johnson, as many did. Later he turned bitterly against the war because he was not told about 34A or about where the *Maddox* might really have been and that McNamara had lied to them. Gruening and Morse were the only two senators to vote against it. On August 7, 1964 Morse said: "I believe that history will record that we have made a great mistake in subverting and circumventing the Constitution of the United States... by means of this resolution... we are giving the President... war-making powers in the absence of a declaration of war. I believe that to be a historic mistake." Johnson put the resolution in his hip pocket and resumed running for president.

Goldwater made America like unctuous, syrupy Lyndon Johnson in spite of himself. Lyndon Johnson the moderate, Lyndon Johnson who was sincerely worried and constrained about an expanded war leading to war with China, worried that it could lead to nuclear war. Getting out wasn't seen as an option. Hobson's choices between "moderation" and "extremism" were the only ones on the table that Johnson, McNamara, and all the rest of his Harvard advisors saw.

In that summer of 1964, Lyndon Johnson campaigned as a peace candidate with his warp speed energy. It was one of the happiest periods of his life. There is nothing quite so exhilarating for a politician as to be twenty points up and have all the trends positive, all the arrows pointing up.

Toward the fall of that election year, however, he was wrestling with real differences among the defense bureaucracy, about the state of our efforts in Vietnam. He wasn't telling the American people about it. Defense Secretary Robert McNamara, General Maxwell Taylor, and advisors McGeorge Bundy and Walt Rostow were all telling him that bombing as well as our other efforts would work against a deteriorating situation. The Joint Chiefs and General William Westmoreland were telling him it wouldn't. Westmoreland wanted ground troops. The Joint Chiefs wanted more of everything plus the nuclear option. Dwight Eisenhower told him to "go all in."

The election of November 1964 went just the way Lyndon Johnson imagined it would in his most pleasant dreams. It brought him out from behind the Kennedy shadow. He would be a great president and have his Great Society. But in order to do that he could not be a war president. He would have to conceal the war from the American people. "Of all the men in public life," said historian Theodore White, "Lyndon Johnson was the most friendless."

The war wouldn't go away. The bombing started. Then Westmoreland said we had to have ground troops to protect our air force bases. That was the start. More bombs were going to be dropped on Vietnam than by all the participants in WWII in all theatres. The bombing, despite the Harvard-educated advisors' conclusions to the contrary, wasn't working. The CIA told him so. Westmoreland wanted ground troops. In increments so modest that inquiries about an expanded war effort could be denied, he got them. An enclave approach taking the peasants off their land was proposed and tried. It failed. Westmoreland wanted search and destroy, wanted to take the war to the enemy. When that didn't work, it was back to different theories, different attempts, including a variation of enclave, pacification. An electronic fence across the country to prevent infiltration was tried. So were hopping rocks (imitation rocks with servo-mechanisms and electronic eyes to determine the location of the enemy). None of it worked. In 1965 troop levels went from 20,000 to 40,000, from 175,000 to 200,000. On the inside, Asst. Secretary of State George Ball told him it wouldn't work. So did old discredited China hands. In the Congress, Fulbright, Morse, and others were becoming more critical. Johnson denied he was expanding the war. The credibility gap turned into a chasm.

# Chapter 29

# GEORGE HALL HAS AN IDEA

George Hall was doing okay in the early 1960's. Out on probation, he was going to school at Lansing Business University in downtown Lansing and working there as a janitor while he did. He was browsing at Arbaugh's Department Store near the school and happened by the toy department where he saw a detective sleuthing tool kits based on the TV series Tightrope. Inside the kit was a realistic toy gun. Knowing that Lansing was a small town he drove to Detroit's Cass Corridor and held up the night clerk of a small hotel there. He was successful. He came back several weeks later with a real gun to the same hotel. The door was locked. He made the same clerk unlock the door and robbed him again. He stopped at a bar on the way out of Cass Corridor and had a drink or two. He left his fingerprints on the glass. He was identified by them. He went back to Jackson Prison for another two and a half years.

# Chapter 30

# TIMES WERE A-CHANGING

On February 1, 1960, a group of black college students from North Carolina A&T University refused to leave a Woolworth's lunch counter in Greensboro, where they'd been denied service. This nonviolent action sparked a wave of other sit-ins across the South. The Student Non-Violent Coordinating Committee, SNCC, was created on the campus of Shaw University two months later to coordinate these sit-ins, support their leaders, and publicize their activities. Vee's buddy Dave Lawson lived on Lantern Hill in East Lansing and was one of East Lansing's own. He was a math genius, started attending U of M in 1960, joined SDS, both befriended Vee and mentored him in politics, knew all the prominent national political radicals of the era. Lawson was also going to get to know George Hall.

Lantern Hill was both street and subdivision, a cooperative real estate development. It was located north of Burcham Rd, an east-west artery that ran parallel to Grand River Avenue about three-fourths of a mile north of the MSU campus. It was east of what would be the new high school and was not part of the more expensive housing of Al White's Whitehills. It got its start when married faculty, forced out of campus housing by a two-year limit on their stay, cast about for alternative housing and found the prices daunting. They went to Hannah and asked for his support for a non-profit cooperative housing development. Hannah, only half joking, said that he'd sat in on many a faculty meeting, and found faculty incapable of agreeing on anything. He declined to support the project.

The faculty, led by Professor Miles Boylan went ahead anyhow, agreed on the basics. The result was Lantern Hill subdivision, constructed in the early 1950s. It ultimately housed many opposed to the war in disproportionate numbers. In addition to student activists like Lawson and Smith, Leonard and Dorothy Rall lived there, as did the Rokeaches, future interim President Walter Adams and his economist wife Pauline, and many others. Maggie Hackett's parents lived there as well. Maggie knew just about everyone in the peace movement in the state as did Dave Lawson. It included the U of M types and Bill Ayers. She did not have an entirely favorable opinion of Ayers and U of M SDS.

Years earlier, John Hannah had told Milton Muelder, "If you leave it to faculty, they'll run over you. You need to respond to faculty but not capitulate." He would not respond the way they wanted. Faculty and students wouldn't capitulate. The result was more division, more protest, with all of Hannah's counter-response that included the Red Squad and other forms of surveillance of faculty and student radicals and antiwar activists.

Dave Lawson became radicalized and half converted the golden Bob Vee. After various freedom rides and voter education projects in the south that resulted in assaults and jailings and killings, the movement with SNCC as the organizing body began to move north in 1962 and 1963.

The group of SNCC-type supporters and sympathizers began to draw the attention, and then the ire of President Hannah and the Red Squad before Vietnam became an issue. When SNCC and Professor Robert Green, and many other pillars of the community began to organize and conduct the open housing marches in EL, it would draw more than the ire of John Hannah. He generally did not go off half-cocked. He'd been through the McCarthy era when the state legislature would have him fire anyone even suspected of being communist or socialist. He thoroughly investigated before acting, usually protecting faculty. In this case he thought they'd crossed the line and didn't do much investigating. At his best, President Hannah was not on the opposite side of SNCC. As Assistant Secretary of Defense for manpower in 1953-54, he'd ordered the integration of the remaining all-Negro fighting units and of the all-white schools at southern military bases. On the strength of that, Eisenhower had appointed Hannah the Chairman of the new US Commission on Civil Rights. Hannah was the one who brought the Asians and the blacks to MSU in the first place. Where did he think they were supposed to live?

## A Blind Eye

Back in East Lansing in 1964, the police didn't pay much attention to the continuous parties that could involve several hundred people with cars parked around the party house for half a mile in every direction, nor did they pay much attention to the thieving that had its origins in the Union Grill. If their effectiveness was rated by how much crime and vice they rooted out among the Grill gamblers and thieves (the two consisted of mostly different groups of guys, and Rick Fowler and Larry Chappell were not part of the Grill thieves), then they were pretty ineffective. Betting on all games continued. High stakes card games still were played all over town. The state's school districts continued to lose their typewriters, and many students or their parents had to buy their books twice.

Political radicalism was a different story. East Lansing Police Chief Charlie Pegg, in cooperation with the MSU Dept. of Public Safety established a political surveillance unit that spied on hundreds of faculty and student activists. The files were made possible in part by infiltrating various activists groups, aided by heavily leaning on marijuana users and small time marijuana dealers. They then shared their files with the Michigan State Police Red Squad and the FBI. The bumboys, many of whom were conspicuously non-law abiding, were conspicuously absent from the files.

Beth Shapiro, a former SDS member, and much later head of the MSU library, said that antiwar leftists and others who were busted for penny-ante marijuana possession or dealing got their charges reduced or eliminated if they would snitch about the goings on in SNCC and SDS and the other antiwar groups. What Beth said was supported by what Charlie knew.

## The Eastern High Guys Weren't Rats

A couple of Eastern guys Charlie knew got involved in a business deal involving a small amount of marijuana. He didn't know if they needed the money or they were just entrepreneurially minded, but as they were completing a transaction, a guy at another table said, "See that guy?" He pointed to someone who looked no different than any of the other students a couple of tables away. "He's a narc and you're going to get busted." And so they were.

Milt Lucas, with whom Charlie was in German class at Eastern High, was one of those arrested and his world came down around him. The police approached him on the same day he got his draft notice. He said he was arrested in the Grill for having six dollars of pot on him. They took him to a state police intelligence officer for a long talk about his radical friends. He didn't have anything to say to them. Milt went to the Ingham County jail for six months instead of to Vietnam.

John McAllen was another guy who got busted. John was more cynical and more resilient and wasn't going to school at the time anyway. John told Charlie later that when he was busted his car was somehow involved and it was impounded. He was given the name of a State Police lieutenant who he was told to go see. He entered the building and was told to go to such and such a room. John thought he was going to get a private audience with the lieutenant. He entered and found himself entering a classroom where there appeared to be twenty or twenty-five "students."

John found that he was going to be part of a "lab" experiment, a white "rat". All the "students" put their heads under their desks. Then the cop said, in front of "the students," that John would get a better deal and get his car back if he could tell them about other dealers and anybody he knew who was involved in political radicalism or antiwar protesting. He declined and spent time in the Ingham County Jail. He didn't get his car back. The reason that those in the classroom hid their heads was because they were all undercover cops, narcs, from MSU and the State Police investigating anti-war goings on. John said his experience made him more curious about what was going on with the war. The police emphasis on political activists, encouraged by John Hannah, partly explains why the fairly conspicuous vice going on in the Grill was not stopped or pursued with much energy. It also offers a partial explanation of why Rick felt like he could pursue his career path with impunity. Anti-war politics was a much bigger offense against the social order than card-playing, thievery and petty vice.

Later, Vee made McAllen's situation even more difficult. They were all at McDonald's, on the east side of East Lansing. Mac's was the place to go, with fifty or so extra cars circling around or through the parking lot trying to find a place to park, while the drivers basked in the glory of showing off their cars to the hundred and fifty people milling around the premises at all times on Friday and Saturday nights. There were some nice cars, too, belonging to either the drivers' parents or the guys who worked at Olds. Somehow McAllen, drunk at the time, had gotten crossways with the heavy-on psychoanalyzing rent-a-cop who got too buddy, buddy, trying to do the favorite uncle routine. John slugged him. East Lansing cops were called. McAllen didn't have a car and was desperately looking for a car to get into. Vee, who had great charm but not always great character, wouldn't let him in his car. McAllen got nabbed and got into even more trouble.

Vee always worried about getting into trouble and what his mother would say. Then when he'd been drinking, he totally forgot about his mother and got into trouble. McAllen was not pleased with Vee. His bail was set at $200, which he didn't have. He asked his mother for the $200, and she said, "You got yourself into it; you get yourself out of it." Circuit Judge Sam Street Hughes, former Mayor of Lansing during WWII, had John spend 120 days in jail while he was awaiting trial to teach him a lesson. John said the lesson it taught him was "Never be without money."

**A House Divided**

A couple of weeks later in early spring, Vee, Sherb, Chal and Charlie got together with Tim Morrison for a card game while he was home from college. He started reminiscing about high school days and his experiences with Rick Fowler: "And then I got burned again (in Burnie, a card game) and my tally with Rick was $800 and he actually thought I was going to pay him." Tim chortled, then guffawed. He was referring to the gambling that he and Rick used to do in back of the class at East Lansing High. It was some time in 1964, "Tim" was short for Truman Morrison III, son of Truman Morrison II, who was Reverend Truman Morrison of Westminister Presbyterian Church. Truman Morrison Sr. was a left-winger, had politics that were pure and sincere, as much from noblesse oblige as from democratic conviction. Morrison Senior was involved in freedom marches in the South, and in the early "open housing" protests in East Lansing, where he began to attract the attention of the Red Squad.

The Michigan State Police Red Squad had established their files at least as early as 1961, Hannah had authorized the university's Department of Public Safety (DPS) to cooperate with them, spy on and infiltrate activist campus organizations and individuals, sending names and photographs to the Red Squad, that had recently been energized by increased funding from the Michigan Legislature. They too were concerned with activist students and the communist menace.

The university also employed as informants reporters from the campus newspaper, the *State News*, to provide tips and photographs of those involved in dissent. Their spy activities included having the Red Squad break into University Methodist Church to copy documents pertaining to local clergy-faculty draft counseling efforts. The surveillance and files included many of the "usual suspects": a future congressional candidate; a future state representative, future county commissioner and Democratic candidate for Governor and a bunch of other left of center and radical individuals and groups. It also included David Stockman, future Republican Congressman and later Ronald Reagan's Director of OMB.

Before long, the dragnet used to identify and sometimes prosecute ostensible subversives started scooping up East Lansing's own, Truman Morrison Senior among others. Years later Charlie talked to an old political friend. 'Old East Lansing", who laughed after reading some of the names in the Red Squad files. He figured the Red Squad must have followed somebody's car to a place like a school bake sale, took down license plate number of the school janitor, and maybe the school district plumber, as Communists worthy of keeping an eye on. Truman Morrison Senior was not alone.

## Communists Not Just Under The Bed, But In The Bed

The deepening divisions in the East Lansing community had some potential for comedy as well, highlighted by some of the social and romantic couplings, that from a political perspective were bad fits. Truman Morrison III, Tim, son of Red Squad File member Truman Morrison II, eventually married Margaret Oates, whose father was the director of the Michigan State Police, under whose auspices the Red Squad Files were held. If the seedling didn't sprout far from the tree, then there was the danger of a Commie not just under the bed but in the bed. Doing one supposes, what Commies do. With all the talk of the campus being infiltrated with those on a "mission from Moscow," did that mean that other relatives, sons, daughters, mothers, fathers were wrapped up in conspiracy? Did it mean that, because Jane Munn, wrapped up in the counter-culture and Vietnam protest politics, and her Father Biggie Munn, the revered football coach and subsequent athletic director, were part of the conspiracy and worthy of surveillance? As he stood side by side with John Hannah making plans about athletics and the university, on a mission from Moscow? No. One thing was certain though, when it came to the rehearsal dinners and other social events surrounding the wedding of Morrison and Oates, the two families probably did not talk about the political situation and Vietnam. Tim and Margaret later divorced.

There is no record of John Hannah's thoughts on the subject of his athletic director's daughter being mixed up with those he was trying to fight, or the black football players becoming involved in anti-war protest, or the state police agency's head having a daughter who was marrying the son of someone regarded as subversive. The daughter of the director of the state draft board was picketing Hannah at his house while he was trying to serve the cause and help with the draft.

Meanwhile, *State News* reporters like Marcia Van Ness were shilling for the pro-war position. They said Hannah never intruded. That may have been true, but they were self-guided. They knew how to pander to Hannah without receiving instructions. They liked what John Hannah and Wesley Fishel liked. Some rebel reporters dropped out of school and started *The Paper*, one of the first five members of Underground Press Syndicate, the first nationwide network of underground papers. Scholarship student Steve Badrich conceived of the idea of a political comic strip in the paper called "Land Grant Man," and the dialogue was written by none other than Jane Munn, Biggie's daughter.

"Inspired by Batman... President "Palindrome" (Hannah) once he thumped a hoe on the floor and shouted the magic word "Poultry," became the inept caped crusader, "Land Grant Man." Gleefully, Munn and the comic strip writers had Hannah's alter ego subjected to acid trips, gang rape by sexually repressed coeds, and assault by his wife who did not recognize him in his "Land Grant Man" costume."

Another radical child of a war supporter was Louise Holmes, the daughter of Michigan Selective Service Director John Holmes. The community beyond the campus, its sons and daughters, were involving themselves in dissent. The humor, and the sometimes lightheartedness, was a hugely redeeming characteristic for those on the sidelines who later joined their ranks by the thousands. It was also a survival mechanism. Those organizing and involving themselves in the protest must have shrewdly understood they would not win any contest against the State Police, or the MSU-DPS, that involved violence. Plus, MSU had a history of staying peaceable and both sides with a few exceptions maintained it.

# Chapter 31

# POLITICS? FOR THE BUMBOYS?

Through the sparkle and lure and allure of the next card game, the bumboys had to be aware that something different was going on outside their world before and after the Presidential election of 1964. Of course there was school and schooling, but nobody gave that much attention. There was sex. After gambling it was a priority. It was easier and looser. But even after gambling, sex, booze, and drugs, something else was creeping into their little corner of the universe. It was politics. It was war.

Transferring the bumboys' game theory into political beliefs meant a system where there was little room for altruism. There was glee and enjoyment in their world of calculation and connivance to win, but it had harsh rules. Most of the guys believed they were the fishermen, that they were better, if not the best, and they looked for fish (sucker-fools), from minnows to whales, someone down the food chain to extract money from.

Underneath their gaming was a free market approach that was the freest of the free where Darwinian rules applied. In the "game" the strongest survived, and the weak, if rational, found something else to do. Of course, poker and the other games were not an exact science, and the weak sometimes took money from the strong. The trend line, though, ran inexorably toward the favor of the stronger players. Fish were not to be given a coup de grace and consumed whole. They were encouraged to come back so that they could continue to be milked, until they got "The Picture," which was that they couldn't win. Some got the picture; others, the compulsive gamblers, never did. That, and the real possibility of their being cheated, made some of them angry.

It was an approach to life that made Ayn Rand seem liberal when applied to conventional party politics. In the bumboys' world view, the poor and less affluent, most of the "schvartzes," as the bumboys called blacks—except for the superior black athletes—would not find their world a hospitable place. Their "game" politics, applied to national politics, would incline them to support someone like Barry Goldwater. Except for the "draft," a small but looming problem for the guys as the mid-sixties arrived. They also adapted the coloration of their surroundings. After all, East Lansing was a college town. Most of the guys Charlie hung around with at the time, as well as the East Lansing guys and the bumboys, were pretty much status-quo-accepting. When JFK and later LBJ said the Vietnam war protected us against Communism, most accepted it.

Lyndon Johnson's famous campaign ad showed a little girl picking daisy petals in the foreground while a countdown to Armageddon, interspersed with nuclear mushroom clouds representing Goldwater's advocacy of using "The Bomb," filled the background. The ad was looked at by many as demagoguing. Johnson himself, especially when the war started going badly, had to wrestle with the Joint Chiefs and the right wing to suppress their desire to consider the nuclear option. At the time he said he did not want a wider war, but that was a lie. He was already preparing for it, already widening it. His "middle-path" approach ruined him politically and took the country to the brink. The Grill bumboys probably didn't vote. If they had, they probably, along with the rest of the country, would have voted overwhelmingly for Johnson and Peace. Or as one conservative wit put it: "I voted for Goldwater because I wanted war, and we got war."

## The Bumboys Start To Listen; Bumboy Sherb Had No Choice

In July of 1965, at General Westmoreland's request, the draft was increased from 17,000 a month, to 25,000 a month. Five months later, US Selective Service Director Lewis Hershey, citing a need for more soldiers, ordered that college student draft deferments be cut by at least 20%. In order to maintain 2-S status at MSU, students had to have a "C" grade point average and score 70% in a Selective Service intelligence examination, an exam largely composed of math questions that favored engineering and business majors and placed social science and liberal arts majors at a disadvantage.

Director of Selective Service in Michigan, Col. John Holmes, responded positively to Hershey's request, Holmes stated that "only 10% of the student body was qualified to be in school. The other 90%," Holmes stated, "were unworthy of a college education and were shirking their patriotic duty in Vietnam." Hannah didn't state agreement with Holmes and didn't go that far, but students were increasingly expelled for low academic performance, qualifying them for the draft. Holmes' daughter Louise, didn't agree, and picketed Cowles House.

In the ranks of the guys at the Grill, there were large numbers of the unworthy. The need for a draft deferment changed lives. In the WWII era those involved got married and went to war because they wanted to. Vietnam was different. Marriage and war wasn't high on anyone's list. It led to marriages that shouldn't or wouldn't normally have occurred, to babies that were regarded as less than bundles of joy. Marriages and babies were get home-free cards. The guys in the Grill were a varied bunch and so were their responses to their threatened 2-S deferments. They ranged from the dutiful and the mundane to the outrageous and the comical.

Several were married already, and expecting children. They included Chal, Bill Chaliman, and his wife Dianne; and Rick, who'd already married Prudy, who was pregnant and was living with him down from the Union. Mike FitzPatrick was called "Toad" because he looked a little frog-like and had something of an odd manner. Some thought he was a homosexual, which he was not. Anyway he went before the draft board and acted his oddest whether with homosexual overtones or not, and the draft passed on him. Forty years later, homosexuals would struggle for the privilege to fight and die for their country. In 1965, few people of any sexual persuasion seemed eager for the privilege.

According to another story, which has been accepted as true, one of the guys with low blood pressure stayed up all night drinking coffee thinking he could raise his blood pressure to an unacceptably high level. That morning he went to his physical looking haggard and drawn. The doc said, "You don't look so good, and your blood pressure is a little low, but I'll pass you." If he hadn't stayed up drinking the coffee, he'd have failed the physical with low blood pressure. Another MSU SDS'er, not part of the grill crowd, reported for induction. During his exam the medical doctor ordered him to drop his pants and bend over. The doctor noticed something protruding from his butt and shocked, asked, "What the hell is that?" Nonchalantly he replied, "Oh, that's my pet rat." He was not drafted.

Dave Lawson, peaceful, cheerful, friendly, told the draft board examiner that if they drafted him he'd "burn the draft board down." "Don't worry," he said they told him, "you'd cause too much trouble." Dave was probably bluffing. The draft board probably thought Dave was bluffing too, but all would be in agreement that he'd have been a lot of trouble. When pushed, Dave didn't give in.

Sherb, slim, with Beatle-style hair was hawkishly alert. He was a rising star in the bridge world and became at twenty-one what a lot of old men could only dream about in the reverie of their afternoon naps. He became a life master. When it came to the University though, he wasn't even showing up. He seemed to be immune to the draft based on some youthful indiscretions

BOB SHERBURN "SHERB"  DAVID LAWSON
EAST LANSING HIGH YEARBOOK 1962   EAST LANSING HIGH YEARBOOK 1960

that included gang membership and car theft. Sherb's parents, specifically his father, Smiley (Vee called him that because he never did), was a late arrival as a hovering helicoptering parent. It could have been a very lethal helicopter. Smiley called the draft board "My son's a bum, he's not doing anything with his life. You ought to draft him." The draft board bureaucracy, ever so responsive to that kind of parental and citizen request started looking into it. He seemed to be worthy, if not of continued attendance at the university, at least of qualifying for the draft. His combined grade point average was about a 1 point, extremely deficient. But there was the problem of his juvenile arrest record. The local draft board in Lansing wouldn't take him. With due diligence the board inquired around to other draft boards. The Chicago draft board, where troubles with the law weren't uncommon for the south side blacks who made up a lot of the pool, gave Sherb the privilege of being accepted into the United States Army in March of 1967.

Like the guy in Mark Twain's story, who was tarred, feathered, and ridden out of town on a rail, "Even considering the honor of it," he said, "I'd have just as soon walked." In those days when life centered around the Union, Sherb was known for his bridge-playing ability, not his fighting ability or his inclination to fight, or for his physical courage. He wasn't that crazy about going, but he knew he wasn't accomplishing much hanging out.

Sherb entered and finished boot camp in Fort Knox, Kentucky. At that time his alertness and intelligence seemed to fail him. Despite being aware of the conventional wisdom of never raising one's hand to volunteer for anything, after boot camp graduation, they asked for a raising of hands for anybody that was interested in jump school. It was an extra hundred dollars a month. Sherb asked if you could still be a clerk or a cook as a paratrooper. He was reassured he could. He raised his hand. He found himself in jump school the next day, part of the Americal Division, headed for the I Corp section of Vietnam. He was sent to Ft Lewis Washington, was given leave to go home for Christmas. There was a big snow storm. He was four days late to return to duty, AWOL. He missed his unit's departure to Vietnam. He was sent to the stockade briefly at Fort Belvoire in Maryland, where he was guarded by none other than Mark Waite, from East Lansing High School, East Lansing, Michigan. Mark had also flunked out and had become MP, military police. As soon as Sherb was let out, he was on his way to Vietnam.

For the US troops in Vietnam, as the sixties progressed and shaded toward a darker and more futile middle-game, the success rhetoric of national political leadership, the can-do attitude of military leadership was in sharp contrast to the increasingly bleak and nihilistic reality in that country. To assuage the difficulty of the life, troops were increasingly turning to powerful Chinese heroin and marijuana. Sherb and his comrades in arms were sent to the same part of the country that contained My Lai where Lieutenant Calley and his platoon killed the locals including women and children. The locals were not friendly; there was some provocation. Sherb said: "it was only the blacks who murdered and raped the peasants." Umhmm. They were in the foothills, transitioning into mountains. They were on a hill that turned into a plateau. They were newbies, had been in the country for less than three weeks. As the leader of his squad on reconnoitering patrol they had stopped for the night and were relaxing. They'd taken their boots off, contrary to training, and were somewhere between relaxed and blasted on marijuana. They heard footsteps on the wrong side of the plateau. A member of the squad, before Sherb could stop him, threw a grenade. Ten more tai-coms, Chinese grenades came back. Sherb said. "There was a guy on my left from Arkansas, a guy on my right from Tennessee, they both had their heads blown off." The remaining member of the group said he didn't want to leave his buddy. They were in a panic. Sherb told the guy "you can do what you want, your buddy isn't coming, I'm leaving." They scattered in different directions, chaos reigned. Barefoot among the nettles, thorns, and poisonous snakes, they tried to find the rest of their comrades in other squads and platoons. "Don't shoot, don't shoot, we're US, we're US" they shouted. They made it to friendly forces. Later when they went back to collect the bodies, one was identified only because he had a University of Tennessee t-shirt on. It was a long way from East Lansing.

After that incident he was made a RTO, radio telephone operator by the lieutenant in his platoon. At night he was placed closer to the lieutenant in what Sherb described as an inner circle when they were out on patrol, more out of harm's way.

Sherb was made a clerk, after a buddy traded a typewriter for him to a sergeant. He changed units, spent the rest of his time out of combat as the company clerk, made himself a sergeant. He looked up everyone's records, found that he had the second highest test scores of any enlisted man in the Army in Vietnam. He often played bridge with the generals and was highly regarded, acting almost like their instructor He also played a lot of poker with the guys in his unit that barely knew more than the rudiments of the game. He won a lot of money before he was honorably discharged. He understandably came out much harder and more cynical than when he went in and he was pretty cynical to start with.

Back in East Lansing, he started attending MSU again on the GI bill, was well paid by Uncle Sam to do so. He took his time, continued to party with Vee and Chal. Chal, uncertain about what he wanted in life besides a party, a fifth, and a gamble, was about at the end game in his marriage with Dianne. Their divorce proceedings had started when Sherb, always alert for the main chance, came in and scooped up Dianne. The Chalimans divorced; Sherb and Dianne married. Chal was not entirely happy about it. Sherb's outlook had changed. He, along with Dianne who gave him a lot of support, was committed to not turning out a bum. Plus he was no longer a boy. Chal kept working.

About the same time Sherb was in Vietnam, Charlie started dating a girl named Sandra Johnson. She was a fine person, from Evanston, Illinois. She had a voice so gentle and sweet that she could charm birds out of trees and make small wild animals come to her. Her fiancé had been an army officer in Viet Nam and seen a lot of action. He was home for six months, then committed suicide. Sandra had black moods because of it. Charlie didn't know anything about Viet Nam and black moods.

# Chapter 32

# THE WALLACES, OF "OLD EAST LANSING"

The Wallace family was "Old East Lansing." Karen Wallace attended Central Elementary School, as did her mother. Her grandfather was an Oldsmobile exec. Her mother was a co-ed and a member of Chi Omega Sorority in 1940. Michigan State College had 4,000 students at the time. Grand River Avenue was a two-lane road and had just been paved. John Hannah would not be president for another year. Her mother met her father at the scene of a minor traffic accident. He was a state policeman at the time. They were formally introduced at the scene by Charlie Pegg, the East Lansing Chief of Police who later helped establish the "Red Files."

As Karen recalls, she didn't have any political awareness and leanings at the time. She did remember a straw poll taken in her class at Central Elementary School for the presidential elections in 1952. Adlai Stevenson got two votes; Eisenhower got all the rest. Richard Zimmer, her classmate, was one of the two Stevenson votes. He was not pleased to have his ballot revealed. Children tended to vote like their parents, at least at the tender age of eight years, so that's a pretty good indication of the political leanings of the community at that time. John Hannah was in synch with it.

KAREN WALLACE, 1962
EAST LANSING HIGH YEARBOOK

## Don't Go Near The Union

As pre-teens and young teenagers, Karen said they could go anywhere, do anything. They rambled through the fields north of town in what later became Whitehills Estates. They went to the horse barns and small animal barns on campus. The only place they were forbidden to go was the Union Building. In the children's book, Flopsie, Mopsie, and Cottontail were told by their mother to stay away from Mr. MacGregor's garden. So too was Karen Wallace told to stay away from the Union Grill. Danger lurked there. From an East Lansing parent's perspective, nothing that a high-school girl would learn or experience there would do them any good. As Karen got older, and she saw her friends going there, she defied her parents and spent a lot of time at the Grill.

She went off to Lincoln College. "Kennedy's assassination in the fall of 1963," Karen said, "was the beginning of a slow political awakening. We had no thoughts on the Vietnam War at the time, no knowledge whatsoever of MSU's involvement in it." She did remember sending out Christmas cards in 1965 that had a peace symbol prominently displayed with a message that said "War is not healthy for children and other living things." She said it was regarded as semi-scandalous within her family.

Around the same time, she went to a march on Washington to protest the war. What impressed her at the time was how "utterly peaceful it was, with few police in sight except traffic cops." That changed; engaged to Dave, her politics got radical. They joined SDS at the University of Michigan, and became friends with the famous radicals of the era. When they brought their VW bus covered with peace symbols and anti-war slogans, they were told to get it out of the driveway and park it down the street. Dave had the first bell-bottom pants and wire-rimmed granny glasses in East Lansing. When he gave the bell-bottoms to Karen's brother, her parents were offended.

### The Enemy is Us

In the beginning, the bourgeoisie stood firm against the "radical element" who were trying to tell them who they had to live next door to with their "open housing marches." They were seen as having communist agendas or being communists themselves. Police Chief Pegg, following in the footsteps of Art Brandstatter, and City Manager Jack Patriarche were the instruments of their reaction. A unified clarion call was made to deal swiftly and harshly with the radical element, the outsiders. Increasingly, as the Vietnam War dragged on, the enemy became their own children, or, as Walt Kelly put it in the cartoon *Pogo*, "We've met the enemy, and it's us." John Alfred Hannah continued his support for the Vietnam War, continued his fight against "us." It confused those in East Lansing who always thought that the "different ones" were outsiders. As time went on it made many tolerant in a confused sort of way. People like David Lawson and Rick Fowler, who broke the mold in completely different ways, became more easily acceptable from the older generation's perspective. At the time, though, in the early days of the anti-war movement, it made for more division.

## Protest Begins With Green, And White All Over East Lansing

Robert Green, an Education Prof and African-American whom John Hannah had recruited, organized the first protest march in East Lansing. It was in the spring of 1965. It was not about the Vietnam War at all. It was about the lack of housing in East Lansing for people of color, for Asians. The bumboys, all white, paid no attention. The authorities did.

The march was part philosophical and part personal. People of color who worked at the university couldn't find housing anyplace in town to rent or to buy, even though they could afford it as much as any other faculty member. Dr. Robert Green decided to do something about it. He'd had experience with the freedom rides in the south, and was an advisor to the Southern Christian Leadership Association. He started looking out at the problems in his own hometown. He was joined in his effort by black pastors from the City of Lansing, Rabbi Phil Frankel from the Jewish Congregation Shaarey Zedek, Truman Morrison II from Wesleyan Methodist Church, other East Lansing churches, assorted students from school, and, of course, the Student Non-Violent Coordinating Committee.

It started, and remained peaceful, like all protests at MSU for the most part. John Hannah did not think it peaceful or reasonable or legal. To Hannah, the civil rights movement should take what it was given, not ask for more. Hannah had been chair of the U.S. Civil Rights Commission under Eisenhower and an advocate of racial integration. He had actively recruited black faculty to the campus, not to mention black student athletes. He integrated campus dormitories. But he was a firm believer in law and order, didn't think marches and protests without permits were lawful or orderly. Of course, the marchers were denied permits. Hannah was not pleased that they marched anyhow. East Lansing City officials including City Manager Jack Patriarche and Police Chief Charlie Pegg were also not pleased. It resulted in the arrest of fifty-nine students. Hannah dispatched three university buses to take the students to the county jail in Mason.

### Cassandra Speaks. The Bumboys Don't Know or Care About Cassandra

Later in the spring of 1965, in a talk at the Union Building, above where the guys were playing pool and planning the location of the next bridge or hearts or poker game, Lawrence Battistini, a Southeast Asia specialist, spoke to a small number of students. He informed his sparse audience that Johnson's Vietnam policy would replicate France's humiliating experience in Indochina, and that the US would be regarded as colonizers as were the French. Americans who believed that the Indochinese conflict was a product of international communist aggression, instead of a civil war, were the victims of presidential and press duplicity, the professor concluded.

After the speech, the Young Socialist Alliance (YSA) and the Students For Democratic Society (SDS) announced plans for a march on Washington. Few students and faculty signed up. The feeling among attendees was that neither students and faculty nor Americans in general were interested. They trusted President Johnson to advance democracy at home and abroad.

Johnson's decision to send the marines to Da Nang on March 8, 1965 changed public opinion. Battistini, Greer, Donoghue, and Milton Rokeach, organized a seventeen-member ad hoc MSU Faculty Committee for Peace in Vietnam. They conducted a "Teach-In" that attracted 2,000 students including one hundred hawkish Democrats as well as the Young Americans for Freedom (YAF), who heckled the anti-war speakers. It was twice interrupted by bomb threats. Hawkish faculty glared at them with hostility, believing that professionals should not criticize their own government. Despite the tense and chaotic atmosphere of the situation, most of the people present felt that it had solid content and clearly defined the issues. It was the first campus-wide anti-war protest and it lent a sense of legitimacy to the participants. One hundred and thirty students signed up or the March on Washington, four times the original number who had signed up two weeks before the teach-in.

The environment against the protesters became increasingly hostile that spring of 1965. Hawkish faculty, led by Fishel, some of the other MSUG veterans, and joined by the YAF, People to People. and other pro-war groups, became a chorus of criticism. In letters to the editor of the *State News*, they accused the antiwar activists of being "cowards, communist appeasers, psychotics, and traitors."

That June, the pro-war group American Friends of Vietnam came to campus. It was an ostensibly grassroots organization but in reality was set up and funded by wealthy friends of Lyndon Johnson who'd helped fund his 1964 presidential campaign. Among them was Sidney Weinstein, a Wall Street financier, and Arthur Krim, a United Artist executive in Hollywood. One of AFVN's first endeavors was a speaking engagement on the MSU campus at Anthony Hall featuring Vice-President Hubert Humphrey. As part of Humphrey's visit, organizers of the peace faculty, including Thomas Greer, chair of the humanities department, challenged Fishel and the pro-war faculty to a debate at the Anthony Hall event, across the circle from the Union. At the debate, Fishel misquoted and dismissed the peace speakers. Of the crowd of four hundred, about forty stood up and gave Professor Greer a standing ovation. Fishel then said: "After that I'm not sure I should address you as the Madman's Society or the Future Beasts of America."

Humphrey's visit was designed to drum up support for Johnson's policies, not to inspire a debate. Following Humphrey's speech, Greer presented him with a "peace petition" signed by several hundred faculty. The professor was good natured about it and said that they did not fault Humphrey for Johnson's wrongheaded actions on Vietnam. According to historian Kenneth Heineman, "Humphrey crushed the petition between trembling hands and sputtered that he had been a foe of Communist conspirators long before Johnson had become President." A friend of Charlie's from Eastern High, Rodger Webb, grabbed Hubert gently by the arm, and more in disappointment than in anger said "Hubert, you sold out." Hubert Humphrey, one of the many self-guiding team players of the era, knew that if he didn't stay a team player, he would be more on the outside than he already was. His temperament and his ambition made him a loyal and somewhat intimidated one. He knocked on Lyndon Johnson's door with the same trepidation as Joseph Stalin's valet and was about as subservient.

Johnson increasingly intervened on behalf of campus hawks nationwide, and ultimately gave nearly $50,000 to Fishel, to organize various pro-war speakers bureaus and information centers throughout the country under the auspices of the Friends of Vietnam, of which Fishel was the first Director.

The increased troop build-up increased the draft. It began to get the Grill guys' attention.

They started paying attention with the most central of interest, self-interest. Viet Nam was first an exotic unknown location. Then it became a place in Southeast Asia where we were fighting a war. Then it became a place where "We" or "I" might very well have to go to fight a war. The guys started becoming vaguely aware that something was going on.

## Marchers For Peace Find It a Slog

The first confrontation between antiwar students and the university occurred in October 1965 when twenty students from SDS set up booths on either side of a Marine recruiting table in the Union lobby and held up pictures of children burned by napalm. First they were threatened with bodily harm unless they left; then they were threatened with arrest. Five didn't leave and were arrested for trespassing.

Alarmed at the growing number of antiwar activists, the YAF, the American Legion, and the MSU chapter of Delta Tau Delta social fraternity that dominated student government collected over fifteen thousand signatures of students, faculty, and community residents on a petition supporting Johnson's Vietnam policy. That event and the ensuing months of increased troop commitments and draft calls rapidly deflated the optimism of those who thought their protests were being listened to and heard. With the winter of 1965 approaching, the 50,000 people who assembled in Washington realized that the struggle was going to be long. At the same time they were being branded by critics as traitors and Communists.

## Jane Munn and Louise Holmes Slog On Too

By 1966, the threat of the draft had grown exponentially and so had the anti-war movement. The movement rallied around the students arrested in the Union the previous fall of 1965. President John Hannah insisted that Ingham County Prosecutor Don Reisig prosecute the students to the fullest. He did. Circuit Judge Marvin Salmon increased the fines given them by the justice of the peace, and sentenced them to ten- to thirty-day jail terms and denied them bail, despite their intention to appeal to the Michigan Supreme Court. By the time their appeal could be heard, they had served their sentences.

In the cold March of 1966, a small contingent of those involved in the movement rallied around the students who were arrested. Following Salmon's ruling, twenty-eight students camped in front of Cowles House, Hannah's residence, across Circle Drive from the Union, and fasted there for three very cold days and nights. Hannah was not happy about the campers. Among them were Jane Munn, and Louise Holmes. The president refused to speak to them, and unfriendly students threw water balloons on them in the cold. On the third day, two hundred students rallied around Beaumont Tower, and the protest became a major story for the state's leading newspapers and television stations. Hannah's role in the event considerably tarnished his image.

## To The Ramparts

The clarion call from the ramparts, sounded by various critical MSUG officials about MSU's questionable involvement in Vietnam had been echoing around intellectual and academic circles for several years with limited impact. Then it happened. Just as the controversy over the arrested students was beginning to subside on the campus of Michigan State, the April 1966 issue of *Ramparts* magazine published an article that linked MSU, the Defense Dept., and the CIA, in a way that was almost unbelievable. It was written by their staff writer Warren Hinckle with an introduction by MSU Prof Stanley Sheinbaum. Sheinbaum had written glowingly about the MSUG Project earlier in the MSU Magazine, but he'd changed his mind now. It was a sensational story that documented and detailed the MSU-CIA ties in the then-defunct (as of 1962) Vietnam Project. The fallout from the magazine article was enormous. The *Detroit Free Press*, the *New York Times*, and the three television networks descended upon Cowles House. State Senator Jack Faxon said he was going to investigate. Fishel called the

*Ramparts* article "a silly, slimy smear," and was "pure fantasy." He apparently was referring to the part of the *Ramparts* article that he was living lavishly in a mansion with a security box. The part about the security box was irrelevant, but later Fishel admitted that some "former" CIA people were connected to MSUG. "Twenty-three people of the one hundred and seven were involved in the [MSUG] police project and five had a CIA connection." If there were twenty-three people involved in policing activities at MSUG when the total MSUG in South Vietnam was one hundred seven, when MSUG grew to over two thousand at its largest, extrapolating, that would put the number of MSUG involved in police and security at over four hundred fifty. Smuckler admitted the MSU-CIA connection. Hannah denied the CIA connection and contradicted Smuckler. Former CIA Inspector General Lymon Kirkpatrick contradicted Hannah, saying, "Only an idiot could not have known that the CIA used the MSU Viet Nam Project as a front."

MSU Vice-President and Dean of Social Science Milton Muelder was hearing the same rumors about the CIA's presence on campus. He said: "I greatly respected Hannah but did not trust him." Muelder, who was responsible for international programs, started asking questions from people he knew who could give him honest answers. He asked two questions about suspect faculty members: "Do they carry a lot of money? Do they have guns?" The answers he got back was "yes" to both questions, Muelder had his answer. As a response he issued a directive to all faculty and staff that all hiring would be done through regular channels with the usual checks of resumes and backgrounds. This directive was brought to the immediate attention of Hannah who didn't like it. Muelder offered his resignation; Hannah didn't take it but sent Muelder to Washington where an Army representative tried to persuade him of the errors of his ways. Muelder said, "I was used to blue speech. I'd been a Naval officer for seven years in World War II. I could take it and I could also dish it out. I didn't change my mind." Muelder said that he "thought Hannah was way too impressed with the Army and couldn't say no to them."

## What was the CIA doing on campus?

The air around Hannah that spring was filled with the same fog of lies that filled the interrogation room of the MSU police station he controlled.

In the Union Ballroom on April 20, 1966, a scant twenty feet above the heads of those who had ears but did not hear down below in the Grill, Wesley Fishel spoke. He was increasing his efforts to convince a thousand curious and suspicious students that his motives were pure and the cause was good. The *Ramparts* article had thoroughly undermined his credibility. Hannah's zealous anti-communism and ties to the defense establishment made it difficult for Fishel, equally committed, to establish any credibility with the students, and made it easier for anti-war activists to make their case.

## Radicals in Our Mist, that is, Midst

It was difficult to tell in 1966-67 which way the protest surrounding Viet Nam was going to go. John Hannah was self-guided, but he was also being pushed by conservative faculty, conservative alums, conservative elements of the state legislature, and corporate benefactors like GM and Dow Chemical. They thought it was going one way, the way of "the Moscow-Peking Axis," to quote Arthur Brandstatter Sr.

There was much soul searching on the left, and great search for a solution that tended toward radical left answers. But the revolutionary, the violent, was not finding fertile ground at MSU. There were several reasons for this. First, the SDS at MSU was kind of a homegrown family affair composed of the community. Second, the University Christian Movement had more of an appeal with leftist but non-Marxist politics, and ultimately eclipsed the more radical violent groups. Third, some very wise, shrewd, peaceful moves on the part of people like Walter Adams kept things calm by involving themselves with the protesters and the left. Lastly, and probably most importantly, "The Movement" was policed from within by several groups with common sense, among them the Vietnam Veterans Against the War (VVAW), the Lansing chapter of which was the biggest in the country. Ultimately the growing anti-war movement would be a peaceful one, not a radical or revolutionary or violent one. It would not be a particularly well-mannered or happy one. It would not be violent. It would make for a lot of dreams that didn't turn out. The non-violent aspect must have had an effect on Rick and Larry. Violence was just not the East Lansing way.

Jack Sattel said his anonymity within the huge MSU community did not bother him after four years in the Air Force. He gravitated toward the YSC (Young Socialist Club) because he thought they had done some good things, including support for education efforts in the south and demonstrating against discrimination in off-campus housing, and that it gave him a sense of purpose and direction. But he thought the YSC was too serious to have much fun, while he enjoyed going out and raising hell with his friends; and they saw discussion of politics as an end in itself. Although he was one of the early founders of MSU SDS, he and his wife had no patience with "rock throwers" in the chapter and especially the chapter from the University of Michigan, whom he described as the "sons and daughters of the ruling class" who "wanted to win this" and bring revolution soon due to their being used to getting what they wanted when they wanted it, and came to MSU in the late 1960s to sow discord in the ranks.

## East Lansing's Own Dave Lawson

One of those people, part of U of M SDS, was Bob Vee's good friend and East Lansing's own David Lawson. He had a much more reasonable and gentle temperament than the U of

M SDS types, but had left the tender mercies of East Lansing, not for the rarified air and exalted education of the University of Michigan, but "for their SDS chapter." He was a math genius and was enrolled in their Ph.D. program. Dave said "I knew I was part of a wider world and wanted to involve myself in it." He was "drawn to black liberation movements and went to hear Malcolm X speak with two black students." By this time, Malcolm was no longer playing football for Mason High School at the Ingham County seat ten miles south of Lansing. He was no longer a busboy at Coral Gables Restaurant in East Lansing. He'd hustled and pimped in New York, been imprisoned, hustled some more, been imprisoned some more, read in prison, found himself. He also found Islam, or the "Nation of Islam," as Islam was interpreted by Elijah Muhammad, and became a leader in the movement. As Sociology Professor Carl Taylor put it, "They took everybody, they took the 'lumpen proletariat,' and made something of them. No other religious group did." One of them was "Detroit Red" Little, from Lansing, Michigan, Malcolm X.

Dave was the only white person in the room the evening that Malcolm railed against all white people, then afterward came up to Dave and said he "had the devil's eyes." Dave's eyes were bright blue. He knew it wasn't a compliment but he was still impressed with Malcolm. Malcolm's views evolved so that he no longer felt Dave was the devil. Dave's also evolved and he became more radicalized by the Vietnam War, became acquainted with political organizers Tom Hayden and Rennie Davis and Bill Ayers, who became part of the Weatherman faction of SDS at U of M. Dave said he did not believe in violence and did not share that part of the SDS philosophy.

Later, Black Panther Eldridge Cleaver and comedian Dick Gregory ran for President and Vice President as candidates of the Peace and Freedom Party. They decided they needed a bodyguard, and because Cleaver and his entourage were convicted felons who could not carry weapons, Dave was nominated to carry the shotgun. Dave Lawson carrying a shotgun as a bodyguard conjures up the image of another romantic radical of the time, Salvador Allende of Chile in a famous picture: at his desk in a suit, with bandoliers of ammunition criss-crossing his chest on his business suit, a shotgun held upright in his right hand. He and Dave, with their shotguns. Both would seem to have about the same amount of threat and menace, which was not that much. Allende was dead 48 hours after the picture was taken. The official explanation was suicide, but he was generally thought to be the victim of the machinations of Henry Kissinger, the CIA, ITT, Augusto Pinochet, and his generals. Charlie said he was glad Dave was never subjected to similar forces. "I think he would have suffered the same result." He ultimately and ironically became a programmer for Texas Instruments, working on rocketry software for the military-industrial complex.

Dave was a close friend of Mike Munn, and Bob Vee. A case could be made that he was too friendly, too democratic, too trusting, too good. He and Rick Fowler both, once they walked through the bubble of East Lansing and into a different world, would not know who to befriend and why, or why not. East Lansing confidence? Ideology? David Lawson was blinded by goodness, Rick by greed. Secure he was walking in righteousness, unafraid and un-fearful, Dave partied with George Hall and Rick Fowler. He was a leftist but practical, not into breaking things, not a ranter, a fine person.

# Chapter 33

# BOB VEE STANDS FOR TRADITIONAL VALUES

Vee's parents' house on Audubon in East Lansing was neat and clean. It was so well kept that it barely looked lived in. As time went on, maybe it wasn't.

Vee's father Russ drove a new red four-cylinder Pontiac Tempest coupe, Martha, Bob's mom, drove a new dark blue Olds convertible with a white top, paid for by the company, WJIM. Both parents were pretty generous about letting Bob drive their cars, which were very well cared for by Russ. He took good care of everything in sight as well as he knew how, including Vee, but increasingly, Vee was out of sight.

In early 1965 Charlie knocked at the side door of Vee's house. Charlie heard him holler "Come on in." Charlie turned the knob, opened the door and entered. He was in the bathroom getting ready, talking to himself in the mirror. "Pretty Bob, pretty boy," he repeated, clucking and preening to himself like he was talking to a parakeet, then moving his fists with thumbs toward his face, back and forth, pointing to himself, emphasizing his greatness. Maybe he was expecting additional acclaim from behind the mirror telling him he was the fairest of them all.

"Vee," Charlie asked, "do you want to go to the Grill?" "Nah, I gotta go pick my brother up at the airport, haven't seen him for half a year, he's coming home from Principia [a prestigious boarding school]" Charlie left, Vee went to the airport, picked

Tommy up, After looking at him, Vee, usually not short of words said nothing. They drove silently home.

The vestibule of the VerPlanck home opened up at the front into an expansive living room with highly polished floors covered by expensive rugs that were, in the heated moment, threatened with becoming scuffed and ruffled. Vee started talking to Tommy about proper behavior in looks and actions. He was mad. "Get a haircut, you son of a bitch, you look like a girl." Tom protested that it was not that long and that it was the style. Tom's hair was about an inch below his collar. "Style my ass, you look a disgrace." Vee said.

Vee's mother arrived home and joined the conversation. She agreed with Bob. She and Bob seldom agreed on anything:

"Your brother's right, Tommy. You need to get a haircut. You can't stay in this house looking like that." Martha said.

"Have you ever looked in a newspaper or magazine and seen how people dress outside of East Lansing?" Tommy countered.

"I don't give a rip. We're in East Lansing and you're going to get a haircut."

"And another thing, get rid of that goddamn marijuana that's in your suitcase," Bob said.

Martha recoiled at the sound of the words.

"Your baby boy is bringing back drugs from that hot-shot school you're sending him to," Bob said to Martha

"Get rid of it, Tommy," Martha said.

Bob pushed Tommy from the dining room toward the kitchen to emphasize the point. Tom, realizing it was hopeless to try and reason with them, opened the kitchen door and slammed it as hard as he could behind him as he left the house to go for a walk.

Before the summer of 1965 was over, Vee was smoking marijuana with Tommy and relying on Tommy as his source of supply. Vee showed no signs of embarrassment at this change of position.

Charlie was never an evangelist for dope, and wasn't ever in the vanguard of the movement, but after a trip to California to visit Anne Cox and others who were working and smoking, he gradually overcame his moral objections. Back in East Lansing he was ahead of some friends who, like he did when he was sixteen, thought it sinful, immoral, character defining, destructive. Dick Giltner's grandfather had a hall named for him at MSU. He and Charlie were at a friend's party over on Kedzie in EL and went into a closet together, partly to be inconspicuous, partly to capture and inhale the second-hand marijuana smoke. If they weren't found out about by the smell, they were found out by the giggling. In a huge melodramatic gesture of moral theater, Charlie's host ordered them out of the closet and out of the house. They had disrespected him, disrespected his house, conducted themselves immorally and on and on. The chain of adjectives continued until they were down the block and out of hearing distance. Six months later the host was smoking more dope in a month than Charlie did in a lifetime.

## Bob Vee Gets A Little Political — Look At Those Fascist Pigeons Strut

The guys were developing their political positions pretty gradually. Vee's father's harshest scorn was for the passivity of draft resisters. "I'm not sending you to school to lie down in the street," he would say. Charlie started developing pretty moderate anti-war positions, Chal's positions were about the same as Charlie's. Sherb was quiet about what he thought about the war, but on race, he was a racist even then, didn't even know any black people, hadn't been around any. East Lansing was all white.

Vee started taking things half-seriously, which was about as serious as he ever got. The time he spent with Dave Lawson, who was already serious, good natured, radical, and anti-war, contributed to Vee's increased political awareness. He practiced what he preached, worked at Olds, worked as a construction laborer-foreman, thought working with his hands was honest and rewarding work. Bob Vee took this part of Lawson's radicalism, the hard work, the work with your hands, make something part, perhaps more seriously than the antiwar part. That maybe was because he was living through his own family what he'd also seen elsewhere in EL. He was not impressed with the moral costs and compromises that came with achieving middle-class success, not impressed with the vanity and delusion of social superiority. Vee too was a democratic unsnobbish person, though he was aware of his good looks, his good humor, and his ability to captivate people.

By this time the word "fascist" had become an overused and depreciated currency. The pro-war militants were all called fascists, as were, of course President John Hannah and President Lyndon Johnson. Vee was the first one to turn the word into a joke. Don't agree with him on a time to get started somewhere: "You're a clock fascist, Charlie," he'd say. Disagree with him about the merits of a particular athletic team: "Fascist." Get an uncomprehending waitress. He'd call her a fascist. The waitress would walk away even more uncomprehending "What is this guy talking about? And what's a fascist anyway? And why am I one?" Somebody over-carded him unexpectedly in a bad-beat hand of poker. "Fascist." He always had a light touch and made it funny.

## In Lansing—Starting In "The Shop"

The people supported by the Oldsmobile factories in Lansing could be a tough bunch. Many turned it into a middle-class lifestyle. If they were wearing a suit and carrying a briefcase they would be indistinguishable from any other middle-class family. Others would be handicapped by scar tissue from the life.

There were fissures and cracks in the foundations of some of those blue-collar middle income families. Into those cracks seeped the sweat and bile of those who had to work too hard to keep up with the line, too hard to pay the mortgage on the new South-side Lansing house with the new Olds, maybe two Olds' in the driveway maybe a Buick, that they got with a factory discount. That driveway had three growing kids playing in it, who had to be kept on the straight and narrow. They had to get through college so that they would have a life that would be better than working on the line.

It was difficult to generalize about those jobs. Charlie was hired in the summer in the mid-sixties as a forklift driver to supply the line in final assembly. A pretty cushy job. A guy he went to Eastern with, Jim Dickey, all he seemed to do was walk around with a clip board and write a few numbers down. Other guys had much tougher jobs than Charlie, like Eddie Lloyd whom he went to Eastern High with. He picked up drive shafts weighing 40 lbs. from a rack above his shoulders, turned around and installed them in the cars chassis down around his ankles, all day every day. Later he was skilled trades as a painter. "Final assembly wasn't that bad," Eddie said, "wasn't that noisy or dirty compared to the engine plant. That was hell on earth there. An oily fog hung in the air, along with metal dust from the boring. There was a chemical vat that some of the parts had to be dipped in and guys wore gloves up to their elbows. Some were starting to get skin rashes, were getting sick. It was urine poisoning. Some were pissing in the vat and on the floor so they could make production. There were big fat rats from the river roaming around. If somebody got sick or had a minor injury, and there was nobody to replace you, you couldn't go. In the 70s OSHA and the union made them come in and clean it all up."

Some of the guys could be tough and hard, and at their worst, belligerent. When guys worked 50 or 60 hours or more in "the shop," keeping up with the line, they often felt like letting off steam, either about factory life's inequities or something else. Foremen had control of their job which meant control of their lives. One friend's father, back during the Depression, had to work on the foreman's farm in the summertime—for nothing—to keep his job at Oldsmobile. They couldn't take it out on the foremen. They shouldn't have taken it out on their wives and kids, though some did. That left the bars. Many walked in with the triggers to their temper already cocked. In World War I there was "Kilroy Was Here" in the bars and bathrooms on the other side of the world. In World War II and Korea there was "North Lansing Against the World." There were bars in Lansing to brawl in, usually nothing worse than that. But sometimes it was worse than that. Bars circled the various GM and Olds plants. Bars lined North Washington Avenue from Michigan to Saginaw. They were interrupted by the housing of Lansing's elite for a few blocks, then picked up again in North-town, now Old Town where if you were looking for a fight you would find one easy. A friend of Charlie's who had another hard job on the line, said "if you went into those bars you'd better be ready to fight."

Charlie remembers the time he was driving by the Mustang Bar late at night with a buddy and he saw a cop beating the hell out of a guy who was lying on his back, spitting what looked like teeth at the cop. It was Charlie's Uncle. His buddies asked Charlie if they wanted to stop. "What are we going to do, tug on the cop's sleeve and tell him to be nice? It's not the first time my Uncle has been in a brawl—or got his ass kicked. I'll bring him some liniment and a six-pack in the morning."

Charlie said his Uncle was a good guy, worked at Olds, was a WWII vet, liked to drink beer, fish, and philosophize. He would also fight about Roosevelt, the Democratic Party, and his union, all of which he supported. He said what was on his mind and would spit in the eye of anybody who disagreed with him. Charlie said "my Uncle talked of the times before the war when it was so hot in the plant that the workers keeled over on the job because hydration wasn't as well understood then, and if they drank too much water they'd have to piss too much, and a bad foreman could be very tight about bathroom breaks."

It could be rough, but it was also candid. Lansing, the Oldsmobile-supported town, had good income, but it was different than East Lansing. The old song "Smiling faces, smiling faces—tell lies." Not that lies weren't told in Lansing and everywhere, but there was a certain transparency of thought and action in Lansing that was missing in higher circles. You found out where you stood in a hurry.

## Oldsmobile and the East Lansing Life

The autos that Ransom Olds and other carmakers wrought were the enemies of the concentrated city. Cars would disperse population to anywhere that they wanted the car to take them. The suburbs expanded. The vitality of downtown Lansing had lessened as the sixties progressed; Frandor hurt downtown more. Frandor was one of the first shopping "malls" in the country that responded to the population shift. It was built on a former golf course between Lansing and East Lansing, on what had been the south edge, perhaps in the south end, of the Chandler swamp. The land was valuable, but not that valuable because it was so low, plus it was cheaper because it was in Lansing Township and the taxes were as low as the land. It was an amalgamation of 'Fran" for Francis Corr and 'dor' for Dora, Francis's wife. Francis was one of the first to understand the exodus from urban centers to the suburbs that was going to happen all over the country and profited by it.

One of the first businesses to leave the urban center was the Lansing Oldsmobile dealership. The Olds dealership skipped from the northeast corner of Kalamazoo and Capitol Avenue in downtown Lansing, to Michigan Avenue between Mifflin and Hayford streets. It was not yet owned by Karl Story, it was Trevellyan Oldsmobile at the time. Their best salesman, Karl Story, bought the dealership from Trevellyan in the mid-fifties. Then, shortly after Frandor opened, so, too, did Karl Story buy

*'49 OLDS WITH "ROCKET V-8," AMONG THE FIRST POST-WWII OVERHEAD VALVE HIGH PERFORMANCE V-8'S. IT ACCELERATED OLDS' SALES IN THE ALREADY HOT POST-WWII MARKETPLACE.*

his parcel and open Story Olds just to the south of Frandor on Michigan Avenue between Lansing and East Lansing in Lansing Township. He too was attracted by the lower taxes. Karl Story, the super-salesman was from the state of New York, as were many of the best people who were part of the colossus that was General Motors.

The Oldsmobile overhead valve "Rocket V-8," introduced in 1949, propelled GM past the competition. It gave GM a market share approaching 51%. The old flathead side valve Ford V-8, dating from 1932, innovative in its time, was left in the dust. The new Olds V-8s made GM and Oldsmobile even more prosperous, and Oldsmobile made Lansing prosper more than ever. It also made Karl Story rich.

Or perhaps it should be said that Karl Story made himself rich. He was also closely connected to the corporation. He could talk candidly to company management about what needed to be fixed and also about what was right about Oldsmobiles. They listened. Olds knew how to make them. Story knew how to sell them. He priced them fairly, discounted them, perhaps more than the competition, and gave fair prices for trade-ins. He was an excellent dealer, an excellent businessman. He paid attention to the details, made sure his salesmen kept the cars' oil and water topped off, the cars themselves clean and shiny. Story and Oldsmobile were perfect for the famished post-war market. The center of that market was Lansing, Michigan. He had the only Olds "stores" in the metro-Lansing area. But there were other reasons why that was so, and why Karl did well.

Up to that time, and continuing into the seventies, destination charges were tacked onto every automobile sold. The charges were more or less based on how far the cars were shipped to the dealership that sold them. This made cars on the west and east coast more expensive than they were in the mid-west where they were produced. There were several ways that out-of-state buyers would deal with the extra expense of having them delivered. One was that they could fly into Lansing where they could actually watch their cars being made, then pick them up for delivery. Another was that they could pay a "drive-away" company to have a driver, often a college kid like Charlie, pick up a car and drive it to its destination. Sometimes the drive-away company would pay all the gas to the driver, sometimes half, sometimes a tankful. The driver got a new car to drive to his or her destination; the drive-away company got whatever the new owner of the Oldsmobile would pay the company. Up until the mid-fifties, Oldsmobile Corporation itself sold the cars to the people who came to Lansing to pick them up or had the drive-away do it to avoid the destination charges. Then things changed. Oldsmobile Division of General Motors got out of the car sales agency business. The cars had to be ordered through a dealership. That meant the Story Olds Dealership. This helped create the Story Olds dynasty. The dynasty and all its beneficiaries were very very grateful. It made Karl Story very very rich. He built an empire, more Olds dealerships in Detroit and Florida, some Datsun dealerships, a piece of Isuzu Corporation, real estate around the city, the state, the world. He became one of the first "mega-Dealers," before Auto-Nation, before Penske, and it was all privately held by Story Corporation. Lansing was the center of his empire.

Charlie had driven his car into Karl Story's Oldsmobile dealership next to Frandor to look at the new Oldsmobiles. He'd traded his '53 Chevy in on a '57 Ford after a high-speed run to the Music Box at Houghton Lake had collapsed a couple of the lifters on the Chevy. He couldn't come close to affording a new Oldsmobile, but the salesman couldn't know that, because if he'd worked at Olds on the line, he could have afforded it.

He was just starting to get out of the car when he heard, "Don't touch that car, you little son-of-a-bitch. Get away from there." A little kid had wandered on to the Story dealership lot. The little kid hadn't said anything. He hadn't done anything. And he hadn't touched the car. He put his hands in his pockets and walked away with his head down. Karl Story would have done it differently because he knew that maybe someday he could sell the kid a car, or, sooner still, the kid's father a car. The person bullying the kid was Leo Jerome, Karl's son-in-law. As Charlie stepped out of the car, he was closer to Leo than anyone else. He went to talk to someone else to answer his questions.

Leo was a football player out of the University of Wisconsin, second-generation Polish. He changed his name to Jerome after Karl suggested it would be easier to sell a car with a name like Jerome than with a Polish name nobody could pronounce or spell. Leo was married to Eleanor Story. He had no money to offer to gain Eleanor's hand in marriage, but he gave everything else he had to give to gain entry into the life that being part of the Story Olds empire offered.

Eleanor Story was beautiful. Her sister Nancy Story, younger by two years, was beautiful. They were Goddesses. If their faces and forms were miniaturized, chromed, and put on the hoods of the upscale cars of the thirties and forties along with swans and Venuses and other symbols of grace and beauty, they would be a tribute to the cars. When Oldsmobile had the new car introductions at the Civic Center, Nancy was there, chatting beside a new 1979 Olds Toronado on the stage. She looked more radiant than the professional models paid to look good and radiate.

Eleanor was dark-haired, Nancy was blonde. They were part of the East Lansing High School elites, not snooty, not unfriendly, just aware of their prerogatives. A good friend of Eleanor's at the time was Prudy Shelley, another member in good standing of the northern European lineage "in crowd" at East Lansing High. Prudy was tall, blonde, buxom and curvaceous, with a face that was chiseled in long strokes, one of God's better creations of an exterior. She was born to the purple, it seemed, or at least to the upper-middle class as that life was lived in East Lansing, Michigan. It was a productive class; it was a competitive class. It was a white-collar class. It was a class that played by the rules and mastered them, or sometimes adjusted them, whether they be left or right wing, business or academic, pro or anti-war, pro or anti-Dionysian age. It was a self-satisfied class, with some right to be. It was dedicated to perpetuating itself through good parenting, good education, good career, and good marriage. For females, both pre-feminist and non-feminist, that meant marrying well. With close to 97% of East Lansing High's graduating class going off to higher education to become doctors, lawyers, and industry chieftains, it would have been easy for Prudy to marry a doctor or a lawyer.

From outward appearances Prudy appeared to have had an upbringing similar to the Story girls and the other boys and girls who were growing up in East Lansing. She had a kind manner and a winning smile that brought her friends and no enemies. Her family lived around the corner from Bob Vee. She and her brother Pete went to Glencairn School. Her father was the director of education for the Michigan Department of

ELEANOR STORY
EAST LANSING HIGH YEARBOOK 1960

NANCY STORY
EAST LANSING HIGH YEARBOOK 1962

PRUDY SHELLEY
EAST LANSING HIGH YEARBOOK 1960

MARCIA WILKINSON
EAST LANSING HIGH YEARBOOK 1962

Corrections, a big prison system with big needs. He also had a private psychology practice. He did not counsel George Hall, #090753, who would be released from prison later and get to know his daughter and future son-in-law, Rick Fowler. Prudy met Rick between classes at East Lansing High.

### Princess Nancy Attends Marcia's Party

Marcia Wilkinson, whom Charlie went to junior college with, had a house not far from Vee's in East Lansing. The Wilkinsons were solid. The dark red brick Tudor was solid. It was on the winding, mature tree-lined street of Roxburgh, in a prosperous neighborhood composed of faculty and business people. Mr. Wilkinson's two Cadillacs fit snugly in his two-car garage. Cadillacs achieved a substantial size at that point, and the house had been built pre WWII, when cars and garages were a lot smaller. He commuted every day to Mount Pleasant, Michigan, seventy-five miles north, where his chemical business was located.

Marcia was the dutiful daughter, one of three siblings. She had a round face, big round brown button eyes, and a curious smile. Marcia was a good person, a good friend, sociable, threw a good party. When Charlie got to her home, he saw twenty or twenty-five people outside talking. Through the glass between the rails and mullions of her very large living room window he could see many more people crowded inside. Most all the scions of the East Lansing bourgeoisie were there. They were good looking, well dressed, carefree. Well, maybe not carefree, surely they all had their cares and their problems, joys and sorrows, but they weren't evident that night. Vee and Sherb and several other guys Charlie knew were there, but no other bumboys; Marcia did not hang out at the Grill.

The scope of their interests and cares, Charlie's interests and cares, were narrow. They didn't extend then to the other side of the world in Viet Nam, or back here with the buildup of the war, where the two issues would soon be joined as one.

A single person, out of all those present at the party, likely was aware of what was going on in that distant world. That was Bob Brandstatter, MSUG operative Arthur Brandstatter Senior's third-born son. His father's absences from this country to Vietnam must have made him ask about the country. There would have been enough talk over the kitchen table for him to know. He likely approved of the efforts that America and MSU and his father were so heartily involved in. Other recent graduates of East Lansing High, like Jane Munn, Mike Munn, and Mike and Vee's buddy David Lawson were going to be just as vehemently opposed. Neither Jane, nor Mike, nor Dave, nor Dave's future wife Karen Wallace was present at the party.

You can't talk about what you're not aware of; oftentimes you can't talk about what you are aware of. There was no political talk at the party. Several people said hello as Charlie arrived, some warmly, some politely polite. Charlie didn't see Marcia right away but knew she was fine that he was there. Charlie saw Vee from across the room. Vee would never miss a party but he was a little standoffish at them, even when he knew everybody really well. He was getting loaded, and whomever he was talking to was laughing at whatever he was saying. You couldn't help not laugh at what Vee was saying.

Charlie made a little small talk with the people he knew, said hello to Marcia's mother, sitting in the living room who remembered him and was friendly. He meandered down to the basement that was finished just like the rest of the house.

Then Charlie saw the Princess. "She was radiant in beauty, sapphire blue eyes sparkling, a smile like the sun coming up in the morning." Charlie said. She was mingling, introducing herself and her fiancé. It was Nancy Story, Oldsmobile mega-dealer Karl Story's youngest daughter. She was low-key and friendly. "Nice to meet you," her fiancé Doug Milbury said, with emphasis on the "You" and a direct eye-lock in the way fraternity and sorority types did. He was a little above average in height, even-featured, well-dressed, not expressed in fancy.

"I thought he was an all right guy, not real loose, but focused, business-like." Charlie said. He would be all business, furnishing the next generation of the business that took it to a new level with the brains that the other son-in-law did not have. Nancy had met Doug Milbury at Syracuse University in New York where Karl's roots were. He moved on for more introductions. Charlie moved on, didn't think much more about it until he talked with Vee and Sherb later. He had a couple more beers, then a couple more after that.

The pop hit "Do You Love Me, Now That I Can Dance" began playing on the record player. Marcia had all the good stuff. Rock n roll was starting to eclipse Motown at that point. Charlie danced some. Sherb danced, not as well as he thought he did. When there was a lull in the dancing, Charlie and Sherb talked, watching Vee who did not dance, talking to someone in the corner who was laughing at Vee's antics of imitating someone or something with a great deal of animation. "Enjoying Vee's performance, Sherb?" said Charlie; "From the first day we met him," said Sherb.

It was a great party, several hours. By the time Charlie noticed the time, it was getting late, The crowd had thinned out; only about thirty or forty people were left. When Charlie walked out the front door he saw five or six people gathered around somebody on the ground. It was Vee. He was retching. He looked horrible. His face was all red and swollen; his throat was swollen. He was struggling to breathe. In his hand was an expensive cut glass whiskey decanter. Charlie'd seen it on the mantle of the fireplace in the basement. It was full of light blue powdered soap. Vee had tried to drink the soap. Mrs. Wilkinson was not in mothering mode. She was pissed, not about Vee's sarcasm and humor, which she'd weathered in the past, or that Vee had made off with the decanter. She was pissed that he could very well be harming himself, not to mention single-handedly turning the scene into something more out of the bowery than what usually was a tony neighborhood. Mrs.

Wilkinson was without pretensions and had seen a lot. It wasn't about appearances. She was double pissed at Vee, out of control.

The next time Charlie saw Vee and Sherb, he didn't ask Vee about trying to drink the soap. If he had, Vee would have said something funny to get out of his embarrassment. Instead he asked them what they thought about Doug Milbury, Nancy's fiance. They both, without hesitation, said they thought he was a jerk. Charlie didn't see it, persisted and asked them why. They couldn't really say why; they just thought so. For Vee, was it that Milbury represented all the striving and studying that he was coming to regret not doing a little more of? Or was there a smidgen of jealousy there, Sherb because he thought he was so smart that he deserved to be with the Princess, and Vee because he thought that he was as good-looking as she was so he ought to be with her. At any rate, her fiancé did not pass scrutiny with the guys.

### Nancy Gets Engaged, Eleanor Too

Charlie ended up at Nancy Story's engagement party at their expansive home on the Looking Glass River by accident. He'd met Nancy at Marcia Wilkinson's party some months before. Nancy didn't know him from Adam. It all started with Marcia. Her good friend was Jill Behymer. Jill didn't have a date for Nancy's wedding engagement party, and apparently dates at these sorts of events were expected. So Marcia asked Jill about Charlie. Jill said okay. Marcia asked Charlie if he would escort her there. He said okay.

As to whether Jill Behymer was psychologically secure or not, Charlie felt in retrospect that there was less there than met the eye. Jill was tall, blonde, beautiful. That she did not consider herself so was a consideration that existed only in her mind. After college she married a man in the steel business, moved to Hong Kong, and circulated in the realms of the rich and beautiful where she moved with imperial ease. Charlie's take on her at the time was that she was pretty insecure. Her take on Charlie was that he was just a minimally socially acceptable vehicle to get her to Nancy's engagement party. You didn't talk to vehicles, you drove them, or in that case Charlie drove her. "She didn't have much to say to me," Charlie said.

Arriving at the Story home was like arriving at the Great Gatsby's. It was a display of grandeur that would rank high anywhere. From the outside it seemed to go on forever, The grounds had lights everywhere, and they sparkled in the night all the way to the horizon. Nancy and her family had moved there from East Lansing while Nancy was still in high school. Inside was filled with Story friends and relatives and acquaintances and business relationships from Lansing and New York, Syracuse, and beyond, everywhere the Storys knew people from their far-flung enterprises.

The party had been going on for quite a while by the time Charlie and Jill Behymer arrived. "Two scenes pressed on, hit me over the head really, as we entered the living room," Charlie said. "The first was seeing Leo Jerome, husband of Nancy's sister Eleanor, on the left side of a spacious living room, drinking his drink and chatting amiably with a guy I didn't know. On the right side of the room was Eleanor, coming out of what appeared to be a bedroom embracing John Brandstatter, Arthur Brandstatter Sr.'s second-born son. Eleanor looked more than a little tipsy, her wig was cockeyed, and her arms were all over John. Art Brandstatter Sr. may have got around the world and to Vietnam, but his son John got around East Lansing."

Leo willingly paid the price. Maybe the reality of it was what Vee had in mind when he rejected the middle-class upward mobility model. Too much striving, too little fidelity, too many compromises.

## More Political Leaders Are Assassinated

On April 4, 1968, Martin Luther King interceded in the Memphis, Tennessee, garbage workers strike. The black workers were paid much less and had much worse working conditions. He was also critical about the Vietnam War. King was shot by James Earl Ray at the Lorraine Hotel in south Memphis. Many white bars in the south erupted in cheers. Major cities erupted in flames. There was a big demonstration at MSU. It remained peaceful.

On June 6, 1968 Robert Kennedy was killed by Sirhan Sirhan in Los Angeles, California after winning the California Democratic primary as a peace candidate with strong establishment and black community support. His motivations? An existential stew of ambition and idealism and opportunism, an eager willingness to represent the Kennedy and Irish tribes. He had a high capacity for avoiding the embarrassment of previous positions. He was an integral part of all the decisions that JFK was part of that got us further into Vietnam, was personal and political friends with people like Robert McNamara and Maxwell Taylor that helped persuade JFK to do so. His death was the death of the anti-war movement's chances in the 1968 elections.

# CHAPTER 34

# THE GUYS GO SEE THEIR STATE REPRESENTATIVE

The guys were dimly aware that political events were a little unusual in the summer of 1968, but they had other things on their mind. Dave "Ratface" Smith, who'd been kicked out of one state office building for stealing stuff from the concession stand of a blind woman in the Mason Building, got a job as a janitor in the Capitol building. He got the job from his mother, who worked in Governor Romney's office. He had the run of the place. There weren't any offices he didn't have the keys to. He also got to know State Representative Dale Warner.

The Capitol Building was one of those grand old post-Civil War capitols designed by Elijah Meyer as knock-offs of the federal Capitol, slimmer and similar. In Michigan's it was more economically-constructed than his later efforts, with a lot of faux-marble columns, paneled wainscoting with faux-mahogany wood-graining over pine. It had a mostly wood and brick frame.

Meyer designed Capitol buildings in Austin, Denver, and other places. Denver's gold leaf dome supposedly inspired Mark Twain's label of the rapacious 1890s as the gilded age. The other states had a lot more money to spend on them. Michigan was his first effort in 1869, and there was a lot riding on it for him. It was an engineering marvel at the time. It had an elevator that rose and fell by counter-balancing it with the amounts of water put in and taken out. A ventilation system kept it relatively cool, pre-air conditioning. Almost all of the executive offices were contained there, from governor to attorney general. If its politicians did not always soar, the building did, with its lofty height and dome, and its elegant rotunda area with gilt and columns and glass tiled floor, with open space that started at the first floor and went far up and away to the top several hundred feet above. The interior of the dome contained eight murals in renaissance-revival style consistent with the architecture of the building. They were allegorical murals illustrating art and agriculture, law, science, justice, industry commerce, and education. It looked like something you'd see by an artist in Rome. It was, and remains, very beautiful.

The rotunda separated its two capacious legislative chambers with large wide hallways, or lobbies. There were legislative leadership offices off the corridors. The floors were of gleaming black and white checkerboard marble laid diagonally. The "lobbyists" congregated there like rats. Instead of being kept away from the legislative granary by chicken wire, they were kept out and away from the legislative chamber entrances by about twenty feet of burgundy-colored velvet ropes held up by chrome stanchions, and were maintained by the sergeants-at-arms. In fact, lobbyists weren't contained. They didn't stop. The mutual whoring was unstoppable, difficult to determine who was on top and who was on the bottom. With politicians it was about survival, money being the mother's milk for election and re-election. There was an old saying about the three rules of politics. The first rule was to get re-elected. The second and third rules were to follow the first. That accomplished, it was also about ambition. Most politicians were hard-wired to "go along and get along." They would do this until they reached the proper level of glory and satisfaction at which time they would then do their job more or less in earnest. Most wanted up, most of the time. Some had obtainable goals like the State Senate or Congress. Others thought by rights they should be president or at least governor. The state was the worse off for it, then as now. Now all the ambition, all the grasping, is compressed and exaggerated by term limits.

The basement of the Capitol where Ratface let Vee and Sherb and Mulligan and Chal into the building was spare and plain. Its floors were gray-painted concrete; the walls painted block. It did not have the grandeur of the upper floors but it did have history. In glass cases, in back of the round, cast iron pillars providing support for the dome above, were the battle flags of the Grand Army of the Republic, many in tatters with bullet holes and dried blood coloring them. Real.

On that night things were a little surreal. The guys weren't concerning themselves with any of that stuff. They had a couple of six packs with them and were looking forward to a unique visit to the Capitol and meeting with their legislator in a most productive way.

First, Ratface took them up toward the top of the dome, the area which is closed to tourists and to just about everybody else. Ratface unlocked the small, obscure hatch door below the wainscoting on the fourth floor. It led to stairs that wound upward and spiraled around the dome, several hundred feet in the air, on what to the ascenders seemed like shaky catwalks and stairs between the outer steel wall of the dome and its interior skin that were used mainly by maintenance and emergency crews. The only lights were dim bare bulbs spaced sporadically along the rough, unfinished wood framing. It seemed like they were being led up into a medieval dungeon tower. At various places, they passed observation holes where they could look out, into the dome. The floor of the rotunda was a dizzyingly long way down. They got no comfort from the view.

They'd had a couple of beers and a little acid, but it didn't relax them. "Let's get going where we've got a place where there's something under us," Vee said. Sherb had seen worse in Vietnam. He didn't say anything. Chal said, "There could be ghosts here." Ratface had done it before and was enjoying their discomfort. "Isn't this cool, guys?" he said; the others said nothing. They finally got near the top where there was a platform with a ladder that had to be climbed the last ten feet up into the cupola. The cupola was about six feet wide with glass on every side. It offered a three hundred and sixty degree view of Lansing, probably the best there could be. The cupola seemed to sway in the wind. The topography of the city loomed far below, a giant patchwork quilt of black velvet, each patch of a block stitched together with diamond threads that were the streetlights. It was a clear starry night with a full moon. The wind whistled through the cracks around the windows.

Vee said, "Ratface, it was awfully nice of you to take us up here on this history lesson and see the sights, but I'm ready to go down now." Mulligan had had his equilibrium and his poise tested many times before when on acid, but it was still a test. He was thinking how much he'd like to have his feet back on firm ground and how much he'd appreciate it when he did, if he didn't die on the way. When they got down, their knees were knocking worse than when they were up there. Nobody said anything for a while.

After the guys got down out of the dome, Ratface took them to the Supreme Court chambers on the third floor above the governor's offices in the east wing. At that time, many of the offices below were honeycombed with added temporary floors to take advantage of all the space of the high ceilings even though the practice put a questionable load on the structure and was probably a fire hazard. Plus at the time, all the frescoed walls of the Capitol had been painted over with flat white paint. The Michigan Supreme Court offices weren't like that. They had their original frescoing with high ceiling and paneled wood all around. Ratface opened the door. The guys followed through. Then he shut it and locked it behind them. The only occupant of the room was State Representative Dale Warner, from Eaton County. Warner was the Chairman of the Special House Committee on Narcotics.

The guys' problem about drugs was that they wanted some. Dale Warner sat in one of the high-backed heavily padded leather chairs used by the Supreme Court judges. The chairs had supported the posteriors and the posturing of many a judge. The chairs had been present while much that was both wise and foolish had gone on in the State of Michigan. This was more of the latter. Chal said he had a "bulging satchel full of drugs." It had a sign on the inside that said "Property of Rep. Dale Warner. For Investigative Use Only." Warner lifted his arm from the heavy leather padded arm of the chair like a pasha. He took all the drugs out of the satchel. In it was everything a drug abuser could want, from acid to amyl nitrate, lots of marijuana, Vicodin. He laid out the drugs in a line on the conference table that had been placed there many years before when the state and the Capitol and the table were newly created. The guys took from the samples like they were picking out hors d'oeuvres from a buffet table. They passed around beer to everyone to wash it down. The room had dignity. Its tall, high ceilings sheltered built-in cabinetry with the rows and rows of law books that contained legal decisions that looked more orderly than they were. The dignity and greatness of the room did not extend to its present occupants.

They popped their pills of choice, talked, and wandered around the offices. The eastern side offices looked out on downtown and Michigan Avenue stretching east. In the light of the full moon, the city stretched east, visible across the Grand River for several blocks, then faded into blackness, with the parallel trails of streetlights on both sides of the avenue being observable nearly all the way to East Lansing and the campus. The streetlights, the Union Building, and the rest of the campus were obscured by the trees and a bend in the avenue.

Looking down below in the front of the State-House square, they could see the posterior of the statue of Austin Blair, Civil War governor of Michigan, looking poised and persuasive standing there in the dark in bronze. A governor's statue would never be seen, unhorsed, in a Southern Statehouse square. Blair didn't need to be on a horse, he got the job done.

Austin Blair was first a Whig, then a Free-soiler, then, under the oaks in Jackson, Michigan, a founder of the Republican Party. He opposed slavery, secession, and capital punishment. He was for the war, women's suffrage, and black suffrage. Within days of the firing on Fort Sumter, he called for volunteers and $1 million to support them. He raised four regiments. The US Secretary of War wrote him and told him to stop, that they couldn't have any more troops from Michigan. He ignored the letter and raised three more, including a sizable contingent of "colored" units.

The guys talked about many things, but not about Austin Blair or politics. They offered observations about life, their part in it, their true friendship, strengthened by the effects of the drugs. At some point in the evening, Rep. Warner excused himself and said if he could help them out again, he was at their service. At this point, the Supreme Court Conference Room and its offices, which had all the stability and dignity that strong architecture could bestow, was starting to seem a little unstable. The room seemed to start moving around a little. With some difficulty they struggled to their feet and said their goodbyes to Warner and shook hands, just like they would do in a conventional Representative–Constituent meeting, except the room was starting to spin. They all sat down, quiet in their own solitary trips. Vee, who'd been up for a couple of days, lay down on the conference table and went to sleep. Mulligan, Sherb, and Chal had another beer apiece and continued to talk. Ratface said he needed to get back to work, and that they should make sure to close and lock the door behind them when they left. Chal and Sherb, who'd taken some Dexamyl, an upper, along with a little acid, were particularly animated. Chal started talking about "new plateaus of consciousness," Mulligan about the possibility of "really touching God."

Ratface came back an hour later, fumbled and stumbled through the door, and said they probably should leave pretty soon because it was getting late. They talked a little longer, then tried to rouse Vee, who was still flat on his back on the Michigan Supreme Court conference table. Mulligan shook him by the sleeve. No response. They talked a little longer. He tried to wake up Vee again. "Seaman Vee, Seaman Vee, Topside" Mulligan pounded on Vee's chest. Vee was working at getting into the merchant marine. "Seaman Vee, Seaman Vee, man stations," Mulligan shouted in Vee's ear. Finally he started to stir. He opened his eyes and was unfamiliar with his surroundings. But Vee had awoken many times before to unfamiliar surroundings. He woke up and acted like he slept on Supreme Court conference tables all the time. "Come on, Vee, we've got to get going," Chal said. Everyone was a little unsteady on their feet. "Go down to the first floor and take the Ottawa Street exit to your left," Ratface said. He thought they'd be less likely to bump into a night watchman.

With concealed confusion they made their way out of the Supreme Court chambers, walked down to the Rotunda area, and took a quarter turn, around the corner to the massive open stairway with marble treads. The treads had concave ovals worn in them by legislators and others who had conducted the affairs of state over the last hundred years. Ascending, descending, transient. Every step a microscopic abrasion of dust on marble. The ovals were a politician's permanent trace in an impermanent political world. The guys placed their feet on the treads, unsteadily made their way down to the first floor, and walked to the north side exit. Mulligan opened the door…

Then they saw the big stained glass window. It was the stained glass mural in St. Paul's Episcopal Church across the street, all lit up, picturing Christ and his disciples. First they were transfixed, then transported, caught up in a Halley's Comet tail of color and light. It swooped down on them, washed over them, tumbled them. Laser strobes of every color of glass in the mural flashed around them, over them, through them. They were taken out and away from their bodies, standing there on the sandstone steps of the Capitol. They were as one with their comet vehicle, leaving earth in the distance, heading for distant galaxies. The mural resurrected itself for a nanosecond in Chal's mind, and St Paul was with him, racing, riding beside him. They were on horses of fire, the flames of their mane brushed Chal's face but did not burn him. Paul was holding his hand. "Explore with me," he said. They bounced off planets and stars in a shower of sparks and cascading colors.

"Hey, you guys, what are you doing? You've been standing there with the door open for five minutes. You're letting cold air in," the night watchman said. Ratface had told the watchman that they were in the building, but the watchman still thought they were acting weird.

"Sometimes it's not as easy to walk through a door as you think," Vee said to the watchman. Mulligan was too far out on the edge of the cosmos to be brought back by the words of a mere mortal. Vee put his arm around Mulligan's shoulder and gently nudged him through one of the massive oak double doors.

They continued to gaze at the stained glass. Vee, who hadn't taken any acid, just some pot and Dexamyl, figured they ought to get out of there because they were attracting attention to themselves. He'd drive—he was the soberest one of them all. It was three o'clock in the morning by now. They followed their eclectic path back to East Lansing. They were going to go to Sherb's apartment in Spartan Village, MSU campus housing for married couples, but Vee was waking up, energized by his nap on the conference room table and stimulated by the Dexamyl. "Let's go over to Fowler's," Vee said. "There's bound to be something going on there." That something meant gambling, but also booze that Rick provided for anybody who played, plus the possibility of more pharmaceuticals that Prudy might have for Vee. Chal was up for it. Sherb grudgingly said okay. If he was going to gamble and give something his mental attention, he would rather do it with bridge. Mulligan was completely out of it due to his confrontation with the stained glass mural at St Paul's that had him wrestling with his Catholic upbringing again. He mumbled an okay. Vee pulled his 65 Mustang into Rick Fowler's driveway...

## THE GUYS PLAY SOME CARDS, AND OTHER GAMES

There was a card game going on with Rick, Larry Chappell, Harry the Horse, Fuzz, and Doug Parker. They stayed up and talked. Sherb started listening to music through Rick's new hi-tech headphones. Over the earphones he listened to The Who's, "Don't Get Fooled Again"

> "Tnktinktnktnktnktnktnktnktnktnktnk—
> BAWHOOOOM...
> We'll be fighting in the streets
> With our children at our feet
> And the morals that they worship will be gone
> And the men who spurred us on
> Sit in judgment of all wrong
> They decide and the shotgun sings the song
>
> I'll tip my hat to the new constitution
> Take a bow for the new revolution
> Smile and grin at the changes all around me
> Pick up my guitar and play
> Just like yesterday
> And I'll get on my knees and pray
> We don't get fooled again
> Don't get fooled again..."

The song could have been Sherb's anthem. It was deeply dubious about positive change, in an era that was desperately hungry for it. Sherb fought in the war without believing or not believing. He would essentially isolate himself from all of it and "pick up his guitar and play, just like yesterday" and would be too cynical to be fooled. He knew he was too stoned to play poker. He listened to the music and didn't pay any attention to the game.

Mulligan just sat on the couch and mumbled. Nobody could tell exactly about what.

Chal and Vee joined the poker game. The game of choice was mostly seven card stud hi-lo. Lots of betting, lots of chasing with almost nobody getting out because everyone had the eternal hope of backing into half the pot with a low hand developing into a high hand and somebody busting on a high or a low so they could scarf a half. The playing and the betting was mostly fairly reasonable, most all the players knew the rudiments of the game. Things were loosening up however, because the hour was late and the beer, freely distributed, did not make for conservative play. The pots were large. This was good for whoever won or split the cash. It was also good for Rick Fowler who was raking a percentage.

Vee played conservatively, folded several times. Then he got in, starting out with a three card straight, jack high, hoping to build a high hand. Everybody was in. The numbers and the color of the face cards on the table indicated that just about everyone else was aiming for a high hand as well. The next card distributed to Vee was another jack giving him a pair of jacks. Whatever their strength the opponents were raising (a maximum of three raises), Vee stayed with them. The next card for Vee was low, Fuzz to his right caught a queen for a pair of queens. This did not make Vee's jacks look good at all. The betting and the raising continued, Vee called because there was so much foolishness going on that it was hard to tell what anybody really had. On the next card Vee caught another jack for trip jacks, a very formidable high hand assuming Fuzz did not have trip queens and there were not straights or flushes building and the up cards on the table indicated that there weren't. Still the betting and raising continued with the high-hand hopefuls now praying that they could back into the low half of the pot because Vee was obviously going high. The low hand hopefuls continued to raise. The high-hand hopefuls lost heart after the seventh card failed to deliver a straight or a flush. The rules of the game were that there was a bet, then a declare (of high or low) then another bet in which there was again a maximum of three raises. The pot was immense. Then Vee surprised all present. "I sweep," Vee said. This was about as un-conservative and ballsy a call as a poker player could make. The best low hand he could have was jack low. The low hand hopefuls were crushed. They couldn't beat the Jack which Vee had figured. The queens up hopeful didn't fill the full-house, the four card straights busted, all of which Vee had figured out, and it wasn't easy to figure it out. Vee raked in the pot, lightened by more than anyone knew or cared by the percentage Rick took out of it. His pants pockets were bulging with the cash, several hundred dollars. Then in an un-ballsy move he said "I quit." Everybody booed. He took much of the money present with him.

Giddy from the win and with the drugs again influencing him he went upstairs to look for Prudy.

"Wake up little Prudy, wake up," he sang to the tune of the Everly Brothers "Suzie" in a pure sing-song tenor that made him laugh and was so infectious that it made everyone else laugh too. "Dear Prudence, won't you come out tonight" he continued from the Beatles. "Where are you Pru? What are you doing?" Prudy, pleased to hear the sound of his voice, woke up and smiled. "I'm sleeping, Vee, what do you think I was doing." "I want drugs Prudy, right now. And I expect you to get me some, Vee giggled. Prudy roused herself from sleep. "Let me see what I've got." As matter-of-factly as if she were making breakfast for little Ricky, she went to the medicine cabinet in the bathroom and brought back some of her prescription medicines that she thought would satisfy him. When the drugs began to kick in, Vee said "There's smelling the flowers, there's watching sunsets, then there's the rush. We must discuss things. The meaning of life in these perilous times. What would Bozo the clown do about war and peace? Tell me your exact thoughts on this, Pru." They settled down on Prudy's bed and talked.

Down below in the basement where the card game was going on, things were not as enjoyable, as least for Chal. He was losing. Chal had just spotted Rick passing cards under the table to Harry the Horse. "What's going on? What the fuck are you doing? I had the winning hand until you got passed the card," he said to Harry the Horse. Chal thew his cards in, picked up his remaining money and got up from the table. "Come on you guys," referring to Sherb and Mulligan, who weren't paying much attention until then, "let's go home." "I thought you guys were supposed to be my friends." Chal said. Nobody said anything. Harry followed Chal and the guys up the stairs and out into the cool night air. "What could I do Chal," Harry said with semi-sincere earnestness, "Rick passed me the cards. I'll give you your money back." Chal didn't say anything and stomped off. Vee stayed up in Prudy's bedroom. It was a short walk home for him up Harrison Road in the morning. The rest of the guys thought that they were too loaded to drive. They let Doug Parker drive. He was eager for the experience because he was legally blind.

Back at the Capitol a couple of days later, Democratic State Senator Charles Youngblood talked about hopheads and out-of-state-agitators being the problem on MSU's campus. With Rep. Dale Warner providing drugs to the guys and taking them himself, he had a hophead and a doper and an agitator, right in the Republican Party, right in his own legislature. The times just weren't like Senator Youngblood thought they should be. Warner was found to be doing a little too much investigation into drugs, and was defeated in his Republican Party primary re-election bid.

# Chapter 35

# MSU GETS UN-RADICAL

Another alternative to the radical and the violent was the University Christian Movement.

It posited that God acted on earth only through political modes, and that fundamental political change could be realized by activist humans. They were only thirty in number in 1966 and were not formed to disavow the war, but based on their deep-rooted home-grown religious convictions, they soon did. Based upon social issues and evangelical zeal, they made common cause with Catholics, Jews, Methodists and Quakers, surmounted their theological differences, and grew. Their reward for their peacefulness was to have the Red Squad break into the University Methodist Church and copy their files.

Economics Professor Walter Adams, later Interim President of MSU, was supporting Johnson and the administration. He was beginning to have his doubts. Initially he thought the war just didn't make economic sense. Later on he would prove invaluable in preventing violence and in creating a climate that resulted in a manifold increase in the size of the anti-war movement at MSU.

### THE UNIVERSITY OF MICHIGAN SDS WANTS IT THEIR WAY

Later on, in 1967, the Viet Nam Veterans Against the War got involved in confronting U of M; this helped keep the peace. They regarded the Weather Underground from the University of Michigan, without concerns about political correctness, as "a bunch of upper-middle class faggots who want to fuck each other" and chased the radicals out of town.

Maggie Hackett, a friend of Charlie's, thought the Vietnam vets had it partially right:

> "The U of M SDS'ers were the people with money, the people with their noses in the air. They were in part reacting against the authoritarian domineering ways of their parents, but were acting just like them, only with different politics."

In the fall of 1966, MSU SDS grew, but in a different direction without most of the extremism from the University of Michigan Chapter. It also grew in the number of its prima donnas. At the time, MSU had more National Merit scholars than Harvard. They were academic superstars, not used to the anonymity and the size of MSU, and didn't like the war. They also didn't like not being listened to or having their insights and conclusions ignored. The Sattel husband and wife duo, being a few years older, functioned as big brother and big sister to the Merit scholars and helped keep things together by keeping them calm.

### Alternatives to SDS Grow Stronger

As SDS grew, so did the UCM. Area pastors and less-radical but still anti-war professors were concerned that a university organization was needed to oppose the war but be less radical than SDS. Their goal was "to reform the university, educate the people about Viet Nam and civil rights, and strive to ensure social democracy in the world," goals the bumboys would have problems relating to, even on acid.

The regional UCM developed an interpretation of the Vietnam War similar to the SDS, though UCM was more concerned with the threat of Marxist dictatorship than SDS. They began to work together and coordinate their activities. Future Reagan budget director David Stockman as chair of the UCM Peace Coordinating Committee, helped draft a proposal for antiwar activists to capture student government in the spring 1967 elections so that student government could challenge the

*BETWEEN VIETNAM WAR MILITARY CONTRACTS AND THE SALES OF NEW OLDSMOBILES LIKE THE 66 TORONADO, LANSING HAD VIRTUALLY FULL EMPLOYMENT IN THE LATTER HALF OF THE SIXTIES.*

University's defense-related research and demand that students be given more freedom and power.

The UCM defined their group as radical in philosophy but moderate in approach. They won the battle for control of student government but lost the war on "The War." The Vietnam war effort continued and expanded.

### SDS Member Benardine Dohrn Comes to East Lansing to Advocate — Sex Sells

The SDS state convention turned surreal. It had sex. It had a circus. Radical attorney and future federal fugitive, future wife of Bill Ayers, Bernardine Dohrn, was front and center. She paraded around the campus in the most minimal of leather miniskirts. Never had so little leather done so much for so many. It wasn't enough to prevent schism or contain the inflated egos. She and Ayers were friends with Maggie Hackett, also friends of Dave Lawson, buddy of Vee.

As Maggie tells it, Ayers was first involved with Linda Evans. Then Dianne Oughton before she was killed in a bomb-making attempt in New York. He then became involved with and married Bernardine Dohrn: "Bernardine was the secretary of the national SDS out of Chicago. She met Ayers in Ann Arbor some time in 1968. Maggie thought that Bernardine would be the perfect person to enlist for support of a women's caucus in SDS to address the way women were treated in the movement. Either because of her connection to Bill Ayers or the power that her overt sexualness provided, she would have none of it. Her base of power was secure. She did have a positive effect on Bill though, Maggie said, and helped tone him down."

Despite that toning though, as the SDS was wont to do, it got more extreme, more foolish, more factional, and totally unrealistic. The "Maoist Progressives" wanted to organize the workers of the world for revolution, while the Ann Arbor-based group wanted to unite with the Black Panthers, the Viet Cong, and other Third Worlders in the struggle against "American imperialism." In addition to all the delegates present, scores of people with crew cuts and wearing suits were presumed to be from the FBI and the Red Squad. Beth Shapiro, a more "moderate," participant, also had the style of the long straight hair, long tall black boots, and short skirt. Later she became head of the MSU Library. At that time, Beth kept her sense of humor. She put together a fake workshop on "Sabotage and Explosives." She said "All the FBI types attended those workshops, pretty much leaving alone the real sessions."

Almost all of the sessions, however, were full of diatribe, cant, and rant, based upon faction or ideological purity, or the fulsome egos of the participants, many of whom thought it was futile to engage in electoral politics and began to refer to and purge from their ranks "baggy-assed liberals." SDS was weakened by all this, and many potential recruits walked away shaking their heads. The antiwar movement was not weakened, though it was shaken by the prospect of what was perceived as two inadequate "pro war" candidates from the major parties. Hubert Humphrey, the heir apparent of Johnson's political base, was hemmed in by that base and could not seem to find a way out. Nixon, being Nixon, said he had "a secret plan to end the war."

# Chapter 36

# THE PRESIDENTIAL ELECTION OF 1968

The Tet offensive was the beginning of the end of belief for the country. A year or so before Tet, Dennis Speck was in his apartment that he shared with Fuzz on Division Street in East Lansing. He wasn't a bumboy but he roomed with them. He was staring at the snow on the TV screen at four in the morning. He didn't want to play poker, he'd tried to study. The boisterousness of the guys playing poker made studying impossible. He couldn't sleep either. He continued to stare at the TV until morning came. Dennis had been the starting quarterback at Detroit Catholic Central High School. He was always kind, always good-natured, always patient. You had to be patient to spend a lot of time around the guys. When he played poker he almost expected to lose but it didn't bother him. He wasn't doing that well in school. He got a high draft number but was drafted anyway. He was dutiful. He believed what our government was telling us. He was inducted into the United States Marine Corps, volunteered for a second tour as a medic. He didn't know whether he'd lose or not. He died in the Tet offensive.

Before Tet, the war was supposed to be going so well. January 29, 1968, was a turning point for Lyndon Johnson, Secretary of Defense Robert McNamara, and the rest of the country. Along with Dennis Speck, more than two thousand American fighting men lost their lives in it, disproving contentions that "victory was around the corner." Johnson's credibility diminished to the point where the public, the establishment, and even he himself wondered about his viability. He still thought the antiwar liberals of the country were weak and he could control them. He was contemptuous of US Senators J. William Fulbright and Eugene McCarthy, thought the former a blowhard, the latter lazy.

The first presidential primary took place in New Hampshire on February 7, 1968. Eugene McCarthy entered. He said that the American people no longer cared about all the bills Lyndon Johnson passed. They cared about the war. He came within a few points of equaling Lyndon Johnson's election totals in New Hampshire. When asked what he would do about the current state of the country he said, paraphrasing Eisenhower, "I will go to the Pentagon." He came to speak at the Union. Charlie and his friends were there, much moved by what he had to say.

On the Republican side, Michigan Governor, and former head of American Motors, George Romney, destroyed by his candid comment about having been "brainwashed on Vietnam" by US generals, did poorly and withdrew from the race after the New Hampshire primary. Presidential candidates are supposed to know better than to be "brainwashed." If he'd phrased that differently would it have been more palatable? Probably Richard Nixon would have played the "soft on communism" card he'd always played in the past against his opponents, and would have defeated him anyhow. We'll never know.

Concerned about increasing over the top radical protest from the Weathermen and others, but also antiwar, many MSU profs joined the McCarthy presidential campaign and did a good job of advancing it. Nearly 400 students joined the campaign as well, to canvass in Indiana and Wisconsin. Charlie was among them. "I couldn't speak for everyone," Charlie said, "we were dovish on the war, but were not really that radical. I got a good response from the people I was canvassing."

In the days leading up to the Wisconsin Democratic primary, Larry O'Brien, the National Democratic Party chair, told Johnson that things didn't look good. On March 31, 1968, Lyndon Johnson said "I shall not seek, and I will not accept, the nomination of my party for another term as your president." Soon after that, Robert Kennedy said he would seek and accept it.

Spring brought the first campus protest against ROTC on the MSU campus. During the May ROTC Field Days, approximately one hundred protesters, mostly Quaker families with their children, marched across campus to Demonstration Hall where ROTC was housed. ROTC students were staging a mock battle in a mock Viet Cong village. When an enemy died, the children placed a cross on his chest.

After the mock battle, when the Green Berets came out on the field and twirled their rifles with bayonets unsheathed, the children ran among them playing ball. A major threatened to arrest them or blow them to pieces. Larrowe, with Walter Adams, went over to discuss the war with an upset captain. Adams dryly recommended that they level one less hamlet. The soldier reluctantly agreed, understanding what a public relations disaster it would be to arrest the clean-cut Quakers and their children. The military did not make a stand at Demonstration Hall.

At this point in the spring of 1968, Hannah had his hands full of draft card burners and SDS-ers attempting to occupy the Administration Building, At the same time state legislators like Democratic State Senator Charles Youngblood were fed up with war protesters and "outside agitators." He suggested that MSU re-evaluate admissions policy for out-of-state students or Hannah's budget would be slashed, which would much reduce his cherished Merit Scholars. Hannah was getting grief from the left and those more rightward than he was. Conservative legislators demanded his resignation "if he knowingly allowed the SDS Convention to take place." (at MSU) The American Legion and the VFW also condemned Hannah and argued that SDS was not entitled to constitutional guarantees of freedom of speech. The SDS convention wasn't stopped. Being President in those days was not easy for John Alfred Hannah.

At around the same time in 1968, the Democratic Party was having its state convention. Charlie was involved in a majority faction that was opposed to the Viet Nam war. The pro-war labor side put forth a resolution blessing everything the Presidents (Kennedy and Johnson) had done with the war. The peace Democrats had the votes to defeat it. The pro-war faction staged a rump caucus, an illegal meeting, to reaffirm their conclusions on the pro-war resolution.

Charlie came into the room and said, "I spoke in idealistic protest, with what I thought was great eloquence." "Al Dutzy was an old Polish-American labor leader, big, burly, bearded, who had paid his dues as an original organizer for the Walter Reuther led UAW. They had paid for their efforts against Ford in blood at the 'Battle of the Over-pass.' Al at the time was the CAP Director, political director, of UAW Region 1-C In Lansing, (that included UAW Local 652, the biggest local in the country at the time), a Lord in the UAW fiefdom. Al picked me up by the seat of the pants and my hair, rammed my head into the wall, then threw me out the door. I weighed less then, and had more hair. He didn't say anything. I called it an example of Al's non-verbal communication. We later became good friends."

## ON TO CHICAGO FOR THE 1968 DEMOCRATIC CONVENTION

"I didn't know the Lawsons all that well, except as friends of Vee's, didn't know at the time that the Lawsons were in Chicago for the '68 Convention. I would not have taken part in the radical stuff, but we were both motivated to be where the action was and that was in Chicago, no doubt about it." Charlie said. The Lawsons were in Grant Park where a lot of the police clubbing took place. Charlie was downtown where the police put the squeeze on protesters in a dead-end street. Chicago would prove to be politically very important as the place that would doom the presidential aspirations of Hubert Humphrey and bring the country closer to civil war than it had been since the last one.

He [Charlie] decided to go to Chicago that August on the spur of the moment. He had a freshly inked degree in Communications and thought he'd try to communicate, try to get credentialed so that he could attend the Convention, then write about it. This was a little naïve. He didn't get credentialed. "I kind of looked the part, so whenever I walked anywhere I was offered a ride by the Chicago cops, who were sort of half-assed instructed to make a good impression. This they did by picking up people like me, who the cops thought were newsmen, and tried to be helpful. What they said to each other within my hearing made it clear that they were not going to be helpful to the "counter cultural element." One of the nicest things they said was a variation on what legislator Dominic Jacobetti would say about hippies and bicyclists coming to his U.P. (Upper Peninsula) district in Michigan: "They come here with one pair of underwear and a five dollar bill, and don't change either one."

The Yippies didn't help with a red on black banner that said "Up Against the Wall Motherfuckers." It wouldn't take much provocation. It was going to be "open season" on war protesters of every variety, from Hippies to Yippies to the more conventional protesters who thought that McCarthy was getting screwed, which he pretty much was. The cops talked like this on the first day, before anything much happened. It was clear that they'd gotten their direction from above and that it was going to get worse. Hizzoner Mayor Richard Daley was not in favor of anybody who did not want to see Hubert Horatio Humphrey amicably placed as the Democratic Party's nominee for president of the United States. Things got bad.

The Lawsons were among those who got treated badly. They journeyed to Chicago with no real agenda but to be part of the University of Michigan SDS delegation that would protest the war. They stayed with a friend of Karen's. Their approach was all a little serious and intellectual for a lot of those present. Upon joining the SDS rally in Grant Park, they became caught up in a maelstrom of shout, and demonstration, fairly good-natured displays of everything that could offend, everything that was sacred to the "silent majority" that was watching events develop on TV.

Charlie had experienced two kinds of police crowd control. One was in the springtime several years before when Vee, Sherb, Waite, John Terris, and Charlie took Terris's tired and exhausted maroon 55 Chevy to Fort Lauderdale, Florida. The little V-8 had been hot-rodded too much, cared for too little. "We first bought oil by the quart, then bulk oil by the gallon. The little Chevy was burning almost as much oil as it was gas. It left a cloud of blue smoke behind us that obscured our rear vision and the landscape. It left a film of oil on us and everything else in and around the car. But we got there, settled in, and a couple of days later joined a couple hundred thousand students on the beach and in the bars. Then we got a little rowdy along with the rest of the crowd, taunted the cops, and, with the mob psychology finding confidence in the cops being severely outnumbered, threw a couple of empty beer cans at them."

"The cops didn't like it. When things got out of hand, the cops regrouped with several hundred of them in blue (and brown for the Broward County Sheriff Dept.). In a broad band they swept the beaches and the oceanfront, and pushed all bipedal life bigger than crabs, jellyfish and, starfish away from the bars and off the beach. They pushed us down the main perpendicular boulevard, for about a mile. Then they raised the drawbridge, kept it raised, and communicated that they were going to keep it raised. The partiers had to walk six or seven miles barefoot under the heat of the sun around the town to get back to the beach on the north end. By the time we got back to our cars and motels, cussing the cops who made us walk around the whole town to get back to where we started on the other end, we'd pretty much walked ourselves sober and reasonable. We had used up the energy that we were going to use on partying, and went to bed."

Nobody got bloodied; the mutual expense of jailing and being jailed was avoided. Commerce was not disturbed, and the students and hangers-on returned to the beachfront and the bars the next day to continue drinking beer and spending money, a little bowed, but not beaten, a little wiser about what behavior was acceptable in Fort Lauderdale. It was all part of a pretty sensible plan of crowd control. The cops would not tolerate having beer cans thrown at them.

Back in Chicago it was done differently. The crowds were not hostile. "It was like it's kind of fun to be in Chicago." Charlie said. "The weather was not that bad, and the steep buildings on both sides of the streets kept us cool by the shade that they gave and the breeze blowing off the water of Lake Michigan nearby. Besides, the demonstrators were not mad at the city of Chicago; they were mad at the powers that be inside the convention center who were waging a war and were in the process of nominating a candidate who the people in the park thought supported the war. It wasn't really disorderly in the beginning. Nobody was cursing at the cops or throwing anything. Any chanting was about anti-war stuff. The exception was the Yippies and those types who were playing to the cameras and trying to be offensive from the beginning. "I don't know what started the cops pushing the crowds back, whether it was some sort of disorder, real or imagined or exaggerated, but all of a sudden I was part of a huge group of people who were being pushed down a dead end street with no place to go."

As Mayor Daley said later, "The police were there to maintain disorder, not to create disorder." Lyndon Johnson gave a speech in Chicago to the Democratic Party back on April 23, 1964, and was feted by Chicago Democrats in Grant Park afterwards. It was the 'Great Society' speech. It was the beginning.

Four years later, in 1968, the Democratic Convention was the end of it. Karen and Dave Lawson were in Grant Park and were being pushed around and abused, shoved, compacted, worried about suffocating. In the open end of the street, to no surprise, the demonstrators started cursing and throwing stuff at the cops. At the front of the crowd close to the cops, they had no choice but to try and run the gauntlet of a couple of hundred cops who either beat the crap out of them with their batons, arrested them, or both. Dave and Karen said "they were more afraid than they'd ever been."

This was all shown on national TV. In the International Amphitheatre where the convention was being held, Senator Abraham Ribicoff from Connecticut decried the violence. Richard Daley cursed Ribicoff, cursed the demonstrators, and said they got what was coming to them. Fatherly Walter Cronkite lamented the deterioration of the situation and everything that led up to it, which was The War. This was not the textbook way to hold a convention and get a presidential candidate nominated and elected President of the United States. This was not the way the smoke-filled room operators usually did it. This was not the Daley way of "Don't make no waves; don't back no losers." Daley and all the rest of the power brokers were violating their own maxims.

Gene McCarthy didn't have a chance to be the nominee. A product of the same Minnesota Farmer-Labor Party that produced Humphrey, he actually was mentored by Humphrey. The MacAllister College professor was everything that Humphrey wasn't and vice versa. He was the 1968 version of Adlai Stevenson in 1952. When a matronly supporter gushed to Adlai that "You're the candidate of every thinking person," Adlai responded, "Yes, I know, but I need a majority." So it was with McCarthy. With a wry joke or a poetic metaphor for every occasion, he was as deep as the well, and as cool as the water in it. In an uncharacteristic moment, after something particularly exhilarating had happened on the campaign trail, he was photographed kissing a baby, but it never was recorded as happening again. HHH could kiss babies all day, every day, shake hands at the same time, and keep up a steady patter in between kisses. He was as voluble and lighthearted as McCarthy was terse and pithy. That light-heartedness also masked a first-rate, practical political mind.

HHH couldn't afford to alienate and distance himself from his base, at least until he had the nomination in hand. But these weren't normal times. Like a chess player who almost had the game won, he was behind in "time" in the struggle that involved power, space, and time. Hubert was forced to straddle, prematurely. He attacked Mayor Daley's handling of the protesters in the streets out front.

This was all on TV, every night. It was like a family fight in front of the picture window for all the neighbors to see, close up and ugly. And the "neighbors," all of America, especially the silent majority, didn't like what they saw. Every personal and ideological difference, all the squinty-eyed vitriol with every open pore in every screaming, sweating, swearing face, was showing up close to the American people. They didn't like what they saw in any aspect. They didn't like seeing the Democratic Convention in disorder. They didn't like seeing the streets outside in disorder. Outside, the anti-war protesters were not like the clean-for-Gene types who campaigned in New Hampshire and Indiana and Wisconsin. They were hairy. They were loud. They were often obscene.

When the Chicago Seven were arrested they became handy symbols for Richard Nixon. Allen Ginsberg, no matter how reasoned and measured and articulate he really was, did nothing but chant "Ommmm." America didn't understand Ommmm. He was not like the boy next door, unless maybe you were from Brooklyn or were Jack Kerouac. Neither was narcissist Abbie Hoffman. They certainly weren't orderly, and Judge Hoffman didn't think they were lawful. The two Hoffmans, on opposite ends of the political teeter-totter, both used their weight in the political theatre that would come. The antiwar side disliked the judge as much as the other side disliked Abbie.

Richard Nixon's campaign on law and order had perfect pitch. Both sides of the proceedings started looking like caricatures of themselves. And the independent and conservative voters wouldn't have liked the Democrats and the left that year, even in unexaggerated form. It meant that Democrat Hubert Humphrey, the nominee of his party to become the president of the United States, had a long way to go. The participants were exhausted. The country was exhausted from watching it. As Bismarck observed a hundred years before, after observing the political process, "It wasn't easy seeing sausage made." Karen and Dave Lawson hated Chicago ever after.

## Back In Detroit

Later on in the summer of 1968, after graduating from college and returning from Chicago, Charlie got a staff job with the Michigan Democratic Party State Central Committee in Detroit.

"It was a low-level staff job, the lowest-level job, a glorified errand boy, but I enjoyed it," Charlie said. "I don't know why Sander Levin hired me. It was his job to make sure Hubert Horatio Humphrey won Michigan's electoral votes in the fall election. He knew I was for McCarthy; maybe that's why he hired me, to make room in the tent for differing views, to make for some balance. Maybe he was secretly anti-war too, and was for Gene or Bobby and couldn't say so." The Michigan Democratic Party, then as now, was heavily influenced by labor and other conservative forces that were for the war. If that's too strong, maybe it would be fair to say that they were for Johnson, and Johnson was for the war. And they were for Hubert because Hubert inherited Johnson's constituency. They both had a long history of being pro labor.

The party offices were rented space in downtown Detroit in the old Lafayette Building, a building where a 1940's detective movie could have been made. It was solid, dated, a little down at the heels, and smelled old and musty. The hallway walls were lined with marble that was starting to yellow and deteriorate. The woodwork and the doors were dark. Over the doors were open-able transoms to compensate for the lack of air conditioning. Detroit was starting to deteriorate too, and would accelerate its toward-the-ashes run. The Detroit riots had happened the year before, and the steady stream of the middle class to the suburbs was becoming a flood. Most of the small shops, the pharmacies, and the grocery stores would go with them, leaving behind empty, barren storefronts. The iconic Hudson's Department Store, where Denny Diamond shopped for and stole his clothes, and where George Hall used his stolen charge plates, would close soon, too. It would look like a beached and abandoned ship when looking north on Woodward, looking more and more like moonscape.

The future was not apparent in the downtown district where Charlie was working that fall of 1968. Detroit was a bustling, swirling place with sidewalks packed with people hurrying from place to place. The landmark Sheraton Cadillac Hotel, was as elegant as ever, with its Greek Revival columns reaching, it seemed, nearly to the sky. There was sparkle and polished brass and glass everywhere. A Shapiro's Drugstore occupied space in the same building where the gentry, effusing prosperity, went for coffee and sundries. Shapiro's was clean and polished. Charlie went to the hotel with an older, more experienced staffer as a "truth squad" to rebut in press release any flagrant untruths stated by the opposition candidates. The two we went to hear were Richard Nixon, with his tightly reasoned logical lies, and later Spiro Agnew, the unchained darker angel-surrogate of Nixon's aspirations, with all his "nattering nabobs of negativism."

## The Night the President Didn't Come To Dinner

The late October 1968 Democratic Party fundraiser before the election was pretty much standard fare, "It was $50 for rubber chicken or gray roast beef. I never could have afforded it if I wasn't on staff and gotten a free ticket," said Charlie. It was held at Cobo Hall convention center in Detroit, which was named after Albert Cobo, a mayor of earlier times. Cobo Hall was big, new.

The dinner took place in one of the bigger halls. Charlie arrived early when it was still unoccupied. It was a sea of white sparkling circles, all the tables covered in white linen with silverware shining, seating maybe seven thousand people. It filled up quickly. "I don't know what the take on it was, but it was good. It allowed TV ads already placed to be paid for, and many more to be purchased at the FCC-mandated lower rate. The Democrats were way behind, money had been a terrible problem, the fundraiser helped." Charlie said.

These events always got started late, and this one was no exception, except that it was late even by disorganized Democratic Party standards. The affair was supposed to start at 7:30, but it didn't even start getting started until nine. The meals came in motion so slow that it almost seemed like the servers were on a slowdown strike. First the salad, then fifteen minutes later the rolls, then the main course slowly followed by dessert. By 10:30 we'd eaten. An hour after that, about the time the families with young children told their baby sitters they'd be home, the speaker came on.

The speaker was the Hon. George Ball, former assistant secretary of state. He'd been the house dove in the Johnson administration. He'd been a Cassandra of great stature and tragedy since the beginning of the Kennedy administration. In 1962, Chairman of the Joint Chiefs Maxwell Taylor had done a quick tour of South Vietnam and had come back to advocate that we send 8,000 advisors. Ball had disagreed strongly. He said they wouldn't remain advisors, and that the 8,000 would be 300,000 in five years. He was almost right. There were 500,000 fighting men there in five years.

He spoke quite candidly, within limits. He said that if we continued to abuse our power in Vietnam we would squander it. It was precious and might be needed for a real crisis. We were bound to fail in Vietnam; it was as much about nationalism as it was communism. The communists were not monolithic and their power was ebbing. South Vietnam was a failed state and always would be. They ought to do their own fighting, though he doubted they would. We'd spent enough blood and treasure. It was time for them to assume responsibility.

His comments were all highly applauded. He wrote all of his own speeches, but he couldn't have written all this down; it would have taken too much paper. He kept talking, and talking. Only Fidel Castro and black pastors could talk that long. He was tiring and boring everyone. Everybody had had a couple of drinks and couldn't walk around. "Nobody drowned by falling asleep in their soup," Charlie said, "but I saw a lot of heads and chins slowly descend, then the snap back before their heads hit their plates."

Then the rumors started to circulate. Ball's never-ending speech was a filibuster to keep everybody there. The president was coming. Ball talked on. Another half hour passed. The president could have gotten on Air Force One or some other plane at eleven o' clock and been there by now. Ball continued. Whether the president's coming would be a good choice would be open to question. For the people assembled he would have been, but for all the people mad about the war and mad about the Democratic Party, maybe not so much. After all the rumors and excitement that woke everybody up, after another hour of Ball, the president never came. The crowd filed solemnly and sleepily out.

## The President Gives Hubert Some Maneuvering Room

The president's visit probably would have been double-edged. The powers-that-be must have recognized that. Maybe Lyndon Johnson recognized that as well. At any rate he never campaigned for Hubert in any active way. Behind the scenes, Johnson was Johnson, a political animal, and he, tacitly or otherwise, finally let Humphrey know that he was going to give him the maneuvering room to try and straddle the great divide between the peace and war wings of the party. And the country.

In a late September Utah speech, Hubert said that he would end the bombing and end the war. The campaign started to show signs of life, then vigor. The Democratic nominee began to come on strong. In the days before the election he inched ahead in Michigan. Then finally came a grudging half-hearted late endorsement by Gene McCarthy. Nixon's lead fell from double digits to middle single digit. The political tents were busy places the week before the election. HHH asked Johnson for a bombing halt. Johnson gave it to him. It became known as the Halloween Surprise. It was more trick than treat, more trick than reality, but it helped politically. By the end of the week, polls were showing a dead heat nationally, and his lead in Michigan widened to six or seven points.

But Richard Nixon wasn't ready to give in to negative momentum. First, Nixon had a superior strategy, and it was working, all negative, but working. It would realign the parties. What became known as his "Southern strategy" would capitalize on southern resentment about civil rights. California was indispensable for both parties, the state with the most electoral votes, He appealed to the "silent majority" there by promising "law and order." He had it covered.

Then, in response to Humphrey's "Halloween Surprise" of the bombing halt, Nixon had a surprise of his own. He sent

Henry Kissinger to South Vietnamese leaders who told them they'd get a better deal with Nixon. They withdrew from the existing peace talks that were stalled anyway but had some appeal to voters. Nixon also had a secret plan to end the war. His secret plan morphed into no plan at all.

## The Election Result of 1968

The election was a squeaker, too close to call. Not until the morning after would the TV networks call a winner. Nixon won the popular vote by less than 1%, 512,000 votes. California and Ohio went for Nixon by less than 3%, and they would have made the difference. He won 3% of the African-American vote, 17% of the Jewish vote, 39% of the Italian vote, won middle income urban votes by 1%, and had an electoral landslide 301 to 191. He carried 32 states including the south and California. Humphrey carried 13, including Michigan by 6.72%. Nixon almost had to win. He too had campaigned to end the war.

# Chapter 37

## AT THE KIT-KAT CLUB

George didn't know Tony "Baloney" Hamilton well but they got along. Tony liked George, George reciprocated. They were playing pool at Ike Johns' Capitol Recreation Club one afternoon. Both played well, were betting modest amounts of money on their games. Mutual competitiveness seemed to raise the level of their play even more. George thought that if Tony could play that well all the time, they could make some money together. George asked Tony if he wanted to make some money hustling pool. Tony said he did. George thought that if they drove to Marshall, Michigan, where there were a lot of players who thought they were better than they were, they could do well.

A couple of days later they agreed to drive to Marshall. The Kit-Kat Club was a local strip joint that had limited charm and not much eroticism but it did have several pool tables. They ran into a couple of young guys, barely twenty-one, obviously off the farm, who thought they were the pool hustlers. Both teams started out slow, both played with comic ineptness, trying to lose to the other, demonstrating their inferiority and their susceptibility to surrendering their cash. After a while George and Tony did seem to convince the two farm-boys that they were as bad as they seemed and suggested and the boys suggested raising the stakes. After mock protest George and Tony agreed. The game, nine ball went from 25 cents a ball to a dollar, to two dollars. They played until almost closing time when the locals decided they'd had enough. George and Tony split $150.

Driving back in George's red Olds Cutlass, Tony said that they should do that more often. George didn't say anything, he was a little drunk and a little tired. Tony said, "I'd really like to play some of those East Lansing guys. They're not near as good as they think they are, have really big heads." George said, "yeah."

# Chapter 38

# JOHN HANNAH TAKES AN EASIER GIG

John Hannah was under siege. The University he built, the University that he loved so much, had spent his life serving, was not loving him back. Students were angry. Two members of the Board of Trustees were openly calling for his retirement. He was giving signals he might retire. By January 1969, he decided he'd had enough. His decision was another opportunity for protest. From the Ann Arbor SDS contingent came Bill Ayers, and his then wife Diana Oughton, with their over the top approach. Six hundred students occupied the Administration Building and picketed Hannah's farewell address. He was pelted with rotten eggs. He started out at MSU with eggs. He ended with eggs. The reality was that the larger world was a much more intractable place than the bubble of East Lansing. Feeding it, perfecting it, curing it of evil, was not easy.

Hannah was appointed Director of the United States Agency for International Development, AID. At that time to a limited but substantial extent, it was a kissing cousin of the US military and the CIA. He wasn't giving up on his vision of internationalism and his fight against Communism. He likely felt the new job would have much less aggravation. He needn't worry about consensus among faculty and students. He had only one boss, Richard Nixon. He wouldn't have to keep both sides of the aisle in the legislature happy, or wealthy alums and donors either. All he had to do was what he wanted to do, and that was to be an internationalist and fight communism. International development was looked at as a cure for cold and hot war. AID was there,

MSU PRESIDENT JOHN HANNAH SHOWING VILLAGE CHIEF AND FARMER HIGH YIELD RICE THAT INCREASED YIELDS 250%.

doing development work, but also acting as a beard for the CIA and working with the military. Hannah knew the drill from the MSUG, had the best of intentions.

Anti-war students occupied the Administration Building. The students and the police didn't see things the same way. Ray Scodeller, the chief assistant prosecutor of Ingham County at the time, was there. The protesters were given a chance to leave or be arrested. They were given a chance to walk through a double line of police with batons and urged to hurry. One girl fell down; another protester fell on top of her. "Stop beating us!" she cried. "Police brutality!" The situation deteriorated. The police and some white football players were not gentle with several. Scodeller, who witnessed a cop get hit in the head with a rock, didn't see the peaceful side of the peace movement. There were minor physical injuries, minor damage to property, nothing serious, unlike the rest of the country.

Around that time Christine Bailey, a graduate student who was taking classes from Wesley Fishel, was walking on Circle Drive near Morrill Hall. Fishel drove by, hailed her, and pulled over to give her a ride. He got out to move some of his stuff out of the front passenger seat so that there would be room for her to sit. While doing so a student came up to Fishel and asked, "Are you Professor Fishel?" Fishel said, "Yes, I am." The student called Fishel a murderer, spit in his face, and walked away. Fishel said and did nothing and carried on like nothing had happened. It was a big change in the way the student body looked at him compared to years past when Excalibur, MSU's honor society, voted him the most effective teacher on campus.

Hannah and his fellow travelers in the big-business community and the Michigan legislature had helped MSU push in a war effort that the students and the country, for the most part, no longer believed in. He took MSU to the edge. He was not literally forced out, but it was logical that he should go. His time was past. Many years after, he said:

> "We never felt any need for the University to apologize for our participation in the [MSUG] project for what we tried to do in Viet Nam. We learned a great deal from that experience and became much more careful that we did not allow ourselves to be put in a position where an outside agency might compromise us.
>
> I think if Michigan State were to face the same choice again, in the same context, it might well agree to assist the US Government as we did then."

Reading between the lines, what he said about learning a lot meant that MSU wouldn't provide faculty or mission cover for the CIA again. The last part is mostly bravado. If he'd put MSU in the vanguard of creating a national tragedy again, have MSU be part of the brain-trust that got us in there in the first place, it would be crazy. The country couldn't go through what it went through in Vietnam again. It would come apart. At any rate, after extraordinary accomplishments and extraordinary mistakes, the "conventional man for a conventional era" was gone.

The MSU Board of Trustees did something uncharacteristically shrewd. They appointed Walter Adams as Interim President of Michigan State University. Adams was the kind of teacher about whom books, movies, and TV series are made. He was smart, tough, dedicated, humorous. Charlie's future wife Marjorie had him for an Econ class and said he was the best teacher she ever had. The folklore was that if you got a "B" in the class he remembered your name forever, and if you got an "A" you were taken to dinner. Marjorie got a "B," and she said when he saw her a year or so later walking on campus he addressed her by her full name.

Adams was late to the antiwar effort, after supporting JFK and Johnson initially, but he became increasingly wobbly about it. He came to believe that "the war was no longer economically and politically viable."

To deal with the irresponsible, and to ward off the backlash that came from them, he advocated co-opting them:

> "Giving people a stake in the system by making them an integral part of the decision-making process is possibly the most de-radicalizing strategy that can be followed. Participation gives them an understanding of the range and complexity of the problems that must be dealt with. It moderates extremist and unrealistic demands. It commits participants to support the decisions that have been made."

The campus antiwar groups, no matter how splintered, could count on Hannah over-reacting or reacting wrongly, on almost everything. It led to greater student and faculty support for the antiwar movement, and for the radicals as well. But as interim president, Adams changed the game. He confronted the radicals with biting and trenchant wit and tried to either convert them or isolate them from the more reasonable in the antiwar movement. He showed up at every demonstration, defused potentially violent situations, and did it without bringing in the police. Angered and frustrated SDS-ers, instead of engaging Adams in dialogue, responded with such profundities as "Eat shit, Adams" and "Fucking son of a bitch." One female SDS-er kicked Adams in the nuts. Their pure "line," their profanity as a substitute for discourse, widened the gap, and frayed the relationship between them and antiwar liberals. In addition, hundreds of students were coming to demonstrations stoned on drugs, alcohol, or both, making them difficult to control, and SDS was not famous for self-control. So the ideological conflicts the personality conflicts, and their general behavior alienated them from the larger student body. Even though the PL faction made it clear that the Ann Arbor faction was no longer welcome, SDS was no longer at the center of, and in control of, antiwar protest. Even though faculty members like John Masterson and Charlie Larrowe came to their support, it was too late. It made Adams' job easier.

Many years later, after Walter had died, Charlie asked Pauline, Walter's widow, why Walter did not seem to covet the presidency of Michigan State University. She said, "Several of the trustees came over to the house one night and tried to talk Walter into running (for the presidency).

Walter responded by saying, "I'm getting a promotion. I'm going back to the classroom." And that was that.

### Peace was maintained in East Lansing

In Washington, Richard Nixon played his cards close to his vest, didn't divulge anything about his secret plan to end the war. He talked about "Vietnamization," didn't give any details. Sent Henry Kissinger to Paris to alternatively cajole and threaten. Bombed Hanoi, then removed some troops. North Vietnam showed no signs of agreeing to any US plans.

How much things had changed was made clear by October of 1969. That fall, Greater Lansing Community Organization (GLCO), a legacy of Viet Nam Summer, joined forces with

UCM, the Wesley Foundation, and the student government to plan a local October 15 Moratorium March Against the War. The group requested that Adams suspend classes and make facilities available for discussion of the war prior to marching on the State Capitol in Lansing. Adams realized the mood of the students was hostile and frustrated, and that, if he did not make some positive gesture, events would pass him by. Also, by not attending classes the students would have shut down the university by unofficial means, which would anger taxpayers and state legislators.

Adams made class attendance optional and university facilities available. There was a mass antiwar meeting at the MSU Auditorium. Governor William Milliken was in attendance, as was US Senator Phil Hart, who had supported the war for years but was now there to denounce it. Perhaps his wife Jane and daughter, who'd been against the war for as long as he'd been for it, had something to do with his change of heart. Adams set aside moral and legal arguments and talked about how it was bad for the economy. Following the speeches he placed himself at the head of a mile-long procession of 8,000 students and faculty for the march to the Capitol. Reinforcing the moderate image of the whole event, and being a master of the moment, he carried a small American flag. Accompanying the marchers and acting as guards were black members of the MSU football team.

There was not a meeting of the minds however. Economists who were further left spoke to MSU and high school students at the East Lansing High gym and attacked Adams' economic analysis of the war. They said the war did profit the nation, at least the defense contractors and multinational corporations. But the march was peaceful. Adams had kept East Lansing peaceful. The only injuries, minor ones, occurred when a drunk came out of Mac's Bar at three in the afternoon. He wasn't used to having any traffic on Michigan Avenue at that time and couldn't tell the difference between a street barren of traffic, and one with several thousand people in it. He ran into the crowd. This explanation did not satisfy the crowd. The police quickly separated him from it. No one was hurt. Other than that it was peaceful, and was the largest peace march there had ever been in the Lansing area.

## More Protest

On the evening of February 17, 1970, 250 students assembled in the MSU Union to discuss ways of protesting the convictions of the Chicago Seven. After their arrest during and after the violence surrounding the Democratic Party Convention, they were charged with inciting to riot, trespassing and conspiracy. With conviction, they would be looking at long prison sentences. Norman Mailer's take on the charge was, "Left-wingers are incapable of conspiracy because they're all egomaniacs," the implication being that they could not surrender or compromise any part of their masterful own plan about Chicago events to anyone with any degree of cooperation and that it foreclosed conspiring.

In late February 1970, Judge Hoffman sentenced the remaining five of the seven to "crossing state lines to incite riot." They were found innocent of the conspiracy charge but guilty on the riot charge in a compromise after the jury threatened to become hung. Hoffman sentenced the five to five years in prison and $5,000 fines. (Later the convictions were all reversed on appeal on November 21, 1972, too late to prevent the rioting and the broken glass in East Lansing.)

## MSU Protest Gets Unruly

Back at the Union, the SDS Weatherman faction were dressed in black leather and carried six foot long steel fence posts. In February Michigan weather, the protesters marched over to the East Lansing City Hall singing to the Beatles' "Come Together" with their own lyrics, "Trash Together":

> We are the Trashmen, we've got
> Rocks and bottles we've got
> Stones and sticks and right on
> Politics!
>
> We fight the pigs. They try to bust,
> One thing I can tell you is the winner
> is us.
> Trash together, right now, off the pig!

Reports that a mob had gathered at city hall brought out a few hundred curious student and faculty spectators. The Weathermen began smashing city hall windows with their fence posts. The sound of shattering glass and cheering attracted even more spectators, bringing the crowd to over a thousand. After a half hour elapsed, the police counter-attacked. They came out of city hall on the run and started clubbing and tear-gassing everyone in sight. After being reinforced by Lansing and State Police, they pushed the crowd down Abbott, back toward the Union Building on campus. Those caught up in the push, not Weathermen, who were either observers or people separate from the spectacle who got gassed without discrimination became part of a still bigger crowd that broke windows in the East Lansing State Bank and Jacobson's Department Store. Bob Wilcox, the manager of Jacobson's, who treated the store and the city like they were newborn babies, was protective of both. He was not happy about the damage. It wasn't the last protest, but it was the least peaceful that East Lansing had ever had, and would have.

MSU protesters stayed mostly peaceful and the police were not inclined to kill anybody, not inclined to have things turn out like they did at Kent State. Another reason it was peaceful was that the far-out left had more or less collapsed, between personal and ideological differences. The leadership had mostly left campus. Brad Lang and Linda Evans had left town earlier in the year. *The Paper*, the alternative to the university-sanctioned publication the *State News*, soldiered on, but the *Bogue Street Bridge*, was more interested in the counter-culture and sex than it was in politics. More significantly, the most popular antiwar organizations after the strike were those that sprang from the area community and were peaceful. They consisted of the Greater Lansing Community Organization and the Lansing-MSU Vietnam Veterans Against the War. The two groups were liberal and peaceful with goals to work through the electoral system to achieve change and peace. East Lansing's Jane Munn, Biggie's daughter, was still working for peace.

## The Peace Movement Expands and Progresses

With the downsizing of the radical left, the peace movement expanded. On the first anniversary of the Kent State killings, 3,000 MSU students peacefully protested against the war. New President Clifton Wharton threatened to dock the pay of any faculty who canceled classes.

Seventy Vietnam veterans pinned their combat medals on a dummy corpse which symbolized the MSU students who had died in Vietnam. Former President Walter Adams, whose politics were evolving, then read aloud the list. Afterward, the sobbing World War II veteran, no longer able to criticize the war in terms of cold economics, delivered an impassioned moral appeal for peace: "…end this war which is destroying this country and that for which it stands. Let us honor the memory of those who have lost their lives by bringing their living brothers home."

## East Lansing Stays Peaceful, Vee Stays Out of It

By 1972 the political climate in East Lansing was changing, both from the top down and the bottom up. Whether there would be a meeting in the middle for the community's and the country's salvation would be a more elusive question. By that time campus anti-war activists had organized successful student voter registration drives resulting in the election of doves to the East Lansing City Council. Then the Council, with great ardor, started passing resolutions such as at their meeting of April 18, 1972 in which a majority called for Nixon "to immediately cease all bombing of North Vietnam and to accelerate the withdrawal of all American forces in Southeast Asia." The new council majority also meant that City Clerk Beverley Colizzi, and City Manager Jack Patriarche's days would be numbered. They were held responsible for suppressing efforts to register to vote, and for the overreaction of police response.

At the same time youthful stylish transplanted Madison, Wisconsin, attorney and Assistant Michigan Attorney General Bob Carr was readying his first run as an anti-war Democrat against the long-term incumbent Charles Chamberlain.

Meanwhile, former MSU President Walter Adams and Economics Prof Charles Larrowe packed themselves like sausages into old uniforms that had not been worn for nearly thirty years and joined forces with Lansing Viet Nam Veterans Against the War to demand that the university trustees go on record against the war. Their patriotism was unassailable, their arguments persuasive. The MSU Board of Trustees adopted a strong anti-war resolution.

With the SDS and other strongly radical groups vacating or evaporating, it seemed that persuasion and change through the electoral system was the way to go, and that the era of mass disruptive protest was over. Not so. In the last days of April 1972, American naval forces were ordered by Nixon to mine Haiphong Harbor, North Vietnam's biggest port. This was regarded as an expansion of the war, not an ending of it as Nixon had promised. The concern was that American mines would sink Chinese, Russian, and other Communist-bloc countries ships, and that it would start another world war. This started another country-wide campus upheaval that included MSU.

In East Lansing, four hundred doves and veterans met upstairs in the Union Building to discuss the latest escalation of the war. The crowd overflowed outside the building. The East Lansing police, thinking they were seeing a repeat of the 1970 strike, promptly tear-gassed everyone in the vicinity of the Union.

Bob Vee had just entered the line of the Union Grill, where the short-order cooking was done in an alcove on its east end. Against the north wall was a conventional kitchen setup with a big cast iron stove with cook top, big enough to fry a small car. All the eggs and bacon and diced potatoes and everything else grillable and fryable were laid out in precise geometric order. All the utensils, bowls, whisks, and other paraphernalia used to prepare and serve them were hung and stacked on either side. Separating the cooking area from the hungry students was a long buffet-type counter, layered with shaved ice, on which sat the basic varieties of salads, little exercises in culinary geometry, circles of pineapple on a layer of lettuce with a sphere of cottage cheese on top, glistening jello rectangles, along with cakes and pies, cubed and triangular, prepared in the big cafeteria kitchen down below. They were set out in orderly framed fashion on the ice chips surrounded by brushed aluminum. Attached to the counter was a forty-foot long length of chromed parallel bars on which people pushed their rectangular aluminum cafeteria trays.

On the wall of the south side of the cafeteria-grill area were life-size color cartoon caricature drawings of happy and smiling Muffy and Biff types. They were in various phases of campus activities that were almost timeless in the depiction of their looks and styles and student occupations. Except at that time and place, hair was often long, students were often bearded, and what was being waved by them were not university pennants. No sis-boom-bah. There were no people of color in the caricatures either, not even of the shade and grade of Delores and President Clifton Wharton. Also, unlike the cartoon characters on the walls, fewer people were smiling.

Bob Vee had picked up his tray, pushed it down along the counter, gotten his order of a cheeseburger with mustard and pickles, fries, and chocolate shake from Minnie the cook, who was everyone's surrogate auntie. He sat down by one of the tall, divided pane windows on the west side of the grill. The windows of the student gothic Union Building looked out onto the tree-lined boulevard with several old brick women's dormitories on the other side of the boulevard. He was getting ready to watch the festivities. People had gathered and were chanting. He removed the food from his tray and sat down to eat. He was with the protesters in spirit, but thought he was a little old to have joined them.

Vee never joined anything. Also, the previous summer he'd been to Saugatuck, a beach community on Lake Michigan's western shore, and had a little too much to drink. His antics had brought the attention of a local gendarme who took him, under protest, to the local magistrate's home for adjudication. He protested more vigorously and dynamically, prompting the police officer to get out his police officer paraphernalia to subdue disorderly persons without shooting them or clubbing them. The cop didn't want to do that to Vee. Nobody got mad at Vee for long. He had a special aura about him that made whatever stupid or excessive things he was doing seem like an aberration, like he was really good natured, and that it was out of character and he'd soon snap out of it and return to being a really nice guy. It was essentially true. The officer didn't hurt him. Living better, policing better, through chemistry. That was the idea. He got out his Mace, pointed it at Vee, and pulled the trigger. Vee with nimble mind and body, even when drinking, ducked. The Mace hit the judge full in the face, with lesser amounts affecting his wife, sitting as clerk nearby.

The judge and his wife, retching, crying, eyes burning, stumbled toward the door and fresh air, along with the cop and Vee. The judge and his wife had to move out of their house for the long holiday weekend until it aired out. Vee, eventually quieted and humbled, spent the long holiday weekend in the county jail.

It could have been worse in Saugatuck, but his memory of it made him want to avoid a repetition. With his mind back in East Lansing and at the Grill, he sat and watched, his only companions in radical political solidarity being his cheeseburger, fries, and shake. Just as he took his first bite, he smelled a smell that reminded him of being back in Saugatuck in the judge's house, one that made him forget about eating and watching the demonstration.

Tear gas had entered the Grill through the ventilation ducts. This was not good for Vee's asthma, his health in general, or anyone else's. People singly and in pairs started heading for the exit in a steady stream. Then they stampeded for the door, out the Grill, and toward the front entrance on Circle Drive, out and away from where the crowd and the police were going at it to where the air was better.

The crowds did not go away. Michigan State University's huge land grant campus and its resilient students had successfully suffered all the barriers and hurdles that all the overbearing factotums of MSU's administrative and academic bureaucracy could place in front of them. There were too many students, too much land grant campus to spread out in, not enough police and tear gas.

The students who had initially fled after the first volley of tear gas came back with reinforcements, three thousand strong. With them they brought laundry carts from James Madison and Justin Morrill colleges and several other dormitories. They positioned the carts at the intersection of Abbott Rd. and Grand River. The Union Building is on the southeast corner. Abbott Rd. is a main north-south road for the city. Grand River, in addition to being the main east-west street between East Lansing and Lansing, was also Michigan Highway 43, before Interstate 69 and other belt-ways and bypasses were built around the city. Much commerce and many people still traveled over it. Traffic backed up.

Governor Milliken had a problem. As would be typical of that time and many others, the governor received contradictory counsel. Some urged him to clear the area by any means necessary. He initially decided to deploy a very visible force. He declared a state of emergency. With disdain for what fellow Republican Governor Rhodes had done in Ohio, and Kent State, not happy with fellow Republican Richard Nixon's foreign policy, he tried only a display of force.

The first part of the display was a vanguard of state police helicopters hovering over downtown East Lansing's Grand River Avenue, now completely blocked off with thousands in the street. Then all available police from Lansing, East Lansing, the Ingham County Sheriff's Dept., and, of course, the State Police were marched in and assembled on the periphery. Many students thought they were living in a banana republic where a coup was taking place.

The second day of the blockade, the students bought out the liquor stocks of all the "wet" jurisdictions surrounding "dry" East Lansing, partied, camped out in the boulevard and thumbed their noses at very unhappy East Lansing police, who'd previously been given reprimands by the dovish city council for the gassing that started it all. Members of the area Vietnam Veterans Against the War circulated among the crowd, talking to police, talking to students, to relieve tensions. They also dealt with some University of Michigan Weathermen who came to East Lansing to try to get the students to get violent. The VVAW had particularly low regard for the their high social status background and chased them out of town. Ray Scodeller, chief assistant Ingham County prosecutor, was there, and said: "Our job was psychological. We tried to understand what was going on. We didn't want to hurt anybody. We just had to clear the Avenue."

Early in the morning of the third day of protest, all the police already assembled, moved in with bulldozers, more tear gas, and clubs and quickly reopened Grand River to traffic. A bit later, several hundred students on bicycles started circling a section of Grand River Ave., until police abruptly pulled them from their seats. The State Police then deployed sharpshooters on the roof of Jacobson's Department Store, where they trained their rifles on the crowd below. Thousands of students carefully stayed off Grand River Avenue and glared silently at the troopers. Suddenly, one of the students threw something upward toward those on the roof, causing the crowd to gasp. The troopers stiffened. One, crouching on the roof, set aside his weapon and caught it. He smiled and threw the frisbee back towards the sender across the street on campus. The rage subsided; the worst of the blockade was over. Calmed by the non-violence of the police, the crowd seemed to sense that at least this protest was over. Prosecutor Ray Scodeller had an unromantic point of view. He said, "The night was very cold." But he allowed that he and the police did try to understand what was going on. They did try to get into the heads of the protesters and understood that they were not trying to foment revolution. The peace was kept. Ray Scodeller didn't quite get how students closing off Grand River was going to affect US foreign policy, but the students did, when joined with other demonstrations throughout the country. In numbers, strength.

The Vietnam War continued, but whether from exhaustion or resignation, there were no more large demonstrations against the war at MSU.

In spite of all the political differences and contradictions, most of the people of East Lansing worked hard to keep the peace and prevent bloodshed. It was in marked contrast to what had happened at Kent State, Jackson State and other places and was, in a narrow sense, a happy peaceful ending.

The era continued to deceive and distract Rick Fowler and Larry Chappell. They continued peacefully down the road that few others thought discrete to travel. But they'd find that leaving East Lansing wasn't easy. John Hannah had made that clear.

# Chapter 39

# RIDING THE HORSES

Eleanor Story and Prudy knew each other from East Lansing High. They had some of the same classes, knew the same people, everybody knew everybody at East Lansing High. They hung out in the same crowd, had the looks, had the clothes, had the money. Prudy's family didn't have as much as the Storys, but they had enough to be comfortably upper-middle class. They became friends. They rode horses together after their friendship developed on some acreage that belonged to friends of the Story family. That particular day was a rare morning in autumn, with the slanting morning sun turning everything it touched into spun gold and copper. The flanks of the bays they were riding looked as though they were glowing. They rode English style with English saddles and tweed coats. The horses matched the changing colors of autumn in the scene. The horses were shiny with sweat after the young women finished galloping. They were laughing, with color in their cheeks from their exertions. They walked their horses side by side for a while and talked some small talk, some serious talk, some about men. Prudy had a nasal voice, but she talked sincerely, without ornamentation. She spoke, as she often did, of trying to find her birth mother. She and her brother Paul had been adopted by the Shelleys at an early age. What was unspoken was, would she find love? Would she be abandoned by others like her birth mother had done to her? Eleanor listened intently and reassuringly.

At this point in their lives they had both met men they cared about, men who cared about them. Both men, in their separate ways, could be regarded as having strength, and patience. Both were big, strong, muscular. Both were athletic. Leo, Eleanor's husband, had been a football player from the University of Wisconsin at Madison. Rick had been a respectable football player and wrestler at East Lansing High. Both showered them with attention that the timid, the less self-certain, would not venture to bestow. Prudy and Eleanor were daunting women to men of average self-confidence. Leo and Rick were not men of average self-confidence.

From a financial perspective, Leo had the easier task. Initially when he was being shuttled back and forth from the University of Wisconsin with Eleanor in the Story family's professionally piloted twin-engine Beech-Craft airplane on weekends, he was beginning to see what life was like for those who were to-the-manner-born. In addition to Eleanor being beautiful, she was very, very rich. Karl would grind off some of Leo's rough edges, like changing his Polish name to Jerome, and Eleanor would smooth off others by her patronizing treatment, but by and large, he was accepted into the Story dynasty as is, a turnkey deal. All he had to do was watch Eleanor turn the key, and follow her through the door into Story-land. All he had to do was hustle a little and be patient with Eleanor. Leo was born to hustle; he'd been doing it all his life. He would become a part of Lansing's financial leadership, not walking side by side with Karl Story like the one son-in-law, walking maybe one step behind would be a better way of describing it. He would never be up to speed in his business sense, but being part of the Story family would make him a lot of money.

Rick would shower Prudy with attention she had never received before. He was everywhere, doing everything. He was tireless. If she wanted to talk, he wanted to talk. If she wanted to drink and party, he wanted to drink and party. If she wanted to be left alone, he would grudgingly leave her alone—but he would be nearby. Prudy's concerns about abandonment by her mother were subdued by Rick. He was there when her demons appeared and could often chase them away. He never, ever showed any signs of abandoning her.

Prudy's ride with Eleanor was not the last, but after that their paths diverged. There were two reasons for this, and they were both Rick. He was becoming a full-time gambler and he was entertaining questionable company. Being a gambler in and of itself did not give Eleanor or the Storys any moral qualms. Karl was known to place a wager or two himself, and he was good buddies with Howard Sober, who spent mega-bucks on gambling. But Rick was starting to troll in very questionable social waters. The second reason was style. Rick didn't have any. Or at least not the kind that would pass in button-down East Lansing in that period. And Rick didn't care about style. His pants were tight, his pullover jersey shirts were tight, and his shirts were always open half way to the navel, revealing sparse chest hair. Later, as he became more prosperous, he would adorn himself with a gold chain or two. Neither pants nor shirt needed or had ever seen an iron. They were stretched tight around his muscles. His style would get him by in Las Vegas or Southern California, but it would not get him by in East Lansing society. He would not care about "making it" in higher-class realms, about fitting in among gentlemen gamblers, even though doing so could have been financially rewarding. He was content to pick the low-hanging fruit among the bumboys, among the poker bums of Lansing and East Lansing and the state of Michigan. He was the one-eyed Jack in the card deck of the blind.

Prudy started seeing less and less of her upper-middle class high school friends and more of Rick's. Fuzz, a friend of Rick's said they had a lot of good times: "As Rick became more successful in his [gambling] business he mellowed out some, became a real good father. Prudy used to play on our softball teams and keep score. Little Ricky played hockey; they went to all his games. My (Fuzz's) son Troy played with little Ricky. We went to the Dells (nightclub on Lake Lansing) together." Later on, after they were married for several years it seemed to one person that Prudy didn't see many of her old friends at all. Chal, who had gone to Eastern High, was into gambling, and had been at Rick's "hundreds of times," said it seem like she had narrowed her friendships down to Vee. "Prudy looked good, but was getting kind of a hard edge, as time went on I don't think she was entirely happy with the situation. She seldom socialized with any of us, with Rick's friends, and he had a lot of them. I could see what Rick saw in her, kind of like an attractive piece of furniture, but I could never understand what she saw in him. It seemed like she had better options at the time than Rick." But Prudy's needs were emotional ones, not social or financial. Rick, in the beginning seemed to meet them, later on, Vee would help too.

## George Hall Wasn't Hustling At That Time

George stayed pretty close to Lansing. "I'd been let out on parole again [in 1969] and was doing well. Married to my third wife, we were fairly happy. I was working for Industrial Welding in Lansing. They repaired the big stamping presses that held the dies. When one broke, Industrial Welding fixed them. They were very heavy, many tons. My job was to maneuver them with various hoists and conveyors to the setup area. It took some thinking and organization to get the presses at the right place at the right time, but generally it was an easy job. I was making decent money. They treated me very well there. I don't know why I didn't stay. I guess I thought I could make more money gambling and hustling. I got away from God."

## Rick Gets His First Hint

Rick Fowler walked the few blocks to the pool hall from LCC after his last class in 1969. He had no political cares or concerns. The depressed state of Lansing's downtown didn't depress him. It had seen better days towards the mid to late sixties. Just a few years before it had been a hustling, bustling place. It was crowded. It was congested. It was noisy. It was alive. The sidewalks and streets were so packed that it seemed like nothing could move, but they did. Nobody complained.

Ten years later the crowds and people were gone, taking cars to the suburbs. The attractions that drew people after five were closed. The pool hall was still there, down the street from Paramount News, across the street from the closed Esquire Theater, up on the second floor. They could have shot the movie *The Hustler* in the pool room. The Union Grill guys treated the book and the film and Paul Newman's part in it with biblical reverence. They wanted to be like that: hustlers. They wanted to be Paul Newman. In some of their deepest waking fantasies, they thought they were. Rick had an appointment to play pool. He wanted to play like Paul Newman. He wanted to be Eddie Felton. He wanted to beat Minnesota Fats.

Rick went quickly up the worn wooden steps. The entrance was between the appliance repair shop and the other store, which was empty and boarded up. He took the steps two at a time with confidence. He had a wife, a son, and a draft deferment. Better still he had a house, a card game, and a book-making business in it. Life was going well. He was going to play Tony "Baloney" Hamilton.

The old pool hall was dim inside except for the dust and cigarette smoke-filled panels of light coming in the front windows from the late afternoon sun. Beams of light also cast downward from the lights above the pool tables where games were being played. Most of them were dark and empty. The Recreations Billiard Hall was not like the ones in the suburbs that were new and shiny with tables that had bright brass fixtures and red felt. The owners were trying to fill those clean places with women and a young demographic. This one wasn't particularly clean and smelled of cigarettes and stale beer and liquor.

The level of play in the hall was the highest. Jim Mataya, John "Dude" Mataya's younger brother, got his start there.

Jim became a world class player, hustler, and world nine-ball champion, moved to Las Vegas, and married Ewa, a Swedish beauty and female world champ pool player from that country.

The caliber of people that spent time there was generally low. There were seven or eight guys hanging. One of them was Tony "Baloney" Hamilton, who was playing nine ball. He worked the day shift at Olds, and had just got out of work. Those lurking on stools against the wall knew and liked Tony. He was of average height, a little over average weight. He wasn't Minnesota Fats, just a regular Lansing guy. The guys didn't know Rick, but they knew he was from East Lansing. Tony didn't know Rick well, but he didn't dislike him. He thought he was a little arrogant and couldn't help but notice his swagger, but Tony had met a lot of people in his life, and Rick was just one of them. But maybe, just maybe the reason why he wanted to play and beat Rick was because of the swagger.

Rick knew Tony had money. He was pretty sure he could beat him. It was difficult to see anything in the semi-darkness, but as his eyes got accustomed to the light, he saw Tony's face in the shaded light of one of the tables. "Life couldn't be better," Rick thought, as if he were in the movie, *The Hustler*. He and Paul Newman were as one. "Let's play, Tony," Rick said, just like Paul Newman said to Jackie Gleason playing Minnesota Fats. Tony said nothing, took a shot at the table he was already playing on and made it, then made another, and another, and another. He missed. He looked up at Rick, and said, "As soon as I finish this game, I'll play you."

Rick did not attempt to hustle Tony. He didn't have that much of a cushion. Rick may have been in the first rank as a poker player, but as a pool player he was not. Rick was better, but he wasn't that much better. He played Tony flat out. The game was nine-ball. Rick made a few, Tony made a few, then Rick finished off the table, making a bank shot on the 9. They played a couple of hours, and Rick was pulling ahead on the wire, strung across the ceiling with the little plastic donuts on them that kept the score on how many balls had been made by whom. They were playing for $2 a ball, and Tony was down $26.

They played another hour, and Tony pulled fairly close to Rick, then missed an easy shot that he had not calculated on losing. He left Rick with an easy leave, and Rick ran the rest of the table. It mildly annoyed Tony, not just because he'd missed the shot, but because Rick was starting to talk.

After that, Tony started playing less well, and Rick, seizing the momentum, played even better. He got hot. He ran the next table, then did well on the next and the next.

The afternoon turned into night and the guys were starting to come in, back from the bars and wherever they'd been, some to play pool, others to have a discreet beer in the rear, or to have a drink from a pint someone had in their pocket. They all knew Tony.

By around midnight, Rick had Tony down more than a hundred dollars, more than half of Tony's paycheck. Rick was starting to annoy Tony with the talk and the fact that Rick always played safe, leaving the cue ball on the rail or behind another ball where Tony would have no shot. It was legal. It was fair in a way, but to Tony, it meant that Rick had no balls. Rick continued to talk.

Rick, exuberant, and mirroring the same style that got Eddie Felton in trouble in *The Hustler*, said, "You can't beat me, Tony." "Shut up and play," Tony said. Rick might have been stating a true fact. He might have been creating his own dialogue in his own movie, but it was also a needle, something to get under Tony's skin and make him play worse, and Tony did play worse. From Tony's point of view, Rick was not just beating him, he was showing disrespect to him and making him lose face in front of his friends.

"Do you want to quit, Tony?" Rick asked fifteen minutes later. Tony's response was a slashing butt end of a pool cue heading for Rick's head, designed to cave it in. Rick saw it coming out of the corner of his eye, ducked, and put his arm up. Tony aimed for his head again and swung again. Rick grabbed the end of the pool cue that Tony still held. "What's the matter with you?" he said. "It's only a game." "You talk too much," Tony said through clenched teeth. Rick faced Tony off in a wrestling stance with his palms out and slightly down. He was preparing to slam Tony down through the floor, and get him headed toward China. Then he thought better of it. Tony's friends had gotten up off the stools and were starting to take an interest in their friend's welfare. Rick thought better of it. Besides, his arm hurt. He headed toward the door, shaking his head and feeling the pain in his arm, which he was pretty sure was broken. He didn't ask for the last $22 that Tony owed him.

After he left, Tony said to his friends, "All that talk, all that muscle, all that mouth, all that swagger, and he can't even back it up."

Rick met Prudy at the emergency room of Sparrow Hospital, up Michigan Avenue ten blocks. They gave the necessary information to the clerk. Then they sat there. The stiff green plastic-covered chairs were filled with those who had fallen from high places and low, the sober and the drunk, and had injured themselves. Others were obviously ill, and had been attacked by various viruses and microbes. Rick was the only one in the bright florescent lit room who had been attacked and injured by another person. After waiting longer than they thought they should have, they saw a doctor who took X-rays. Rick's arm, broken in two places, was set and placed in a cast. They pulled the white Olds Cutlass into their driveway at four o'clock in the morning. He did not press charges.

## The Fire Gets Too Hot

Charlie was driving down Michigan Avenue and saw Fuzz hitchhiking, pulled over and picked him up. "Charlie," Fuzz said, "I haven't seen you in ages." "Good to see you, Fuzz; I been in California." "How are the guys?" "Good," Fuzz replied. "I'm on my way to Ike's place to see them." It took just a couple of minutes to get to the southeast corner of Michigan and Grand in downtown Lansing.

Ike's place was the Capitol Area Recreation Club, known as the CARC. It was an illegal card room and bookmaking joint, one of several sprinkled throughout town, fueled by the human inclination to gamble, and the plentiful paychecks of autoworkers, turbocharged by the massive amounts of bets made by Lansing trucking company magnate Howard Sober that benefitted all bookmakers. Ike Johns was owner and proprietor.

Fuzz said, "Come on in. Say hello to the guys." Charlie'd never been in there before. A little bird on his shoulder told him not to go in. He thought, what the heck, what harm could it do, so he followed Fuzz through the white door with red trim and into a dark corridor.

Ike was soft-spoken, dressed conservatively, conducted himself conservatively, except for his generosity, with his money, which he had a lot of, and his advice. He was friendly and respectful to everyone, especially to wives and girlfriends of the gamblers, was the first one to pick up the check when he met someone in a restaurant. He exuded family values and counseled the guys to "settle arguments with your wife before you go to bed" and "Be honest; pay when you can." His favorite lament was, "I got enough bad checks to provide kindling for my fireplace for the whole winter."

Ike Johns had a lot of friends and no known enemies; Ike had a lot of business interests and was rumored to have run the numbers games in the Olds plants for several years. He mentored many guys, including Dave Godby, a good poker player whom Charlie'd gone to junior high with, and who ended up marrying Ike's daughter. Ike wasn't greedy, but he did like to get paid.

Ike staked George Hall and hired him as a bill collector. George had a look, a confidence in his physical power that made Ike's debtors feel very un-confident. That, and George's reputation which preceded him, made guys pay up quickly. One of Ike's customers who owed him money was Wing Dot Lum. Wing Dot ran the Foo Ying Café, a good-quality Chinese restaurant on Washington Avenue near the Michigan Arcade. The Café had booths with locking doors which sealed them from prying eyes, such that other pursuits besides eating could be indulged. Wing Dot owed Ike several thousand dollars, but when he saw George coming he got out his money.

George and Ike Johns knew what the guys who owed Ike money did not, that nobody can make money and pay up when they're in a hospital bed. George didn't hurt anybody.

Ike also had contacts in the form of friends in a gray world where the word friendship was more often honored in the breach. Contacts were needed because Ike was a very successful bookie that handled large amounts of money. Other bookmakers' help was needed because of the way betting worked, which was that bets needed to be laid off to balance the "action." If they weren't laid off and a bookie got sentimental and thought that he knew more than lady luck, then the bookie was no longer just a businessman; he was a gambler too, a sport. Sports lost. He knew enough people in Detroit and elsewhere so that laying off bets was not a problem. He and Mataya and other bookies needed to lay off the action because of Howard Sober.

## Howard Sober, The Biggest Loser

Howard Sober brought all the bookies prosperity, but he also brought them problems, big problems.

Sober and his wife Letha were brilliant businesspeople. He was a self-made multi-multi-millionaire, a winner in business. But as a gambler he was the biggest loser. He spent a lifetime looking for the same rush in gambling that he got in business success. He and Letha developed an idea that became nation-wide, then worldwide. He started working for Reo in 1919, delivering Reo cars and trucks by personally driving them to various dealers and individual purchasers rather than having people pick them up at the factory. That was the first step. It would save the factory time. Time was money. Their effort was strong and faithful; their service was excellent.

In the late 1920s he and Letha figured it would be more efficient to truck them, and so they did. Then Letha invented a hydraulic mechanism on the vehicle haulers that could haul more of them, efficiently and safely.

By 1935 they had branch offices in Buffalo, Springfield, Cincinnati, and Fort Wayne. The company was delivering 50,000 vehicles a year in the fifties, 100,000 a year in the sixties, more than a million in the seventies, even more in the eighties. Their clients extended beyond Reo and Olds to all of the big three plus White, Federal, Duplex, and the Defense Department in World War II, Korea, and Viet Nam. Terminals expanded throughout the country and to the east and west coast where they started doing import and export business.

In a January 19, 1970, *Time* magazine article it was estimated that Howard lost approximately $1,000,000 to Dice Dawson from 1967 to 1970 in Detroit after Hall of Fame Pitcher Dizzy Dean introduced Sober to Dawson in 1967. That was just one bookie. He also lost significant amounts to Lansing bookie Ike Johns.

The problem started with a phone call. While rushing to catch a plane at O'Hare In Chicago. Sober tipped an airline clerk $50 to place a $2,000 bet. The IRS was following him and got hold of the slip of paper with that phone number. That slip led to more phone numbers, of all the bookies and gamblers, horse owners, jockeys, and trainers whom Sober and the bookies interacted with, totaling more than 1,000 phone calls. The horse that Howard bet the $2,000 on at O'Hare lost.

Howard was at the top of everyone's list with the amount of money he was betting. He had to be calling attention to himself and those he interacted with. He played gin and cheated and still lost, he was so bad at it. (One exception was the "gift" of his house. With the connivance of the Governor and legislative leadership, he gave his white-elephant house on Cambridge in Lansing to the people as a mansion for the Governor, supposedly for free. In an unrelated item, hidden in the budget, he got $250,000 for the furnishings, a princely sum that was more than equal to the value of the house. He got the tax deduction and the $250,000. The legislators and the taxpayers were easier to scam than the Detroit mob.) He played the horses with all the bookmakers, not just the Lansing guys. He also played them with the Detroit mob. The odds were overwhelming that Howard would lose, but they made sure he lost.

The reasons why the mob cheated were purely from self-interest. The owners and trainers and jockeys cheated because the most they could profit from a win was 50% of the handle, or the purse, resulting from the total bet on a given race. The mob guys would pay them an amount of money exceeding the handle, to lose. The owners and trainers and jockeys won because they got more money losing than they did winning. The mob guys won because the amounts of money that Howard bet way exceeded the 50% of the purse, so it was a win-win for everybody except Howard Sober. With some understanding, and guile, Sober would go to the owners and the jockeys and the others and try to fix the races back in his favor, but the mob bookmakers would pay more and bring them back to them. The Nixons and Kissingers of gaming. The ones with the horses also knew it was probably in the interest of their physical well-being as well as their financial interest to stay with the mob. Sober was playing a dead hand. He was cheated in every way possible.

The IRS and the FBI were interested in Howard Sober for the same reason the bookmakers were. It was all the money. Starting with the phone call in Chicago spreading to Detroit with Dice Dawson, in a ripple effect it spread to Lansing for the same reason. The amounts of money were simply too large to ignore. They started investigating the Lansing bookies connected to Howard.

On the sunny afternoon when Charlie and Fuzz passed thru the door at Ike's place and came inside, many representatives of law enforcement were on the outside, also getting ready to come in.

Charlie was in the Capitol Area Recreation Club for two or three minutes. "I said hello to the guys, then left." Charlie said. "Ten minutes later, all hell broke loose in the place. After reading the next day's papers, it seemed like every representative of every federal law enforcement agency in the federal bureaucracy descended on the place, FBI, Alcohol Tobacco and Firearms, the Internal Revenue Service, the works. Everyone was arrested. Big newspaper headlines, big story, big charges, felonies. Big legal bills."

One of the lasting consequences of the raid and Ike's forced departure to Las Vegas was there was one less place for the Lansing gamblers to gamble. It nudged the Lansing gamblers and the East Lansing gamblers closer to each other, with all their differences in outlook. It brought Rick Fowler and George Hall closer together. Rick encouraged George to come to his place to gamble. "There's a lot of treats there," he said.

# CHAPTER 40

## OLD ENOUGH TO FIGHT, OLD ENOUGH TO VOTE

In 1962 the U.S. Supreme Court had made a decision on "one man, one vote," or Baker vs Carr at that time. It mandated that the state of Tennessee follow its own constitution. It had to do with the every ten year apportionment of legislative districts following the census mandated by the US Constitution. Existing districts favored the status quo, which favored preexisting political power arrangements which had it in their interests to discourage student voting. It also favored rural versus urban, and white versus black. The pre-existing "rotten boroughs" had many legislative districts that were a half or a third the size of some of the urban districts yet had the same or more representation. Baker v Carr's stipulating "one man, one vote" eliminated the disparities in the size of districts. This turned the worlds of the Congress, the statehouses, the courthouses across the country, upside down. In addition, the Michigan Supreme Court stipulated that one did not gain or lose residency by attending college—that one could establish residency at the university they lived in, and also vote there.

As the sixties wore on, and hundreds of thousands of 18-year-olds were drafted to go overseas, the cry began to be heard, "Old enough to fight, old enough to vote." This culminated in the 26th Amendment to the U.S. Constitution in July 1971 which allowed 18-year-olds to vote. That, and prior redistricting, changed the political world in college towns like East Lansing. No longer could the East Lansing establishment keep the barbarians out. It was the foundation, along with Agnew's resignation in 1973, and Nixon's looming Watergate problem, for huge Democratic Party political success that responded to antiwar sentiment of the student population.

The City of East Lansing had long discriminated against its student population. This was especially true after the open housing protests of 1965, when the enemies of the status quo made themselves apparent. City Manager Jack Patriarche and City Clerk Beverly Colizzi were at the gates, stopping the outsiders, the students from voting.

Bob Carr, the young political whiz kid attorney out of the University of Wisconsin, had been poking around the political universe ever since he ran, unsuccessfully, for prosecuting attorney in Madison, Wisconsin as Milton R. Carrelli. After a couple of attempts, he caromed between there and Washington, worked for Wisconsin US Rep. Les Aspin for a while, anglicized his name, moved to Michigan and landed as an assistant attorney general in Lansing. He unpacked his carpet bags, and got ready to run for Congress. He ran hard in 1972 but lost, narrowly; he'd run harder in 1974 as an antiwar candidate and win.

### WESLEY FISHEL REVISES, DISSEMBLES, DELUDES. WHO?

At about this time Wes Fishel started reinterpreting the events about the war that were in startling contrast to the factual history that he himself had helped create. The facts were that he was an original cold warrior, however well intentioned; a team player, in dedicated service to the policymakers that were waging it. He appeared in a June 11, 1972, *Detroit Free Press* article like a man of peace, pessimistic about all military options. He wanted it both ways, East Lansing's Henry Kissinger. Did he do this to try to persuade himself, or to try and persuade others in academic and intellectual circles, persuade writers of history that he was not the abjectly dutiful handmaiden of the government and the military that he always was? We'll never know:

"I did not create [the police and CIA part of MSUG when he was head of it], I inherited it. I tried to get us out of it because I did not think that it was a proper university function."
—WF

There is no record of him ever attempting to put forth any political solution, whether circumscribed by his harsh cold war thinking or not. He was the first Director of MSUG. There is a long record of him reinforcing Diem and speaking glowingly of what Diem was accomplishing throughout the time he was director of MSUG.

"We snatched defeat from the jaws of victory."
—WF

The implication here is that there was some easy way to bring peace and harmony to Vietnam, perhaps a "political solution" that evaded four Presidents, their advisors and their generals. No discussion of 'the elephant in the room' which was we shouldn't have been there in the first place.

## THE GUYS AT THE GRILL SIT DOWN WITH WES FISHEL

One night in late 1973, Fred Lustig and Fuzz and a couple of other guys saw Bill "Smokey" Boss sitting with Wesley Fishel talking about the world situation down in the Union Cafeteria. Smokey was a grad student in Sociolgy at the time, with more intellectual curiosity than a lot of the bumboys. Fred was an accounting major. Fuzz had no known major. Fred knew vaguely who Fishel was, how intelligent he was, how he never seemed to be in a hurry and would talk as long as anybody wanted to talk about anything they wanted to talk about. That day Fishel wanted to talk about Vietnam and how badly things were going. He talked so familiarly and casually about the situation that Fred didn't even stop to think it was unusual that an MSU political science professor was that close to Vietnam events. He remembers Wes Fishel complaining about his lack of success in getting the State Department to do anything about getting people he knew in Vietnam out. He said Fishel said that it was the State Department that had asked him for the names of people who needed help with exit visas, green cards, and other documents that would help them escape the deteriorating scene in South Vietnam and now State wasn't doing anything about it. He was frustrated. They were in danger, he said.

## THE FALL

> "What happens when the US is gone? Nothing dramatic, Theiu has to stay in power. North Vietnam is not going to move down with a full scale invasion across the 17th parallel.... neither side is in a position to conquer the other."
> —Wesley Fishel, June 12, 1971

Wesley Fishel was in his office in Case Hall, frantically working the phones in the days leading up to the fall of Saigon on April 30, 1975. The South Vietnamese Army was making a stand at Xuan Loc, twenty-six miles north of Saigon. It was the gateway. They held out against the approaching Viet Minh, and the communist North Vietnamese army for eleven days. During that time, Fishel was working day and night trying to get his friends and associates whose lives were at risk, out of the country.

On the day Saigon fell, there were pictures on national news of people on rooftops, scrambling and clawing to get aboard the last helicopters leaving Saigon. Wes Fishel was very quiet that day. He'd had the best of intentions. The artificial nation and the artificial government that Michigan State University had done so much to help create had come to an end.

A couple of weeks later, Christine Bailey, one of his grad students, was in his Case Hall office on the MSU campus when he was checking with the State Dept. on the status of those he was trying to help. He read off names. Coming back would be the replies: "Executed, executed, exiled, exiled, exiled, executed." Wesley Fishel quietly wept.

As acting MSU President Walter Adams told it, "Once Wesley Fishel could no longer 'deliver the bacon' [on meaty contracts for MSU], the University abandoned him. The University had profited financially from Fishel's friendship with Diem in a huge way, but the MSUG program was long over. Fishel had become a problem, not a cash producer. Thereafter his salary increases were very modest."

Friends believe that he had been denied advancement because of the *Ramparts* magazine article. Former MSUG head Ralph Smuckler maintained, "Fishel was physically broken by constantly having to defend his actions in Vietnam." But Smuckler was part of MSU's actions in Vietnam too, might also have been a little defensive, a little self-pitying about his own involvement as well as Fishel's.

Fishel was grading papers in his office in Case Hall one evening in early April 1977, and the pain of a ballooning aneurysm made him know that he was in trouble. He immediately drove home and collapsed in his wife's arms. Fishel died of intra-ventricular hemorrhage on April 14, 1977, twelve days after onset.

Among his virtues, punctuality was not one of them. Christine Bailey said that he would get so wrapped up in conversations at the Union Building or some local café, he would end up being very late to class. One time, she said, he showed up when his class appeared to be half over. He responded by saying, "There's a guest lecturer; he'll know enough to start talking when I don't show up." So it was often said that he would be late for his own funeral and he was. The hearse that brought his body to the synagogue got lost and was half an hour late. The many mourners there smiled in appreciation. It was standard Wesley Fishel lateness—in many areas.

The FBI and the CIA cordoned off his office and carefully went through his files. The autographed picture of Diem remained on his desk. It was several months before his last students got their grades.

When he lived there would never be a mea culpa from him on MSU's Vietnam gambit. When he was asked why he so believed in our efforts in Vietnam, there was never an admission of error, that things had not gone as he thought they would, never an admission of all his revisionism of events and his rationalizing of them, never any acknowledgement that he contributed to all the division of the country.

Ditto John Hannah. The Vietnam gamble had been a hard way for John Hannah to have MSU make easy money with lots of federal dollars.

There was no collective insight on the wrongdoing from those at MSU who got us involved in Vietnam, no repercussions for their actions.

The door quietly closed on that era.

# Chapter 41

# GEORGE HALL COMES TO EAST LANSING

Dave Lawson had a political side. He also had a social side. Earlier in the year in 1974 Karen Wallace Lawson and George Hall's wife Diana became neighbors and friends on Lansing's southwest side on Risdale St. Their husbands also became good friends. Karen said neither she nor Dave saw the menace to George that others saw. Was it their friendliness and openness that made them overlook it, the East Lansing confidence? Or did George just show a different side of himself to those he knew well and liked? Karen said Dave enjoyed George's intelligence. Dave described George as his best friend. The Lawsons knew the Fowlers because all went to East Lansing High and as adults they socialized some. Rick knew George thru gambling circles.

Dave didn't know about George's background, but if he had known he wouldn't have cared. Dave effused kindness and goodwill. He received kindness and goodwill back from George. George had a big fish tank in his apartment. They used to buy wine made by Mike Munn, Biggie's son, which Mike sold to them for 25 cents if they brought the bottles back. They always brought the bottles back. They'd sit in front of the fish tank, talk, watch the fish, drink some wine. George took Diana's kids and Georges kids out for Halloween, they exchanged small Christmas presents. George described it as one of the happier periods in his life.

"I thought George had his life on the right track," his wife Diana said. "It was the longest he'd ever been out of prison. He tried to have a normal life. His mother impressed me as a woman full of hate and anger, couldn't have been easy to live with. She'd had a hard life. Wasn't the kind to put her kid first. George always had great expectations, always needed more money. He started gambling more."

## THE BUMBOYS GET A HINT

Several of the bumboys were at the Dells nightclub on Lake Lansing with their wives and girlfriends. They'd split off from Rick and Prudy earlier in the evening. A black guy came up to Union Grill bumboys Fuzz and Bancamper and said, "I understand you guys are gamblers." Their eyes lit up. They said they were. The guy said that there would be a game going on shortly in downtown Lansing at the Motel 6. The Motel 6 was a seedy place by the intersection of I-496 and South Washington Avenue. It was across the street from where the R.E. Olds Mansion used to be before the Interstate was built. Nothing good had been going on at Motel 6 for a long time. Any light left on at Motel 6 was pretty dim.

Fuzz and Bancamper drove there and parked their car. Fuzz had uncharacteristically won $300 at the track. He hid the $300 first in his shoe, then behind the mirror in the bathroom. They played for a-while. Then they played some more. Things weren't going well. By four o'clock in the morning they figured out that they were the fish, not the fishermen. Bancamper got down $300 and couldn't pay. He started talking his best smooth talk. It wasn't working. "Is this a trick?" the guy who ran the game asked. It had an ominous overtone.

"We thought about jumping off the second floor balcony and running for it." Fuzz said, but decided not to. Bancamper figured out it was in the interest of his personal wellbeing to get serious. He showed the guy his pay stubs from Harryman's Shoe store where he worked, farther north on Washington Ave in the middle of the downtown business district. It was a very good shoe store patronized by the white and black community. The game operator carefully scrutinized the pay stub. He asked for additional identification. They made arrangements for him to pay $50 a week until the debt was paid. Bancamper made his weekly payments promptly for two weeks.

He opened up the paper the third week and saw that the guy he was paying money to had been arrested on an open charge of murder. He'd killed a guy after a card game in which the other guy didn't pay. The black guy was running numbers and women as well. It was discussed around the Grill. Rick's reaction was not known. Bancamper's reaction was that the guy's arrest saved him $200.

### Karen Gets A Package

Karen saw George pull into his driveway through her kitchen window where she was doing the dishes. She was very fond of George. She waved hello. He was so good to Diana, so good with the kids, both Diana's, and hers and Dave's. They babysat for each other frequently. George saw her wave out of the corner of his eye, and waved back. He paused, went into the house, came back with a package, and knocked on her door. Karen answered and greeted George warmly. They talked for a couple of minutes, then George asked Karen if she would keep the package for him. As Karen accepted, always aiming to please, some of the warmth went out of her smile, but as she said "sure George, I can." There was a momentary sense of foreboding. She could feel the heft of the package, feel the metallic clicks as they rubbed against each other in the package. She didn't have to look into the package to know they were guns before she looked into the package and saw they were guns for sure. She and George talked for another minute or two, then George said his good-byes and went into his house. Karen thought to herself that George was a little different, but was a good man. She put the guns out of reach of the children in a basement closet and went back to her dishes. She didn't tell Dave.

## Ratface, A Very Bad Bedfellow

At about this time, Vee, at his most democratic and undiscriminating, moved in with Ratface Smith. Ratface was a survivor; Vee was struggling. The amount of drugs that he was taking was turning from recreational to dependency. Vee was working on getting into the merchant marine and out of Lansing. But at the time he was doing with Ratface what Ratface did, which was to take a lot of drugs. He was also seeing more of Prudy, which Rick didn't entirely appreciate.

Ratface had a system for doctor shopping and obtaining pharmaceutically pure drugs. He went to see a doctor, complained about having kidney stones, very painful. The textbook symptoms of kidney stones, because of the friction on the urinary tract and the pain, was blood in the urine. A urine sample would be asked for. Ratface knew the routine. He would prick his finger while in the bathroom giving his sample, and would mix a small amount of blood with his urine. The outcome was that he would get enough heavy painkillers like Oxycontin and Demerol to peddle on the street, make good money selling them per pill, and have enough left over for personal consumption and to share, in this case with Vee. Vee never met a drug he didn't like.

The guys had changed. The youthful exuberance was gone; their hail-fellow-well-met aspect was diminished, replaced by something that seemed more forced, less genuine. They didn't look very happy unless they were under the influence, especially Vee. He'd put on weight and the smooth look and bemused. handsome face was being replaced by that of a puffed up one. A face that had spent too much time in bars and not enough in the sunlight. A face affected negatively by all the drugs. Paul Revere's Bar was the number one hangout at the time, standing room only, a good time had by all. Sherb said Vee shot up with something in the bathroom. Vee wasn't an addict, but he sure was abusing. It was beyond the recreational. It would be easy to say that everyone who tolerated it and encouraged it and laughed at it was part of the problem. "They were supposed to be his friends, we were supposed to be his friends," said Charlie, "and should have done something about it." But they were all doing more or less the same thing. Except they had more of a sense of limits than Vee, a better developed sense of surviving. Perhaps fewer demons were pursuing them.

Charlie told Vee several years earlier before he left for California. "Vee, the party's over." He didn't appreciate it. "Our friendship was never the same after that".

There was commitment, but nobody seemed to think they had a problem that was that serious. For Vee, there wasn't anyone around who could or would force the issue. Vee just wasn't that close to his mother. Did he wonder if some girl was going to come along and rescue him like his mother did with his father, only with a happier ending? It was obvious that he'd had a problem for a long time that went beyond teenage hell-raising. Was it obvious to him? In a way it was, or he wouldn't have left town and joined the merchant marine.

Chal talked about going with Ratface to buy some kilos of marijuana from some Chicanos on Lansing's North side. Ratface made the deal. At Ratface's apartment, they sifted it for seeds, weighed it, repackaged it for Ratface to sell. This was after the time that he'd already spent in the Ingham County Jail for dealing. Plenty of stuff around.

There was a ritual of sorts about the drug taking. Chal said that the three of them, he, Vee, and Ratface, would take some acid, stay in the apartment until they knew what effect the acid would have, then take a couple of six-packs with them and drive around East Lansing. They had done it lots of times. Except then, under acid, it was a new frontier, a dream-world of delights that they could all relate to, all with the same outlook, all affected by the same hallucinogen at the same time. Wondrous.

With the "party over" and most everybody graduated and gone, some, like Chal and Mulligan, had come back again for school. But there were fewer places to hang out. One was Rick Fowler's. It was in Rick's interest to have his place be a hangout, partly because it increased the odds that a game could be got up for the rake certainly, but also any game he played in he was more likely than not, to win. He also liked having people around. Vee would play once in a while, and could entertain those gathered with his humor. More often than not he would huddle up with Prudy and they would talk and talk and talk.

### Denny Diamond, the Pied Piper Toots Away, and the Guys Follow

By the early seventies, a lot of the guys had scattered. Chal and Dianne had divorced, Dianne had married Sherb, and they'd moved to Grand Rapids. Chal had come back from Detroit, graduated, and was working in the Department of Social Services for the State of Michigan. Chal was the most conscientious of the guys, always worked and paid his bills. He did have a weakness for gambling, alcohol, and recreational drug use.

About this time, Denny Diamond, who as a senior Union Grill bumboy who used to hang out there and be charming, had lost most of it. He came back to town from New York. Charlie saw him out at Paul Revere's some time in that fall of 1973 after Charlie got back from California. He was with Vee and Woody White. The guys had changed and no longer looked youthful, especially Vee, who'd put on weight. Mulligan had come back to town. He'd lost weight. He didn't eat. He just drank. Denny in his bumboy days used to cut a fairly impressive figure in his mohair suits however acquired. They had impeccable fit. He was perfectly barbered. Now he looked like a hippy as depicted on the *Ironsides* TV program. He wore a floppy-billed hat that could have been ripped off a golfer in 1890, and his hair was long and stringy. He acted more aggressive even than usual.

He was always cock-sure and know-it-all, but previously it was always semi-good natured with enough humor to not be offensive. Now he was clearly whacked out on something, and there was menace and edge in his voice if you even disagreed with him a little bit. Charlie said, "I thought he looked ridiculous but I didn't laugh. I stayed clear of him."

Chal and the rest of the guys partied with him. Woody White's Uncle Al White, the Whitehills developer was always increasing his holdings and his buildings. He'd purchased a tidy little house near the northwest corner of Hagadorn and M-78, where he later put up an office building. He had no immediate use for the house, and Woody had no immediate place to stay except his mother's, where he would retreat over the years more often than not. Al rented the place to Woody on reasonable terms and a half dozen of Woody's closest friends, including Chal, who were without housing at that particular time moved in.

Denny was one of them. Denny with a straw up his nose was not exactly as charming as the Pied Piper with his flute, but with all the drugs he brought with him, a comparison could be made. The guys followed the drugs. The girls, some hip, some neo-hip, with tie-dyed tee shirts and tie-dyed minds, some grad students, some bar-flies, all culled from Paul Revere's at closing time, followed Larry Chappell and the drugs to Woody's Uncle Al's house. The result was a non-stop party. Lots of short term chemical romance. Chal, as usual, was working, nobody else was. Mulligan would come back to the university sporadically over the years to pursue the one credit more that he needed to get his accounting degree. His current attempt would also be unsuccessful, To take time away from partying and give the one credit a top priority was just something he couldn't or wouldn't do. Larry was there frequently, but still lived on the other side of the tracks at his parents' home in Tower Gardens. He was the bait, along with the drugs, that got the girls to come to the party. Rick did his minor share of drinking at the party, but was not really into the drug scene. Prudy increasingly stayed home with little Ricky.

Charlie saw Chal at Revere's: "How's it going?" "Lots of parties, not much sleep," Chal said. This was seconded by Vee, who was gaining a lot of experience in such matters and had taken Quaaludes, one of the many different drugs Denny brought back from New York, including cocaine and Dexamyl. Taken in excess, which all the drugs were, just made them crawl around the room and struggle to get into chairs.

On a night when Quaaludes were not consumed and a lot of dex and cocaine were, things got very animated. It started over baseball. Denny was trying to convince the rubes in the hinterlands that it was going to be all Yankees in the future, that the Tigers were a team for schvartzes and farmers, he said, and that the Yankees had George Steinbrenner, who may be a crook but he had his money. The Tigers had won the World Series a few years before and the guys weren't buying what Denny was saying. They started hooting and giving Denny the raspberry. "We've got Kirk Gibson, too," At this point, with righteous indignation, and weary of suffering what he thought were fools, he got out his .38 pistol, pointed it at Chal's head and said: "I'm tired of arguing with you fucking idiots. The Tigers aren't going anywhere." This move got instant attention from the guys who were beginning to understand that even talking sports had its hazards in an uncertain world. After calming Denny down and changing the conversation, Chal left for the night and left Woody's place as a domicile.

The next day, after a more pleasant evening and a lot of girls had come over, Denny talked about relocating his drug-dealing business from New York to Michigan. The guys, in their most earnest and diplomatic con, told Denny there wasn't that much market or much action locally, and that New York was more befitting a man of his stature and ambitions. Chal moved in with Larry Chappell. Chal didn't like guns.

## Larry "Handles" Al

Al Patterson was in the same class as Larry Chappell at East Lansing High School, Class of 1964. Al was a friend of both Larry and Rick. He'd struggled to win the affections of Dee Trakas in a contest with Woody White during their community college days. He'd lost the contest, but he was good looking, charismatic, and had a sense of humor second only to Vee's in the EL crowd. People gathered around him, including the girls. He was quick-witted and a little cocky, but without swagger, and did not give offense. People laughed with him. He also had a sense that he ought to do something with his life that put some distance between himself and the guys who hung out at the Grill and increasingly at Rick's. Plus he wasn't a gambler.

Al remembers going over to Larry's parents' place in Towar Gardens without anything preconceived on his mind, certainly not a lecture. It was just a social call, just to say hello. He had a job selling, was making good money, but was on the road a lot, and hadn't seen much of the guys. Larry was always somebody he found easy to talk to.

When Al pulled into Larry's driveway that afternoon, Larry's parents were out. Al knocked on the side door of the modest bungalow and Larry answered. "Well, hello, stranger," Larry said. "Come on in." They talked of many things, how Al was doing, the money that could be made in sales, the craziness that was going on at the house that Woody had rented from Uncle Al. Then all of a sudden, so spontaneously that Al didn't really know where in his mind it came from, Al said, "I'm worried about you. I'm afraid something's going to happen. Rick's got some guys hanging out there that…"

Larry grabbed Al's tie and pulled Al close to his face. "What the fuck are you trying to say?"

"The first thing I'm trying to say is that my head is not a pot and my tie is not a handle. If you want to fight about this I guess we could, but you must let go of the tie right away—soon."

Larry slowly let go.

"All I was trying to say, Larry, is that I'm wor…"

Larry interrupted. "Mind your own fucking business."

There was silence for some seconds. Al said, "At this particular time I don't believe we are going to be able to carry on a conversation about subjects of mutual interest. We certainly can't pursue this one any further. I am going to say good-bye to you. I hope we can have a more pleasant conversation under more pleasant circumstances soon." Al slowly rose and left the house. Larry said nothing.

## CHARLIE'S LAST TRIP WITH VEE

"I saw Vee sometime in the winter of 1970-1971, out at Revere's. I was home over Christmas to see my Mom. It was before I'd moved back from the Los Angeles area. We drank a couple of beers and talked about old times. I was getting ready to leave. Bob was in the merchant marine then, and I wasn't sure he had a car. I asked him if he needed a ride and he said he did. It had started to snow, a soft gentle snowfall, the first of the season, and it was just cold enough for the snow to stay. To a neutral bystander it must have been a lovely lilting snow, with big flakes that seemed to hang in the air before settling on top of each other on the whitened landscape. It made East Lansing look like a Christmas card scene where chestnuts were roasted on an open fire in the All-American home. To me it was just the first of a lot of snow that was going to come down over a long Michigan winter. Vee had dropped a couple of tabs of acid. I asked him where he wanted to go. He was a little vague. He said turn this way, then turn that way. I wasn't in a particular hurry or anything, but it seemed like we were going around in circles. Vee didn't say anything; he was just watching the snow fall. With me it was the destination. With Vee it was the journey. I was his tour guide-driver. After what seemed a long while I persisted in asking him where he wanted to go. There was a long period of silence."

From Vee's perspective East Lansing was now truly a wonderland. Around every corner was a new scene in a vibrant new world, reborn and cloaked in soft white. Quiet. Peaceful. Then he heard a distant voice. The voice became more predominant, relentless, irascible. It was that fool Charlie. The voice kept asking him something that grated against all the pleasantness. Something unanswerable. What was the voice asking him? It wouldn't stop.

"Vee," Charlie said, "where do you want to go?" After what seemed a long silence, Vee said, "Just let me off downtown." Charlie did.

Charlie never saw him again.

On February 17, 1973, Bob VerPlanck, Bob Vee, able-bodied seaman, was sailing on a merchant ship owned by US Steel bound for Chicago from Duluth. They encountered very bad weather. Vee was on duty. Neither he nor any of the other sailors outside and on duty were tied in. A freak wave of the storm hit the entire side of the ship on the starboard side. He was washed overboard. Vee, subjected to the predations of an unfathomable world of people, drugs, storms, and waves, was gone. The water was 36 degrees. The grace and talent, handsomeness and humor, the infinite possibilities were all gone. He was no more. He died in his twenty-ninth year.

All the sailors working on deck were supposed to be tied in. None was provided with the equipment. A lawsuit was filed. Vee's heirs prevailed. He was still gone.

The memorial services were well attended. Vee had a lot of friends. Prudy was there. She'd taken her usual psychotropics and then some to prepare herself. She was still out of control, unconsolable, hysterical. No longer would she and Vee curl up, nestle together in her bedroom and talk and talk, like two motherless kittens mewing, giving each other comfort. She, perhaps more than anybody, appreciated how much we had all lost.

A couple of months later, Sherb was having a beer at Revere's with Fred Lustig and a couple of other guys, and the bartender shouted: "PHONE CALL FOR VERPLANCK." It was for Vee's younger brother Tom. Sherb shouted back, "SEND IT TO LAKE MICHIGAN." No development was too miserable for the bumboys not to make a joke out of.

### Dude Mataya, A Four-Flusher?

George Hall's willingness to fight for justice was demonstrated one evening by an altercation he had with John "Dude" Mataya. Dude was the older brother of Jim, the great Lansing pool player, and Dude got much of his modest fame and notoriety from being Jim's brother.

Dude had a card room and betting parlor underneath Vic's Bar on South Washington north of the railroad tracks in South Lansing. The sign on the door said: "Money's Light, Carry Some." Inside were a couple of rooms, spartan, basic. One room was to conduct private business; the other had a hot plate on an old formica-topped table with chrome legs. Beside it was a small refrigerator with soft rounded edges and a yellowing white exterior. A big round table with a green blanket draped over it was used for card playing. In the far side of the room was a regulation pool table that Dude had recently purchased from Karl Pierce. It was Karl's 49 Olds that, many years before, Clinton and Dave Cliff had loaned to Charlie and he had junked.

The economy of the pool room did not extend to Dude Mataya's exterior or his transportation. Excessive exaggeration could not be used. He was a caricature of a stereotype bookie. Damon Runyon could not have overdone him. Las Vegas types could not out-dazzle him. Ultimately he moved to Las Vegas, was pre-adapted to the coloration of his surroundings, and fit right in. In Lansing, Michigan, in that period, he stood out.

Dude drove a new metallic red Cadillac Eldorado convertible with a white top. It was long, wide, big, a one-car procession. Upon examination, an observer had to move their head to take it all in, from quad headlights in front, to angular tail-fins in the rear. When Dude got out of the car, he was not overshadowed by it. Dude resplendent, dressed in all the colors of the spectrum that glowed: greens, reds, blues, oranges, sometimes all at the same time. He wore a ring on every finger and gold chains and medallions around his neck. Some rings were diamonds, others big and heavy gold, still others big and black and gold. He had all the apparatus and appurtenance an aspiring "big shooter" could wish for. Howard Sober, the trucking magnate, helped with Dude's prosperity, as much as he helped every other bookie in town.

Dude was also not bashful. Stood up beside him, braggadocio turned to introversion. "Come gamble with me," he'd say. "I'll give you a couple of points. I'll give you all the ties. I'll help you out. You wanna play cards? The rake is only 5%… maybe 10% on the big ones only…, Come on, let's bet, let's play."

George joined the card game at Dude's early in the afternoon. It started out as a five-way game. As the afternoon continued into evening, the players started dropping away because they were tapped out, tired, or losing interest. At ten o'clock, the third person dropped away, leaving just Dude and George. George was happy; he was winning. Dude wasn't. The game was down to two, heads-up, which meant the rake was over and he was down. It would be out of character as host to quit before a customer wanted to; besides, he'd lose face. They played on for another 45 minutes.

The trouble started in a hard-betting hand of seven-stud, when George had a pair of red queens showing, with his other face cards also red. George bet, Dude raised, George called after the down card. Dude declared a diamond flush, showed his hole cards quickly, pushed his cards and his red hand into George's all-red hand, and scooped the pot. "Hold on, hold on," George said. "I don't see the five diamonds." "They're right there," said Dude pointing to the various diamonds on the table, and counting to five, then blending the cards and returning them quickly to the deck for a shuffle. "That was my eight of diamonds," George said. Dude disagreed. "You had the three of hearts and I had the eight of diamonds." "Now why are you in such a hurry to shuffle, Dude?" "What are you talking about." "Don't do me this way, Dude. Give me the pot."

George got angrier, Dude tried, with diminished patience, to calm George down. He declared the game at an end and announced that he was closing up for the night and "going upstairs to Vic's for a drink" (and for the protection of friends). He knew George's reputation. Dude closed and locked the front door, entered Vic's, and got a back table. George was right behind him. "That was a $25 to $30 pot, Dude. I want my money." "Relax, George. You weren't seeing things clearly," Dude said. The argument escalated. Dude's friends were in the place as he had hoped. One of them was Dick McKim, the head of the International Brotherhood of Teamsters local, whose offices were across the street. Dick was short and barrel-chested. He was accompanied by two big, muscular members. The Teamsters weren't known for being bashful or being reluctant to fight. They walked over to Dude's table and said hello, as a sign to Dude that they supported his side of the argument. This was a conspicuous hint of menace that George understood and ignored. He'd had it. "Give me my money, you son-of-a-bitch—right now." Dude didn't say anything. "I'll take it out of your ass right now," George continued. At this, McKim and his buddies conspicuously took a half step forward. George looked the Teamster leader in the eyes and said, "I'll take you all on." This wasn't the expected response. With the display of force failing, both Dick McKim and his inadequate brotherhood plus Dude fell back on diplomacy. "Nobody wants any trouble, George," Dude said. George said, "Fuck you, and you, and you, and you," looking them each in the eye, and walked out.

## Two Dogs Together Get Into A Lot More Trouble Than Two Dogs Separately

Charlie's father used to say that "two dogs together get into a lot more trouble than two dogs separately." So it was with Rick and Larry. Larry at this time in his life, spring of 1974, was starting to see its limitations. He had worked for Olds, Culligan water softeners, Sohn Linen, and other employers, and found them unsuitable. Women were still plentiful but life was so-so. It was softened by excessive drink. He had no immediate prospects for gainful employment when Rick Fowler made him a proposition. It would prove to be more than an employer-employee relationship. Larry would become a participant in Rick Fowler's "movie." Larry was to be the minor partner, but still get some of what Rick booked and raked. It sounded good to Larry.

For Rick, it looked like Larry was an excellent casting choice. In *East Lansing World* they would be the biggest, smartest, toughest duo around. They could swagger, they could strut, they could flash rolls of cash, they could have the girls, or the attention of the girls, the attention of everybody. It was all act, and it did not extend to violence. Well, maybe just a little intimidation, maybe a little bit of threat. This was true because Rick and Larry came to the same conclusion from two totally different perspectives. Rick was non-violent simply because it was not part of his DNA, not part of his makeup. It wasn't because it was illegal and immoral. Rick was amoral. To him it just wasn't rational—it didn't compute. It wasn't necessary. He was big enough, strong enough, smart enough to not have to cross that line. Larry, on the other hand, had some different life experiences than Rick. He knew what was illegal and immoral, had some foresight about danger, knew violence could be just around the corner.

Despite not being as smart as Rick, Larry had a much better grasp of human nature and reality than Rick did. Despite the risk, Larry figured he was tough enough, reasonable enough to get by, and agreed to play his part in Rick's "movie." Everything went well for some time. The money that Rick was giving Larry was more than enough to meet his needs. He was even saving a little money playing his part in Rick's fantasy. That was the state of things when Rick and Larry took their show on the road to Lansing that morning.

It was a bright spring afternoon when they passed over the Grand River bridge on Michigan Avenue in Rick's white Olds Cutlass and started looking for a parking place near the Capitol Area Recreation Club. They were looking for George Hall. They'd called earlier and were told he was there. The reason they were looking for George was that they'd heard that George was spreading rumors that Rick was cheating. This was not the most shocking rumor to be heard about any gambling house. It could have a degree of accuracy either large or small, about most any card room. The accusations could involve an allegedly obscenely high rake, or the passing of cards, or someone dealing off the bottom of the deck. Not much was holy in card rooms. But that's not the way George saw it. He thought they should be honest. That's not the way Rick saw it either. Rick could cheat, and he would cheat, but he didn't need to cheat, and that's probably what offended him the most. The accusation of cheating offended his pride, his sense of his own skill at the game, his sense of professionalism, his reputation.

They opened the white front door with the red trim and entered the Capitol Area Recreation Club. Their eyes adjusted to the dim light. They asked where George was. Somebody pointed to the back room. Several people were sitting at a card table, including Ike Johns, Dave Godby, Ike's son-in-law, and George. They entered the room, Rick first. His body was wide enough, muscled enough, that there was not a lot of room between the doorway's sides and his shoulders. Larry stayed inside the doorway.

Rick had his swagger, his confidence, and his self-conscious sense of his own toughness and what he believed to be his menace. George looked up at Rick and his airs. To him, all the tough guy attitude that Rick was wearing was like a suit of clothes that fit badly. A joke.

"We understand you're saying that we cheat at cards?" Rick said. "Well," said George. Rick decided to push the "menace" button a little more firmly. He took a half-step toward George and leaned over him. Larry stayed by the door. "You can't go saying that about us." "Just a second." George laughed and leaned over, grabbed his briefcase, and opened it. He retrieved a gun and pointed it at Rick. "Now, what did you say?" said George smiling. Rick and Larry took one step back and put their hands up in unison. "We don't want trouble, George. We just don't like having things said about us that aren't true." "Why don't you leave," George said. And they did.

"What the hell are you doing, George?" said Ike. He'd stopped dealing the black-jack game. Godby said, "You better leave, George. They're going to call the cops." George tossed the gun to Ike lightly. Ike caught it like a hot potato. He needn't have. George said, "It's plastic. It's a toy gun." Ike shook his head and laughed. Then everybody had a good laugh. That was George.

Rick and Larry didn't know about the joke. Rick called the cops. The cops came, talked to Ike. Ike said he hadn't seen anything. Rick mentioned some other guys at the table. The cops talked to them. They said they were out of the room. The cops sent the information to the Ingham County Prosecutor. Assistant Prosecutor Frank DeLuca, now Judge Deluca wrote George a letter saying he can't do that anymore. Naughty, naughty.

After calling the cops, Rick and Larry drove back to East Lansing in silence, Rick not attaching too much significance to the situation, just thinking that he'd handled the situation reasonably and mastered it by leaving. It wasn't a good read. Larry brooded about it with a sense of foreboding. He didn't like having a gun pulled on him. He didn't like George Hall. He was angry and worried at the same time

## Gambling, a Hard Way To Make An Easy Living?

It didn't occur to any of the bumboys at the time, that gambling was a hard way to make an easy living. Certainly not Rick. To him every day was like Christmas. The definition of problem gambling: "Any gambling that causes harm to the gambler or others," didn't seem to fit Rick; most of the definition was about financial harm and the spindown that affected family and social relationships. Rick was doing quite well financially. As to "harming others," Rick was in tune with satisfying a market, not with anything concerning the good or the bad or harm. That was up to government and religion. He was a gambling fanatic, but he was, above all, a businessman. He had a businessman's disregard—a good gamesman's contempt—for all the personal foibles that poor and weak compulsive gamblers continuously brought to the table. The bumboys had enough addictions and personality disorders to provide full employment for a host of mental health professionals, except, especially in the early days, they were genuinely gleeful, and were enjoying life more than any counselors that would want to help them. For Rick, the "hurting himself" part seemed to be far away possibility.

# Chapter 42

# THE END GAME

As a result of the Watergate break-ins, Richard Nixon was impeached for high crimes and misdemeanors. He resigned as President of the United States. A lifetime of scheming, plotting, pandering and demagoguing, more than most presidents, was over. He had all their intelligence and some of their good aims but none of their sense of restraint and limits. He had less foresight than an average county commissioner about when he had lost, or, more importantly, when he had won. August 8, 1974 was the end of his political life.

At 11 pm on January 29, 1975, George Hall entered the Driftwood Bar near downtown Lansing, and had several drinks; it was not his first bar or his first drink. The bartender, Tommy Champis, whom he knew well, asked him what he was up to. "Going to play at Fowler's, we're going to bank our money together." George said. "Are you sure that's a good idea, playing at Fowler's?" asked the bartender. "There's no problem," said George, self-assured, buzzed. He had a couple more drinks, left after about an hour, drove to Rick Fowler's, and joined the game.

The Fowler house, just down from the MSU Student Union was quiet on the evening of January 29, 1975. Upstairs in their living room, Prudy wasn't paying much attention to what was going on in the basement below. Their marriage was not a match made in heaven, but an equilibrium had been reached. She took care of little Ricky with Rick's help, took care of the house, and did most of the conventional things and a few unconventional things that housewives did. Some light had gone out of her life when Vee died. At the funeral service, Prudy, who was not the kind to lose control in public, had been out of control with grief, screaming and crying. She had thought of ending it all, of going to a bridge to jump, going like Vee had gone. But she had Rick and little Ricky to take care of. Besides, he was a good kid, a fine boy, who seemed to have the best of both of them. Smart, good, good-hearted, athletic, he was the apple of her eye, and of Rick's eye as well. When Rick took Ricky to his little league ball games and hockey games and Ricky did well, they were all home runs to Rick, he was so proud. It was even better than doing it himself—and there wasn't even any money riding on it. With the practiced eye of an athlete himself, he gently told Ricky what he could do better, adjust his stance there, move back more quickly on defense. As a handicapper, he quickly came to a conclusion about which team would win and which would lose, but there wasn't any money on it so the thought left his mind. Prudy was happy with little Ricky, and so was Rick, which made her feel a little better.

That night started much like any other night. It placed Rick and Prudy on different schedules as it often did. Frequently, games in the basement did not get started until late in the evening, sometimes ten or eleven o'clock, sometimes not until the bars closed after two in the morning. If Rick played and raked all night, which he often did, he would then sleep most of the day, get up, and do it again the next night if the guys were interested in the action. He had done this two, three, four nights a week for as long as they had been married, many hundreds of times.

This night was noisy, but they were often noisy and filled with laughter. Prudy thought it a little curious that there was not much laughter. Little Ricky was in bed. Prudy had been up playing backgammon with Mike "The Toad" FitzPatrick, and Happy Jack. But after Charlie Bovinette and Curley Gauldin arrived, everybody went downstairs to the basement to gamble. She went upstairs to bed, further insulating her from the sounds below. She slept soundly, aided by her usual dose of Thorazine taken earlier in the day.

Down in the recreation room, the night and the game started routinely. There were eight people to begin with. Play started around midnight: Curley Gauldin, Charles Bovinette, brothers Euell and Larry Chappell, and George Hall. A sixth, The Toad, always more short of money than even the always-short-of-money poker bums, thought the stakes were a little steep for him and stopped playing. Happy Jack did not play. From the beginning, Larry and George were arguing.

George was drinking, was losing some, was complaining. "Shuffle the deck some more and give me some cards," George said. "Take the cards as they're played, George. You're a big boy," Larry said. "Why don't you keep your nose out of my discussion, sport?" George said. "Take it easy, everybody. This is just a card game," Rick said.

The game was blackjack. Rick was dealing. Most everyone was playing conservatively. Some were up; some were down. George was playing less conservatively than the others.

A six-pack was broken and passed around. Everyone had beer except for Rick and Larry. Rick drank little when he was "working." Larry was on the wagon. George was the only one drinking from the fifth of whiskey that was present. He'd had much too much to drink before he got there. George was known for his mood swings, and his mood was swinging, bragging about his expertise and at the same time complaining about his cards and his luck. Larry didn't want to hear it. He'd been at Revere's earlier in the evening and had met a nice girl with long, dark hair and a nice body. She liked him as they nearly all did. He was feeling irritable. He couldn't have a beer. He didn't have the girl with him. He wished he was wherever she was instead of listening to this shit-bag George Hall complaining about nothing. Larry had had a problem with George ever since the time when George had pulled a gun on Rick and him at Ike's. It made Larry angry. It also scared him. But part of working for Rick was to show up at all these games for a cut of the rake. He had to be there. He had to play. Besides, Rick described George as a treat with a lot of cash. Larry didn't see all that cash, didn't see the treat. All he heard and saw was George. He didn't like him.

After a couple of beers everything seemed to calm down for a while. They talked about sports. They talked about the Super Bowl. They never talked about the Lions making the playoffs. They were realists. Rick, the master of all these occasions, steered the conversation from topic to topic, keeping things light. George continued to lose.

"How about another deck, Rick?" George said.

"If you think it will help, George, no problem." Rick got out a new deck.

George got a new deck but not a New Deal.

"You think you're the only one that's lost hands in a game of black-jack?" Larry said.

"Why don't you keep your nose out of it, Muscleman?"

"Enough muscle to put you down, Fool." Larry said.

"We'll see about that." George said.

"Very tough man when you've got a gun." said Larry.

The arguing continued.

At three in the morning, Joe Edwards and Bob Huss arrived at Rick's house after "closing up" Paul Revere's. Bob was Joe Edwards' roommate at an apartment on Hamilton Road in Okemos. Joe was the son of Al Edwards, the area Lincoln-Mercury dealer. His sister Patsy was married to Art Brandstatter Jr., who also played football at MSU after his father. East Lansing was a really small town.

Joe was not a gambler. Bob Huss was.

He waited in the car for Huss, who had said he was not going to play. He waited for longer than he wanted to, then thought he heard arguing. He got out of the car and entered the side door where he saw Huss and Rick trying to calm down a really ugly argument between George and Larry. He understood why Huss had kept him waiting.

"You're no good without a gun, George," said Larry.

"We'll see about that, tough guy," said George as he reached to grab Larry.

"Come on, you guys, this is ridiculous," said Huss as he and Rick got between George and Larry.

The argument continued, then seemed to settle down. Larry wasn't saying anything. Then Euell, Larry's brother, stopped the awkward silence and filled it with more support for Larry.

"Why do you go around with a gun threatening people. Can't you just have a clean fight?" Euell said to George.

George lunged for Euell; Euell picked up one of Rick's athletic trophies to ward off George and struck George in the forehead.

George got out a pocket knife, opened the blade and pointed it at Larry and Euell. Bob and Rick said in unison, "Come on, George, put the knife away." George eventually did but they continued to argue. Bob Huss went upstairs to the kitchen. Toad and Happy Jack, both no longer happy with the friction, especially unhappy about the knife, followed Huss up the stairs, but left the house by the side door.

Huss could hear the arguing upstairs so he went back down.

"Come on, George," Larry said, "Let's go outside without your guns and knives and let's settle it."

"We'll see about that," George said.

Larry and Euell and George continued to shove and punch each other.

"Come on, you guys. I'm not going to have that here," Rick said.

"Do you have a gun, George?" Rick said.

George didn't answer. He didn't have one.

There was an awkward silence. Rick broke it by saying, "Come on, let's play cards."

Huss, at Joe Edwards' urging, wanted to get going. He called for Larry to come up to the kitchen before he did, thinking that Larry and George were just going to get into it again and he would try to talk Larry into leaving.

Larry came upstairs.

"You guys can put up with this shit," he said, "but I'm not going to. The rest of you can get pushed around and have a gun stuck in your face, I'm going to beat the shit out of him so bad he can't do anything to anybody."

Huss at this point thought that Rick should have broken up the game and everybody should have gone home. Rick never had a game he didn't like. Huss thought he could at least talk Larry into leaving. Larry said, "As long as Rick's playing I've got to stay. Plus, one more threat from George and I'm going to beat his ass so he'll remember."

Things seemed to be calmed down when he got back downstairs. Euell had had enough, thought things were under control, so he left.

Huss and Joe Edwards left.

Everybody else was a little shaken. George was fuming. The game continued. George was silent.

The game was black-jack, with Rick, of course, dealing. The dealer had a slight edge. The guys played, still conservatively. George started losing more. When he told Rick he wanted to increase the size of his bets, Rick obliged. He lost still more. Then, instead of continuing to bet their own hands, the other players took obvious note that George was starting to lose more and began placing side bets against him. He glared at Larry and said, "All you guys are playing against me." Rick, with his usual equanimity, told George "It's not against the rules to place side bets. There's nothing wrong with it." George kept playing, kept losing. He said something about being cheated and Larry said, "Get a life."

Rick was at his calmest, smoothest best. "No one's trying to cheat you, George. You can cut the cards any time you want to." George didn't answer. He seemed to calm down. On the outside he seemed to acquiesce, resigned to playing in the only game in town. In his mind he would not be bullied. He would not be cheated. He lowered his voice and resumed play. He won back a little money. Then he stayed pat with 19 and the dealer pulled a smooth 20 with a black jack. He could feel the blood pulsing in his temples. He'd seen Rick put a black jack from the discards on the bottom of the deck. He grabbed at Rick's wrist to lift up the deck and see the bottom card, but with a flick of his wrist Rick muscled George's hand away. It was all in the wrist. George thought he saw that the jack was gone. He quietly said, "I've had enough for tonight," pushed the chair away from the table, exited the room, made a turn to the left, and climbed the stairs out of the basement and the house. Nobody said goodbye. The only tell-tale clue of his state of mind was that he slammed the door.

Prudy heard the door slam and the dog bark and roused briefly. She heard no other noise and fell back into a deep sleep.

Euell Chappell called the Fowler house and asked how things were going. They told him George had left. He went to bed feeling better.

George in his fury was barely self-aware. What was he doing? Where was he going? He went to get Leo McGill. He told him he'd been cheated, been beaten up.

It was 5:30 in the morning when a very un-peaceful George Hall knocked on the door of his friends, the peaceful home of Dave and Karen Lawson. He hadn't come to drink wine and discuss the world situation with Dave. The little house was on Risdale, a housing project on Lansing's far southwest side.

George lived across the street. The house slowly came awake. The two eyes of the upstairs windows lit up and cast rectangular panels in the yard that glowed white on the snow. Then there were light footsteps and the hallway and living room lights came on which revealed a sleepy, tousle-haired Karen in bathrobe and slippers approaching the door. She looked out into the half-light and recognized the figure as George Hall, her neighbor. She opened the door. He looked terrible. He had a cut above his eye and the right side of his face was puffy. "Get me the package," George said. Karen was no longer sleepy: she was scared. George did not seem in his right mind. This was not the man she knew, not a man to be argued with. Without inviting him in, she told him to wait, went to the basement and got the package that she'd been keeping for him. She'd kept it for George because she liked him. She wanted to please. Now it was no longer just a package that was being kept for a neighbor friend. She knew George's purpose was not good. She gave it to him, hoping for no further conversation. She hurriedly closed the door, almost in George's face. She re-locked the door, turned off the lights, and went back upstairs to the bedroom. She woke up Dave. He'd worked late the night before in his construction job. She told him about the package for the first time. They got back in bed and stared at the ceiling, eyes wide open.

George and Leo drove George's red Oldsmobile convertible with the black top up Pleasant Grove to Logan, then north and east to East Lansing. They pulled into the driveway of the brown-shingled house at 1023 West Grand River, ten blocks west of the Union Building. It was quiet as only a college town can be at 6 o'clock in the morning.

George didn't know how he got there. He knocked on the side door and Charlie Bovinette answered. George asked him if they could play and Charlie hollered the request down. Larry flinched. Rick hollered back, "Yes, if they have cash." George hollered back, "Yeah, I got money." Bovinette, Hall, and McGill descended the stairs. George had come to get his money back.

At the bottom of the stairs, Leo McGill, devoid of conscience and restraint, brave when he had an overlay, saw Charles "Bobo" Bovinette nervously reaching for a cigarette; McGill thought he was reaching for a gun. McGill shot him once in the head, fatally. The rest happened quickly.

A fundamentally honest man, George Hall was honest with himself. He'd been struck and beaten, bloodied up, drugged up. He'd drunk way too much. But even in the upside-down inside-out state of his consciousness, he knew that as Leo shot Bovinette at the foot of the stairs, his life was changing, instantly. He was sucked into it, down it, through the vortex, through the whirlpool. Once through it on the other side, he would kill, kill more, and know it wouldn't matter anymore after the first.

George, in his fury, said, "Put your hands up." Rick put his hands up quickly as did Larry and Curley Gauldin. Rick had never really been afraid before. He'd always been in control. Where he sat was the head of the table. Where he gathered was the center of attention. Where he played was where the action was. If he wasn't completely in control he thought he was. Even when he wasn't the biggest, the strongest, the toughest, the smartest, he would most often win his game. When he wouldn't win his match he would be smart enough to know it. He would say to himself, "I'll work it out next time."

This time was different. This was his game, his house, his world. He'd always been in control. He'd always won. He had Larry to back him up, as sure a bet as there could be. Now he was afraid. He was a good enough odds-maker to know that things were not in his favor, afraid they would end badly.

"Keep your hands in the air," said George.

Curley's and Rick's hands were very, very high in the air.

"Give me my money back," George said.

Everyone put their money on the table.

"Lay down on the floor and put your hands over your head," George said.

Curley laid down on the floor "right quick," even though a bad leg made it difficult for him to get down.

George turned to Rick. Rick was the system that George hated. Larry was the law enforcement of that system that he hated even more. In a confused siren song of red and bile flooding his brain, he shot Larry, shot him in the head, again and again. One bullet destroyed his brain and another lodged beside his spinal cord, stopping his ability to breathe. Others hit him in the wrist and arm as he tried to ward off the bullets. The handsome, confident face with the tired pale blue eyes that had looked down on the faces of a thousand women eager to love him was no more. To George it was the face of Rick's world, rigged against him, to stop him, to mock him. He destroyed him.

The two men killed quickly. Curley, down on the floor, heard the shot, then felt the pain in his back, another shot, more pain. He did not move. He heard more; they were of Rick being shot. The sound of the large-caliber gun filled the basement and echoed off its concrete walls. This is payback for all the arrogance, all the cheating, George thought to himself.

Prudence Fowler heard the dog bark and the first shot. It could have been a car backfiring, could have been a firecracker, but she was enough of a realist to be pretty sure what it was and wasn't. Then she listened and heard George and knew the noise came from a fired gun. The sounds George was making were somewhere between a scream and a shout, noises that animals make. They were different than the loud and garrulous talk of the East Lansing guys. The only one talking was George. A little later, more shots followed. She urgently went to little Ricky's room.

He was almost ten years old. She shook him awake. She placed her finger vertically across her lips to shush his sleepy protest at being awakened. She quickly led him to the bathroom, locked the door, and pushed a bookcase in front of the door. She held Ricky close and stayed there. It was their refuge; that was where they stayed.

On their way out, Leo asked George, "What about his wife upstairs?" George mumbled "They're not part of this." They left behind the nearly $1,000 in cash that Rick had on him as well as the three wristwatches Rick had on one arm, then exited the house by the side door. On the floor with life leaving or left were the bodies of Rick, Larry, and Charlie. Covering the walls and the floor were their blood and their brains. Strewn among the tipped-over beer bottles and beer cans, among the unmoving bodies, mostly covered with blood, were the cards they had played with earlier, some red, some blue, some face up—the devil's calling cards.

Curley waited on the floor and stayed still. He heard gurgling and groaning. Finally he thought, "if they're going to come back and kill me, they're going to come back and kill me." He crawled through the carnage to the white Princess phone in the corner. He lifted up the phone but could not read the numbers without his reading glasses. He struggled to get them out of his pocket. He dialed the operator. "Call the police. There's been shootings. George Hall did it." The police came.

Prudy stayed put. She did not leave the bathroom until the police came ten minutes later and shouted up the stairs.

In the basement, everything that Rick was, or dreamed he would be, was coming to a dead stop through the bullet holes in his body.

## THE END

# INDEX

## A

Adams, Pauline . . . . . . . . 34, 158, 243
Adams, Walter
   in Lantern Hill. . . . . . . . . . . . . . . 158
   Interim President . . . . . . . . . . . . 242
   on Hannah. . . . . . . . . . . . . . . . . . . 31
   protest. . . . . . . . . . 185, 224, 242, 247
   supporting LBJ . . . . . . . . . . . . . . 218
Avanzato, Glen. *See* Fuzz
Ayers, Bill
   with U of M SDS. . . . . 186, 220, 239

## B

Babineau, Raymond
   with VBI. . . . . . . . . . . . . . . . . . 92–93
Badrich, Steve
   *Land Grant Man* . . . . . . . . . . . . . 164
   *Secret Agent Man*. . . . . . . . . . . . . . 90
Bailey, Christine
   with Fishel . . . . . . 240–241, 270–271
Ballam, J. . . . . . . . . . . . . . . . . . . . . . . 34
Ball, George
   in Detroit . . . . . . . . . . . . . . . 233–234
   on Viet Nam . . . . . . . . . . . . . . . . 155
Bancamper
   and gambling. . . . . . . . . . . . 274–275
Barke, Charlie
   and Democratic Party 225, 231–234
   and marijuana . . . . . . . . . . . . . . . 190
   and Sandra Johnson . . . . . . . . . . 173
   as reporter . . . . . . . . . . . . . . . . . . . 88
   at CARC. . . . . . . . . . . . . . . 261–266
   at Marcia's party . . . . . . . . . 200–203
   at Morrison's . . . . . . . . . . . . . . . . 162
   at MSU . . . . . . . . . . . . . . . . 117–118
   at Nancy's party. . . . . . . . . . 204–205
   at Story Olds . . . . . . . . . . . . 197–198
   at the Grill . . . . . . . . . 106–108, 139
   at Vee's . . . . . . . . . . . . . . . . 188–189

childhood. . . . . . . . . . . . . . . . . . . 3–4
delivery routes. . . . . . . . . . . . . . 63–69
in California . . . . . . . . . . . . . . . . . 92
in Chicago . . . . . . . . . . . . . . 225–228
last trip with Vee . . . . . . . . . 282–283
on Diamond. . . . . . . . . . . . . 278–279
on Vee. . . . . . . . . . . 65, 119–122, 277
on Viet Nam . . . . . . . . . . . . 190, 223
summer job . . . . . . . . . . . . . . . . . 192
with Miss Jones . . . . . . . . . . 115–116
Barke, Eleanor
   and Charlie . . . . . . . . . . . . . . . . . . . 3
Barke, William
   as a father. . . . . . . . . . . . . . . . . . . . . 3
   with Vee . . . . . . . . . . . . . . . . . . . . 123
Barratt, Gerry
   on Mulligan . . . . . . . . . . . . . . . . . 150
Beed, Douglas
   in Viet Nam . . . . . . . . . . . . . . . . . . 92
Behymer, Jill
   at Nancy's party. . . . . . . . . . . . . . 203
Blink, Nancy
   and Charlie . . . . . . . . . . . . . . . 3, 119
Blosser, Henry . . . . . . . . . . . . . . . . . . 34
Boles, Emerson
   wrestling with Rick. . . . . . . . . . . . 41
Bovinette, Charlie . . . . . . . . . . 292–301
Boylan, Miles
   in Lantern Hill. . . . . . . . . . . . . . . 158
Brandstatter, Art Jr.
   at MSU . . . . . . . . . . . . . . . . . . . . 294
Brandstatter, Art Sr.
   at MSC . . . . . . . . . . . . . . . . . . . . . 18
   in Viet Nam . . 71, 81, 86, 89, 92, 108, 184
Brandstatter, Bob . . . . . . . . . . . . . . 108
   at Marcia's party . . . . . . . . . . . . . 201
Brandstatter, John . . . . . . . . . . . . . . 108
   at Nancy's party. . . . . . . . . . . . . . 204

302

Brodsky, Irv
 as bumboy .................. 99
Brown, Bill
 at *Lansing State Journal* ......... 66
Bullough, Hank
 and football ............. 147–148
 and recruiting ........... 124, 139
 and the Grill................. 147

## C

Caner, Charlie
 as newsboy................... 67
Carillot, Vince.................. 43
Carr, Bob
 for Congress............. 248, 268
Carrelli, Milton ................ 268
Chaliman, Bill
 at Morrison's ................ 162
 at the Capitol............ 208–213
 getting high ............. 277–280
 marriage/divorce......... 168, 173
 on Larry Chappell........ 104–105
 on Prudy..................... 257
 poker at Rick's ........... 215–217
 summer work ............... 112
Chaliman, Dianne
 divorce and remarriage ... 173, 278
 first marriage................ 168
Chappell, Euell
 at the Endgame .......... 293–296
Chappell, Larry
 and drugs................... 279
 at the Endgame .......... 293–301
 at the Grill ................ 2, 105
 childhood............... 103–104
 poker at Rick's ............... 214
 with Al Patterson ........ 281–282
 with Rick ............... 287–289
Churchill, Winston
 Iron Curtain speech ........... 49
Ciaffoni, Bob
 and gambling................ 124
Clevenger, Ray
 on Tonkin resolution ......... 153
Cole, Esau
 with George.................. 52
Colizzi, Beverley
 as EL City Clerk ............. 248

Colizzi, Beverly
 as EL City Clerk ............. 268
Coomes brothers
 with Rick ..................... 36
Craft, Terry
 with George................... 61

## D

Dai, Bao
 abdication ............. 24, 70, 78
 as figurehead .............. 72–73
DeLuca, Frank
 and George Hall ............. 289
Denison, James
 in Viet Nam........... 71, 81, 134
Diamond, Dennis
 later life................. 278–280
 lifestyle...................... 98
Diem, Ngo Dinh
 as President ............... 70–71
 at MSU ........... 76–78, 125–127
 downfall................ 132–135
 political control......... 80, 83–96
 with Wesley Fishel ......... 75, 80
Dohrn, Bernardine
 at MSU ..................... 220
Dulles, John Foster
 on southeast Asia .... 70–73, 86–87
Dutzy, Al
 on Viet Nam ................ 225

## E

Edwards, Joe
 at the Endgame .......... 294–296
Eisenhower, Dwight
 on Cuba .................... 129
 on Viet Nam .......... 70, 86, 154

## F

Faxon, Jack
 on MSU in Viet Nam ......... 182
Findley, Florence May
 with Rick .................... 42
Fishel, Wesley
 and protests ..... 179–180, 182–183
 as a teacher.............. 240–241
 at MSU/in Viet Nam. . 70–77, 81–82,
  84, 88–92, 126–127

303

at the Grill ................ 2, 140
last years................ 268–272
on the coup ............ 130–135
**FitzPatrick, Mike**
at draft .................... 169
at the Endgame ......... 292–295
**Fowler, Christine**
as a mother................ 35–41
on Rick ..................... 29
**Fowler, Rick**
and gambling............ 162, 290
and George.................. 266
and Larry Chappell....... 287–289
and Prudy............... 255–257
arm-wrestling ........... 111–113
at the Endgame ......... 291–301
at the Grill ..................... 1
early life ..................... 29
growing up................ 35–43
hosting poker........ 214–217, 278
playing pool............. 257–261
**Fromer, Dave**
at the Union................... 43
**Fuzz**
at CARC................. 261–266
at the Grill ................. 269
gambling................... 274
on Rick ................. 256–257
poker at Rick's ........... 214–215

## G

**Gauldin, Charlie**
at the Endgame .......... 292–301
**Gent, Pete**
on Fishel................ 130–131
on Hannah.................. 143
on the Grill.................. 147
**Gillengerten, Mary Lou**
at the IM pool ................ 99
**Giltner, Dick**
at the Kedzie party ........... 190
**Godby, Dave**
at CARC............. 262, 288–289
on Rick................... 38–39
**Goins, Levi**
with Gerry Horton ......... 59–60
**Green, Robert**
in housing marches....... 158, 177

**Greer, Thomas**
on Viet Nam ............ 179–180
**Gross, Hal**
at WJIM.................... 120

## H

**Hackett, Maggie**
and anti-war activism...... 90, 158, 219–220
**Hall, Diana**
on George............... 273–275
**Hall, Frank**
as a father................. 11–12
in Kansas City ............... 48
**Hall, George**
and Gerry Horton/prison ... 59–62
and Ike Johns............ 262–263
and Karen................... 275
and Rick ........... 266, 288–289
at Dude's................ 284–286
at Kit-Kat Club .......... 237–238
at the Endgame ......... 291–301
birth ....................... 12
childhood................... 19
growing up.................. 44
in Lansing .......... 109–110, 257
in prison................... 156
in the Army/prison......... 51–53
with Dave Lawson.... 187, 273–274
**Hamilton, Carson**
as professor ................ 101
**Hamilton, Fred**
at the Grill ................. 101
**Hamilton, Tony**
at the Kit-Kat Club ........... 237
with Rick .............. 258–261
**Hannah, John**
and Biggie Munn ........ 141–144
and Diem .................. 126
and housing................. 157
and protests ..... 143, 158–159, 161, 164–165, 177–178, 181–185, 224–225
and Viet Nam .... 71–73, 76–77, 88, 91–92, 95–96
at MSU ...... 2, 6, 13, 30–34, 56–58
on Oldsmobile................ 55
on recruiting ........ 124, 139, 143
to AID.................. 239–241

Hart, Philip
   at MSU . . . . . . . . . . . . . . . . . . . . 244
Hauer, John
   with Rick . . . . . . . . . . . . . . . . . 35, 40
Haynes, Sherwood . . . . . . . . . . . . . . 34
Heinz, Rosie
   and George. . . . . . . . . . . . . . . . 60–61
Hilsman, Roger
   on the coup in Viet Nam . . . . . . 134
Holmes, John
   and the draft . . . . . . . . . . . . . . . . 168
Holmes, Louise
   anti-war activities . . . . . . . . 165, 182
Hooker, David
   Secret Agent Man. . . . . . . . . . . . . . 90
Hornberger, Jim
   with Rick . . . . . . . . . . . . . . . . . . . . 36
Horton, Geraldine
   with George . . . . . . . . . . . . . . . 59–60
Humphrey, Hubert
   at MSU . . . . . . . . . . . . . . . . . 179–180
   campaign . . . . . . . . . . . . . . . 235–236
   in Chicago . . . . . . . . . . . . . . 226–230
Huss, Bob
   at the Endgame . . . . . . . . . . 294–296

## J

Jacobetti, Dominic
   on hippies. . . . . . . . . . . . . . . . . . . 226
Jaffe, Adrian
   on Viet Nam . . . . . . . . . . . 88, 95–96
Jerome, Leo
   at Nancy's party. . . . . . . . . . . . . . 204
   at Story Olds . . . . . . . . . . . . . . . . 197
   with Eleanor. . . . . . . . . . . . . 197, 255
Johns, Ike
   at CARC. . . . . . . . . . . . . . . . 262, 288
   with George . . . . . . . . . 109, 262–263
Johnson, Lyndon Baines
   as Vice President . . . . . . 128, 135–136
   in Viet Nam . . . . . . . . . . . . . 135, 152
   TV in Texas . . . . . . . . . . . . . . . . . 120
Johnson, Sandra
   with Charlie. . . . . . . . . . . . . . . . . 173
Jones, Miss
   getting beer . . . . . . . . . . . . . . . . . 115

## K

Kately, Julian . . . . . . . . . . . . . . . . . . . 34
Kennedy, John F.
   as candidate . . . . . . . . . . . . . . . . . 128
   as President . . . . . . . . . . . . . 129–130
   assassination . . . . . . . . . . . . . . . . 151
   on Viet Nam . . . . . . . . . 78, 132–134
Kennedy, Joseph Sr.
   and FDR. . . . . . . . . . . . . . . . . 14–15
Killingsworth, Charles
   in Viet Nam . . . . . . . . . . . . . . . . . . 71
Kirkpatrick, Lymon
   on Viet Nam . . . . . . . . . . . . . . . . 183
Kramer, Roy. . . . . . . . . . . . . . . . . . . . 43

## L

Ladjinsky, Wolf
   on Viet Nam . . . . . . . . . . . . . . . . . 84
Lafferty, Bill
   as bumboy . . . . . . . . . . . . . . . . . . 99
Larrowe, Charles
   as anti-war activist . . . 224, 243, 248
Lawson, Dave
   and George. . . . . . . . . . 273, 297–298
   and the draft . . . . . . . . . . . . . . . . 169
   anti-war activities . . . . . . . . 185–187
   at the Grill . . . . . . . . . . . . . . . . . . . . 2
   in Chicago . . . . . . . . . . . . . . 225–231
   with Vee . . . . . . . . 122, 158, 190–191
Lloyd, Eddie
   working in Lansing. . . . . . . . . . . 192
Lucas, Dorothy
   at the Union. . . . . . . . . . . . . . . . . . 43
Lucas, Milt
   busted for marijuana . . . . . . . . . 160
Lum, Wing Dot
   and George. . . . . . . . . . . . . . . . . . 263
Lustig, Fred
   at Revere's. . . . . . . . . . . . . . . . . . . 284
   at the Grill . . . . . . . . . . . . . . . . . . 269

## M

Malcolm X
   in East Lansing . . . . . . . . . . . . 27–28
   in Lansing . . . . . . . . . . . . . . . . . . 186
Mansfield, Mike
   and Diem . . . . . . . . . . . . . . . . . . . . 78

Mataya, Dude
   as gambler .............. 263, 284
Mataya, Jim
   at the pool hall............... 258
McAllen, John
   busted for marijuana ..... 160–162
McCarthy, Eugene
   as candidate..... 223, 226, 229, 235
McGill, Leo
   at the Endgame .......... 297–301
McKim, Dick
   with George ................. 286
Mesta, Perle
   in Viet Nam .................. 80
Milbury, Douglas
   at Marcia's party ......... 201–202
Miller, Jim
   with Rick ..................... 36
Milliken, William
   and Mary White ............. 100
   and protests ................. 252
   at MSU ..................... 244
Morgan, Joseph
   on Fishel..................... 74
Morrison, Truman II
   and housing marches . 162–163, 177
Morrison, Truman III
   hosting card game............ 162
   marriage................ 163–164
Morse, Wayne
   and Tonkin resolution .... 154–155
Muelder, Milton
   at MSU ... 32–34, 57, 158, 183–184
Mulligan, Tom
   and casual theft .............. 150
   at MSU ..................... 279
   at the Capitol ............ 208–213
   poker at Rick's ........... 215–217
Munn, Biggie
   and protests ............ 141–145
Munn, Jane
   and protests . 141, 144, 164–165, 181, 201, 247
   at the Grill .................... 2
Munn, Mike
   and protests ............ 143, 201
   at the Grill .................... 2
   making wine ................ 273

# N
Nhu, Madame
   political control....... 89, 132, 135
Nixon, Richard
   and Viet Nam ........... 243, 248
   as Vice President............... 71
   campaigns .. 128, 221, 223, 230–232, 235–236
   impeachment................. 291
Norfleet, Fred
   as bumboy ............... 99–102
Norris, Gladys
   as a mother................ 11–12

# O
Oates, Margaret
   marriage and divorce ..... 163–164
Olds, R.E.
   in Lansing ........ 7–10, 16, 27–28

# P
Parker, Doug
   poker at Rick's ........... 214–217
Patriarche, Jack
   as EL City Manager... 146, 176, 178, 248, 268
Patterson, Al
   and Larry Chappell....... 281–282
Pegg, Charlie
   as EL Police Chief 146, 159, 174, 176, 178
Peña, Gloria
   at ELHS .................... 119

# R
Rajala, Kenny
   at Western Union .......... 67–69
Rall, Dorothy & Leonard
   in Lantern Hill............... 158
Reese, Gordy
   and Rick ................ 112–113
Reisig, Doland
   and protests ................. 181
Rokeach, Milton
   in Lantern Hill............... 158
   on Viet Nam ................ 179
Romney, George
   as a candidate ............... 223

Roosevelt, Franklin
  as President . . . . . . . . . . . . . . 14–16
**S**
Salmon, Marvin
  and protests . . . . . . . . . . . . . 181–182
Sattel, Jack
  at MSU . . . . . . . . . . . . . . . . . 185, 219
Scheer, Robert
  on Viet Nam . . . . . . . . . . . . . . . . . 72
Schokloven, Joel
  *Secret Agent Man* . . . . . . . . . . . . . . 90
Schwarz, Ron
  as bumboy . . . . . . . . . . . . . . . . . . 99
Scigliano, Robert
  in Viet Nam . . . . . . . . . 81–85, 92–93
Scodeller, Ray
  and protests . . . . . . . . . . . . . 240, 252
Seelye, Alfred
  in Viet Nam . . . . . . . . . . . . . . . 95–96
Shapiro, Beth
  and SDS . . . . . . . . . . . . . . . . 160, 221
Sheinbaum, Stanley
  on Viet Nam . . . . . . . . . . 92–93, 182
Shelley, Prudy
  and Eleanor . . . . . 198–200, 254–257
  and Rick . . . . . . . . . . . . . . . . . . . . 41
  and Vee  118, 122, 216–217, 278, 283
  at the Endgame . . . . . . . . . . 291–301
  at the hospital . . . . . . . . . . . . . . . 261
Sherburn, Bob
  and the draft / Viet Nam . . 168–173
  at Marcia's party . . . . . . . . . 200–202
  at the Capitol . . . . . . . . . . . . 208–213
  at the Grill . . . . . . . . . . . . . . . . . . . 2
  cards at Morrison's . . . . . . . . . . . 162
  poker at Rick's . . . . . . . . . . . 214–217
  to Florida . . . . . . . . . . . . . . . . . . 227
  with Vee . . . . . . . . . . . . 190, 276, 284
Smith, Bubba
  and Rick . . . . . . . . . . . . . . . 111–112
  at the Grill . 140, 141–142, 148–149
Smith, Dave "Ratface"
  and drugs . . . . . . . . . . . . . . 276–277
  at the Capitol . . . . . . 64–65, 206–213
Smuckler, Ralph
  on Fishel . . . . . . . . . . . . . . . . . . . 271
  on Viet Nam . . . . . . . . . . . . . . . 183

Sober, Howard
  and gambling . . . . . . . . . . . 262–266
Sober, Letha
  and trucking . . . . . . . . . . . 263–264
Speck, Dennis
  in Viet Nam . . . . . . . . . . . . . . . . 222
Spellman, Fancis
  and Communists . . . . . . . . . . . 76–77
Stein, Arthur
  in Viet Nam . . . . . . . . . . . . . . . . . 92
Steinbacker, Judge
  and George . . . . . . . . . . . . . . . . . . 60
Stockman, David
  at MSU . . . . . . . . . . . . . . . . 163, 219
Story, Eleanor
  and Leo Jerome . . . . . . . . . . . . . . 197
  at ELHS . . . . . . . . . . . . . . . . . . . 197
  at Nancy's party . . . . . . . . . . . . . 204
  with Prudy . . . . . . . . . . . . . 254–255
Story, Karl
  and Leo Jerome . . . . . . . . . . . . . 255
  and Olsmobile . . . . . . . . . . 194–197
Story, Nancy
  at ELHS . . . . . . . . . . . . . . . . . . . 197
  at Marcia's party . . . . . . . . . 200–202
  engagement party . . . . . . . . 203–205
**T**
Tanenbaum, Maurice
  and Charlie . . . . . . . . . . . . . . . . . 68
Taylor, Arthur
  in Viet Nam . . . . . . . . . . . . . . 95–96
Taylor, Carl
  on Malcolm X . . . . . . . . . . . . . . 186
  on protests . . . . . . 141–142, 144, 146
Taylor, Maxwell
  on Viet Nam . . . . . . . . 133, 135, 154
Taylor, Milton
  in Viet Nam . . . . . . . . . . . . . . 87–88
Terris, John
  to Florida . . . . . . . . . . . . . . . . . . 227
Toshimura, Tosh
  as bumboy . . . . . . . . . . . . . . . . . . 99
Towar Gardens
  and Larry Chappell . . . . . . . . . . 103
  socio-economic . . . . . . . . . . 102–103
Truman, Harry
  and southeast Asia . . . . . . 31, 49–50

## V

Valenti, Jack . . . . . . . . . . . . . . . . . . . . 88
Van Ness, Marcia
   at *The State News* . . . . . . . . . . . . . 164
VerPlanck, Bob "Vee"
   and Charlie . . . . . . . . . . . . . . . . . 3–4
   and John McAllen . . . . . . . . 161–162
   and Mr. Barke . . . . . . . . . . . . . . . 123
   and the Munns . . . . . . . . . . . . . . 144
   and Woody . . . . . . . . . . . . . . . . . . 101
   at Marcia's party . . . . . . . . . 200–202
   at Morrison's . . . . . . . . . . . . . . . . 162
   at Saugatuck . . . . . . . . . . . . . . . . . 250
   at the Capitol . . . . . . . . . . . . 208–213
   at the Grill . . . . . . . . 1, 107, 249–251
   death . . . . . . . . . . . . . . . . . . . 283–284
   family . . . . . . . . . . . . . . . . . . 118–122
   last trip . . . . . . . . . . . . . . . . . 282–283
   poker at Rick's . . . . . . . . . . . 215–217
   to Florida . . . . . . . . . . . . . . . . . . . 227
   with Dave Lawson . . . . 122, 157–158, 190–191
   with Denny Diamond . . . . . 278, 280
   with Ratface . . . . . . . . . . . . . 276–277
VerPlanck, Madeline
   and drugs . . . . . . . . . . . . . . . . . . . 189
   and WJIM . . . . . . . . . . . . . . 118–121

## W

Waite, Mark
   and Rick . . . . . . . . . . . . . . . . . 39–40
   and Sherb . . . . . . . . . . . . . . . . . . . 171
   to Florida . . . . . . . . . . . . . . . . . . . 227
Wallace, Karen
   at the Grill . . . . . . . . . . . . . . . . . . . . 2
   growing up . . . . . . . . . . . . . . 174–176
   in Chicago . . . . . . . . . . . . . . . . . . 229
   on Towar Gardens . . . . . . . . . . . . 103
   with George . . . . . 273, 275, 297–298
Wall, Dick
   as bumboy . . . . . . . . . . . . . . . . . . . 99
Warner, Dale
   at the Capitol . . . . . . . . . . . . 206–211
Webb, Rodger
   with Humphrey . . . . . . . . . . . . . . 180
Westmoreland, William
   and Viet Nam . . . . . . . 154–155, 168

Wharton, Clifton
   and protests . . . . . . . . . . . . . . . . . 247
White, Albert
   and Towar Gardens . . . . . . . . . . . 103
   and Whitehills . . . . . . . . . . . . . . . 100
   and Woody . . . . . . . . . . . . . . . . . . 279
Whitehills
   development and style . . . . 100–103
White, Marshall
   health . . . . . . . . . . . . . . . . . . . . . . 100
White, Mary
   and Milliken . . . . . . . . . . . . . . . . 100
White, Woody
   activities . . . . . . . . . . . . . . . . . . . . 101
   at Revere's . . . . . . . . . . . . . . . 278–279
   at the Grill . . . . . . . . . . . . . . . . . . 100
Wickert, Fred
   in Viet Nam . . . . . . 73–74, 80, 82–84
Widener, Ed
   in Viet Nam . . . . . . . . . . . . . . 71, 81
Wilcox, Bob
   and protests . . . . . . . . . . . . . . . . . 246
Wilkinson, Marcia
   party . . . . . . . . . . . . . . . . . . . 200–205
Williams, G. Mennen
   and Diem . . . . . . . . . . . . . . . . . . . 126

## Y

Yaffe, Roberta
   at *The State News* . . . . . . . . . . . . . 149
Youngblood, Charles
   and protests . . . . . . . . . . . . 217, 224

## Z

Zimmer, Richard
   and Karen . . . . . . . . . . . . . . . . . . 174

# Acknowledgements

Special thanks to my cousins Suzanne Frank, for her early encouragement, and Paula Giroux, for convincing me that the manuscript had to be greatly reduced and more focused. Thanks also to Tom Klunzinger for his all-around help.

Thanks to my editor David Barker, wise beyond his years, who wielded a sharp two-bladed axe to the manuscript and also brought order to it.

Thanks to Sam Speigel and Julie Taylor at Partners Book Distributing for making the manuscript a reality.

Pauline Adams
Glen Avanzato
Christine Bailey
Phil Ballbach
Gary Barratt
Hank Bullough
Bill Chaliman
Ray Clevenger
Dave Godby
Pete Gent
Maggie Hackett
George Hall
Jim Hornberger
Laurence Kestenbaum
Jim Klein
Bill Lafferty
David Lawson
Charles Lindell
Eddie Lloyd
Fred Lustig
Milt Lucas
Clinton Mayes
John McAllen
Karen Wallace Lawson
Winifred Motherwell
Milton Muelder
Mike Munn
Al Patterson
Neil Staebler
Bob Sherburn
Carl Taylor
Rodger Webb
Fred Wickert
Rich Wiggins
Kent Wilcox
Mike Wylie
Roberta Yaffe
Chuck Young

# About the Author

Lingg Brewer was born and raised in a strong blue-collar neighborhood on the east side of Lansing, Michigan. For better or for worse, he was a product of the Lansing Public School System. He attended Lansing Community College and graduated from Michigan State University in the turbulent sixties. He did graduate work in political science at California State University-Los Angeles.

Lingg hitch-hiked around the United States several times in his youth; has worked as a tree trimmer, auto worker, truck driver, reporter for Variety in Hollywood, college teacher, county elected official, member of the Michigan Legislature, and as a small real estate developer.

He knew most of the people involved in the stories quite well, was a good friend of two of the people that died young. He knew nothing about MSU President John Hannah and Prof. Wesley Fishel's involvement with MSU in Vietnam at the time.

Lingg played just enough poker to realize he was not a player, spent enough time in card rooms to know he ought to stay away from them. His biggest gambles were in politics where he mortgaged his house to run for his first office. He had some winners and losers since. Politics was and is his first love. He has profound respect for many of the people, all the political institutions, and the process, despite popular opinion to the contrary.

Lingg continues to live in the farmhouse in southern Ingham County where he has lived for more than thirty years and raised his four children with his former wife Marjorie.

He plays with old cars and old motorcycles in his spare time.